Stones Alive! 2

_____

Listening More Deeply
to the Gifts of the Earth

Marilyn & Tohmas
Twintreess

Presented by

AhhhMuse

2340 US Hwy 180 E. #171

Silver City, NM 88061 USA

800-585-9389

www.ahhhmuse.com   ahhhmuse@juno.com

We give thanks to the Stonespirits who so lovingly share their wisdom and ways with us. This book is simply one of the co-creations they offer us in a life filled with unimaginable and ever growing abundance.

First Edition

Printed in the United States of America

ISBN# 1-890808-17-2

Photography by: Tohmas Twintreess

Graphic Design: Charlotte Krebs/Salmagundi Design Studio

We offer the information in this book, based on intuition and personal experience. We do not intend for you to use it to replace your own judgment or your doctor's prescriptions and/or advice. Honor this book and yourself by utilizing it to explore more deeply your own life and your own connection to the earth.

Other Titles by Twintreess

"Stones Alive!, Volume 1: A Reference Guide to Stones
for the New Millennium"

"Stones Alive! The Rituals of Manifestation Deck"

"House as Teacher: Building the Future Now, Creating Sacred Space
in the New Millennium (by Twintreess and Ursela Gurau)

"Ogallalah de Oro: My Life with Humans"

"Etheric Songs from the Children of Earth"

"The Heart of Matter"

Table of Contents

Reference Index to the Energetic Qualities
   of Stones and Stonecombinations viii
Invitation xiv
Our Thanksgiving xvii

How to Journey with this Book . . . 1
Listening More Deeply to the Gifts of the Earth 3
How to Read / Listen to the Individual Stones 6
Tools for Your Journey with this Book 10
One More Word 11
A Word about the Pictures that are NOT in this Book 14

Stones A-Z 21
Stones A-Z 21
Welcome to the second half of the Journey 179

Stone Families 183
Listening to the Families of Stones 183

Amethyst Family 187
Calcite Family 199
Fluorite Family 206
Phenakite Family 214
Pyrite Family 219
Quartz Family 226
Rose Quartz Family 242
Selenite Family 246

Stone Combinations 253
Listening More Deeply to Stone Combinations 253
More about Stone Combinations 255

Amazing Journey 256
   Wolframite, Aquamarine, Phenakite
Blessed Responsibility 258
   Rutilated Quartz, Azurite, Celestite
Bountiful Harvest 260
   Copper, Malachite, Emerald

Center Stillness 262
  Herkimer Diamonds, Una Oportunidad Sagrada Stonessence
Conscious Joy 265
  Amazonite, Aquamarine
Concrete 267
Disease into Vitality: Allergy Support 269
  *Snowflake Obsidian, Moonstone, Desert Snow Quartz, Herkimer
    Diamond*
Disease into Vitality: Attention Support 269
  Brookite, Malachite, Azurite, Turquoise
Disease into Vitality: Bone Support 273
  Red Calcite, Strawberry Quartz, Malachite, Azurite, Howlite
Disease into Vitality: Dream & Sleep Support 275
  Brookite, Smokey Quartz, Sodalite, Fluorite
Disease into Vitality: Growths Support 277
  Brookite, Apache Tear, Desert Snow Quartz, Crystal
Disease into Vitality: Heart Support 279
  Sunstone, Malachite, Tourmaline, Peridot
Disease into Vitality: Hormonal Support 281
  Crocoite, Amblygonite, Peridot, Brookite
Disease into Vitality: Nerve Support 283
  Hematite, Blue Lace Agate, Phenakite, Silver
Disease into Vitality: Pancreas Support 285
  Realgar, Sunstone, Chrysoprase, Rhodonite
Disease into Vitality: Respiratory Support 287
  Tourmaline, Lapis Lazuli, Iolite, Blue Lace Agate
Disease into Vitality: Stamina Support 289
  Black Garnet, Carnelian, Iolite, Desert Snow Quartz
Earth Magic 291
  Pine Needles, Chrysocolla, Rubellite
Evolutionary Grace 293
  *Boji®, Green Obsidian, Ajoite, Japanese Cherry Blossoms (some of
    these are in essence form)*
Gathering Respect 295
  Ruby, Turquoise, Herkimer Diamond
Innocent Child 297
  Kunzite, Blue Apatite, Amazonite
Leading with the Heart 298
  *Herkimer Diamonds, Peridot, (Una Oportunidad Sagrada
    Stonessence)*

Loving Family 302
    Kornerupine, Aventurine, Rose Quartz
Perfect Purpose 303
    Tibetan Tektite, Azurite, Himalayan Quartz, Astrophyllite
Perfect Release 305
    Smokey Quartz, Turquoise, Amethyst
Respectful Welcome 306
    Ruby, Hematite, Herkimer Diamond
Reality Creator 307
    *Wolframite, Crocoite, Sulphur, Green Apatite, Neon Blue Apatite,
        Amethyst, Amblygonite, Evolutionary Grace Stonessence*
Sacred Companions 309
    Stibnite, Topaz, Selenite
Spontaneous Manifestation 310
    Kornerupine, Chrysoprase, Aventurine, Raw Silver Diamond
Sweet Clarity 312
    Galena, Desert Snow Quartz, Himalayan Quartz
Volcano Juice 314
    *Neodymium, Praseodymium, Hawaiian Calcite, Argentinian
        "Herkimer", Argentinian Meteorite*
Welcome Home 316
    Calcite/Cuprite, Aqua Phenakite
Wheel of Life 318
    Sulphur, Cinnabar

About Us **325**

Tools and Services **326**
    Welcome 326
    Tools and Services for your Listening and Support 326
    Please Watch for Stones Alive! 3 328

Index **331**

Reference Index to the Energetic Qualities of Stones and Stonecombinations

In listening to Stones, you no longer need to identify them by their geography and geology, alone. You listen to them and receive their energetic gifts as well. That's why this index allows you to find Stones and Stonecombinations according to the energetic needs that they can support and fulfill.

These Stones/Combinations offer assistance with the issues, below. They are no means the ONLY ones that do so. Just feel these suggestions, as a friendly guide in your Stone adventure. Keep listening and listen ever more deeply, as you read. What truly matters is YOUR OWN energetic connection with the Stonebeings: *How do these Stones and these issues, together, feel to you?* That's what will support you and that is what forms the foundation of all your conversations/work/play with Stones. May you enjoy the wondrous adventure, and one day, tell us your amazing stories!

(Note: The Stones/Combinations with the page in parentheses are listed in the original "Stones Alive!" Vol.1):

Abandonment— Barite, p.35; Carrolite, p.40; Evolutionary Grace, p.293; Gathering Respect, p.295; Obsidian, (p.141); Turquoise, (p.206).

Accidents— Amazing Journey, p.256; Blessed Responsibility, p.258; Bloodstone, (p.36); Center Stillness, p.262; Disease into Vitality: Bone Support, p.273; Focused Grounding, (p.260); Huebnerite, p.94.

Addiction— Amethyst, (p.23); Amethyst Cathedrals, p.27; Blessed Responsibility, p.258; Conscious Joy, p.265; Desert Snow Quartz, p.62; Erbium, p.73; Prehnite, p.129.

Allergies— Ametrine, (p.25); Dioptase, (p.70); Disease into Vitality: Allergy Support, p.269; Dravite, p.69; Lepidolite, p.98; Seraphinite, (p.178); Yttrium Fluorite, p.174; Zeolite, (p.220).

Anger— Blue Lace Agate, (p.38); Covellite, p.57; Center Stillness, p.262; Dumortierite, p.71; Kunzite, (p.103); Lepidolite, p.98; Violence into Compassion, (p.311); Wheel of Life, p.318.

Animals— Earth Magic, p.291; Mookaite, p.108; Sacred Companions, p.309; Selenite, (p.177); Topaz, (p.199); Ulexite, (p.211).

Balance— Boji®, (p.43); Crystal Pleiadean Pyramid Alignment, (p.242); Deva's Gift Singing Bowls, p.64; Disease into Vitality: Attention Support, p.271; Disease into Vitality: Growths Support, p. 277; Fluorite, (p.80); Lithium Crystal, p.101; Rhodozite, p.138.

Beauty— Emerald, (p.75); Gathering Respect, p.295; Goshenite, p.85; Opal, (p.142); Rose Quartz, (p.164); Sapphire, (p.172).

Career/Work— Aventurine, (p.31); Blessed Responsibility, p.258; Epidote, (p.77); Gathering Respect, p.295; Zincite, (p.221).

Change— Boredom into Choice, (p.233); Columbite/Tantalite/Niobium, p.53; Copper, p.55; Evolutionary Grace, p. 293; Innocent Child, p.297; Kornerupine, (p.102); Leading with the Heart, p.298; Moldavite, (p.129); Rhodochrosite, (p.161); Samarium, p.146; Unimaginability, (p.308); Volcano Juice, p.314; Wavellite, (p.214); YAG, p.172.

Chemical Sensitivities— Coral, (p.63); Cuprite, (p.64); Environmental Toxins, (p.255); Hessonite Garnet on Smokey Quartz, p. 92; Moss Agate, (p.134); Perfect Release, p.305; Sahara Sand, p.143; Zeolite, (p.220).

Chronic Disease— Crystal Pleiadean Pyramid Alignment, (p.242); Disease into Vitality, (p.252); Disease into Vitality: Pancreas Support, p.285; Evolutionary Grace, p. 293; Garnet, (p.84, 159); Immortality, (p.268); Lightning Stones, (p.120); Malachite, (p.125); Sahara Sand, p.143; Yttrium, p.173.

Co-Dependency— Desert Snow Quartz, p.62; Disappointment into Responsibility, (p.250); Erythrite, p.74; Freedom, (p.261); Guilt into Perfection, (p.265); Infinite Intimacy, (p.271, 273); Turquoise, (p.206); Welcome Home, p.316.

Colds— Cinnabar, p.51; Disease into Vitality: Respiratory Support, p.287; Impatience into Presence, (p.267); Peridot, (p.147); Yttrium Fluorite, p.174.

Communications— Aquamarine, (p.28); Citrine, (p.61); Galena, (p.83); Herkimer Diamonds, (p.90); Respectful Welcome, p.306; Rutilated Quartz, (p.169); Sacred Companions, p.309; Sweet Clarity, p.312; Topaz, (p.199).

Confusion— Confusion into Focus, (p.238); Desert Snow Quartz, p.62; Huebnerite, p.94; Reality Creator, p.307; Rhodozite, p.138; Spontaneous Manifestation, p.310; Sweet Clarity, p.312.

Connection to the Earth— Ajoite, (p.19); Celebration of Faeries, (p.236); Chrysocolla, (p.59); Earth Magic, p.291; Lingam, p.118; Mother Earth Spheres, p.113; Pipestone, p.27.

Creativity— Azurite, (p.33); Copper, p.55; Gold, p.83; Innocent Child, p.297; Raphael's Rays, (p.291); Spontaneous Manifestation, p.310; Zoisite, (p.222).

Family— Green Kyanite, p.86; Loving Family, p. 302; Rhodonite, (p.163); Silver, p.149; Welcome Home, p. 316; Wheel of Life, p.318.

Fatigue— Carnelian, (p.55); Cinnabar, p.51, Disease into Vitality: Dream & Sleep Support, p.275; Disease into Vitality: Stamina Support, p.289; Regeneration, (p.293); Rutile, p.140; Volcano Juice, p.314.

Fear— Ajoite, (p.19); Apatite, p.32; Disease into Vitality: Heart Support, p.279; Fear into Love, (p.259); Pectolite, p.125; Petalite, p.123; Smokey Quartz, (p.179).

Flexibility— Calcite, (p.53); Disease into Vitality: Bone Support, p. 273; Kornerupine, (p.102); Lithium Crystal, p.101; Wheel of Life, p.318.

Focus— Beta Quartz, (p.35); Cassiterite, p.41; Confusion into Focus, (p.238); Focused Grounding, (p.260); Wolframite, p.166.

Fun— Apatite, p.32; Conscious Joy, p.265; Innocent Child, p.297; Moqui, (p.133); Turkll Delight, (p.306).

Generosity— Astrophyllite, p.33; Bountiful Harvest, p.260; Charoite, (p.57); Gabriel's Dawn, (p.263).

Grief— Botswanna Agate, (p.45); Chrysoprase, p.49; Conscious Joy, p.265; Death, (p.246); Evolutionary Grace, p.293; Perfect Release, p.305; Transformation, Prosperity & the Goddess, (p.305).

Guidance— Aurora's Dream, (p.231); Celestite, p.44; Connecting to Your Guides, (p.240); Iolite, (p.95); Kyanite, (p.107); Lapis Lazuli, (p.111); Sacred Companions, p.309; Sugilite, (p.186); Uriel's Wisdom, (p.310).

Happiness— Amazonite, (p.20); Andalusite, p.30; Apophyllite, (p.26); Bliss, (p.232); Disappointment into Responsibility, (p.250); Guilt into Perfection, (p.256).

Hearing— Blue Moonstone, (p.40) Dumortierite, p.71; Unimaginability, (p.308).

Home— All of the House as Teacher Stonecombinations; Welcome Home, p.317.

Indigestion— Crocoite, p.59; Disease into Vitality, (p.252); Freedom, (p.261); Judgment into Trust, (p.276); Mangano Calcite, p.105; Perfect Release, p.305; Yttrium, p.173.

Infertility— Cinnabar, p.51; Infinite Intimacy, (p.271, 273); Loving Family, p.302; Reality Creator, p.307; Respectful Welcome, p.306; Sunstone, (p.187).

Injuries— Arms of Michael, (p.230); Chrysoprase, p.49; Disease into Vitality: Bone Support, p.273; Guilt into Perfection, (p.256); Immortality, (p.268); Obsidian, (p.141).

Inner Child Support— Apatite, p.32; Faith's Embrace, (p.257); Hope's Call, (p.266); Innocent Child, p.297; Ivoryite, p.96; Lepidolite, p.98; Mary's Wonder, (p.280); Stillbite, p.156; Yttrium Fluorite, p.174.

Inner Communication with the Body— Allanite, p.23; Evolutionary Grace, p.293; Rainbow Boji®, p.134; Scheelite, p.148; Sweet Clarity, p. 312; Tourmaline, (p.201); Yttrium, p.173.

Kidney— Orpiment, p.120; Realgar, (p.158); Relationship into All, (p.292); Yttrium, p.173.

Learning Difficulties— Amber, (p.22); Disease into Vitality: Attention Support, p.271; Focused Grounding, (p.260); Lazulite, (p.115); Lithium Clay, p.100; Volcano Juice, p.314.

Loneliness— Leading with the Heart, p.298; Loving Family, p.302; Petalite, p.125; Relationship into All, (p.292); Rose Quartz, (p.164).

Love— Fear into Love, (p.259); Heliodor, p.90; Kunzite, (p.103); Morganite, p.111; Roselite, p.139; Watermelon Tourmaline, (p.213).

Lungs— Chrysoprase, p.49; Disease into Vitality: Respiratory Support, p.287; Neptunite, p.117; Should into Acceptance, (p.296); Yttrium Fluorite, p.174.

Meditation— Center Stillness, p.262; Disease into Vitality: Attention Support, p.271; Elestial Quartz, (p.74); Focused Grounding, (p.260); Tibetan Tektite, (p.192).

Memory— Gathering Respect, p.295; Lithium Clay, p.100; Wheel of Life, p.318.

Menopause— Crocoite, p.59; Disease into Vitality: Hormonal Support, p.281; Infinite Intimacy: Female Version, (p.273); Vanadinite, p.164.

Motivation— Allanite, p.23; Anatase, p.28; Disease into Vitality: Stamina Support, p.289; Hematite, (p.88); Rutile, p.140; Volcano Juice, p.314.

Nightmares— Arms of Michael, (p.230); Disease into Vitality: Dream & Sleep Support, p.275; Selenite, (p.177); Xenotine, p.170.

Pain— Hessonite Garnet with Smokey Quartz, p.92; Mother Earth Spheres, p.113; Pain into Fulfillment, (p.285); Yttrium, p.173.

Peace— Center Stillness, p.262; Chrysoprase, p.49; Earth Magic, p.291; World Peace, (p.312).

Power— Quetzalcoatlite, p.132; Reality Creator, p.307; Rhodozite, p.138; Sphalerite, p.151; Stibnite, (p.184); Sulphur, p.158; Zincite, (p.221).

Prosperity— Citrine, (p.61); Earth Magic, p.291; Gold, p.83; Lack into Allowability, (p.277); Pyrite, (p.154); Transformation, Prosperity & the Goddess, (p.305).

Puberty— Disease into Vitality: Hormonal Support, p.281; Faith's Embrace, (p.257).

Magnetite, p.104; Psilomelane, p.130.

Purpose— Aurora's Dream, (p.231); Chalcopyrite, p.47; Lapis Lazuli, (p.111); Perfect Purpose, p.303; Welcome Home, p.317.

Relationships— Fuschite, p.81; Infinite Intimacy, (p.271, 273); Larimar, (p.113); Loving Family, p.302; Raphael's Rays, (p.291); Relationship into All, (p.292).

Sadness— Hope's Call, (p.266); Larimar, (p.113); Leading with the Heart, p.298; Snowflake Obsidian, (p.181).

Safety— Arms of Michael, (p.230); Heliodor, p.90; Immortality, (p.268); Obsidian, (p.141); Tiger eye, (p.195).

Spirituality— Copper/Gold/Silver, p.56; Crystal Pleiadean Pyramid Alignment, (p.242); Evolutionary Grace, p.293; Hawkseye Velvet Tourmaline, p.89; Labradorite, (p.110); Nepalese Crystals, p.116; Phenakite, (p.150); Pipestone, p.125; Shamanic Dream, (p.295).

Strength— Calcite with Realgar, p.38; Disease into Vitality: Stamina Support, p.289; Europium, p.79; Hematite, (p.88); Ruby, (p.167); Spinel, p.154; Terbium, p.161.

Stress— Amblygonite, p.25; Center Stillness, p.262; Disease into Vitality: Nerve Support, p.283; Should into Acceptance, (p.296); Stress into Centeredness, (p.301).

Struggle— Covellite, p.57; Eudialyte, p.77; Freedom, (p.261); Impatience into Presence, (p.267); Innocent Child, p. 297; Jade, (p.97).

Trauma— Chrysoprase, p.49; Innocent Child, p.297; Perfect Release, p.305; Welcome Home, p.317; White Moldavite/Elestial Calcite, (p.216); Yttrium/Fluorite, p.174.

Travel— Amazing Journey, p.256; Faith's Embrace, (p.257); Meteorite, p107; Moonstone, (p.131); Respectful Welcome, p.306; Thulium, p.162.

Truth— Arms of Michael, (p.230); Diamond, (p.68); Lapis Lazuli, (p.111); Papagoite, p.122; Sodalite, (p.182); Tanzanite, (p.189); Zircon, p.176.

Vision— Danburite, (p.67); Herkimer Diamond, (p.90); MacEarl Crystals, (p.123); Nepalese Crystals, p.116; Papagoite, p.122; Sphene, p.153; Unimaginability, (p.308).

Weight— Disease into Vitality: Growths Support, p.277; Goshenite, p.85; Perfect Weight (p.287); Rose Quartz, (p.164).

Worry— Euclase, p.75; Guilt into Perfection, (p.265); Heliodor, p.90; Should into Acceptance, (p.296).

Invitation to Evolving Humans

What if you could sit on top of the world,
what wouldn't you see?

Every day would majestically unfold its treasures for you:
the colorexplosion of every dawn's hope
the dancing green waves of trees-in-forest.
the aroma of the wind's sigh after a rain.
the whale's call mapping out the ocean.

What if you could sit on top of the world,
what wouldn't you know?

People-borders would lose themselves in the glory
of mountains and rivers:
Animals, plants and stones all vibrating with one heart—
the heart of the earth—
following its love to know where to eat,
to sleep, to mate
in a grandness that fits with everything else,
perfectly balancing need with harmony.

You are at the mountaintop.
You ran all the way up it
creating your technologies
to make the climb as fast as you could.

From there, do you see yourself on the earth?
Do you see the trail of trash tracing your hurry to the top?
Do you see the places where you eat, sleep and mate?
How do they fit in with the trees
the winds
the whales
and the hopes of all others?

How do they not?

You are blessed.
to see from the highest point of your world
it teaches you everything.
It takes you beyond your single, separate wishes
right into the wonder of life
the dream of belonging.

You do belong here,
didn't you already see that everything fit on the earth?
Yes, you saw it
and you can keep on seeing it.

This is your invitation.

This is the mountaintop.
Every desire, every hurry, every sigh
has brought you here.

Accept that;
though you have left a trail of pain, too,
accept it.

Take it into your heart and love
that everything that you have done
has ascended you to this peak
where nothing of life can be hidden from your endless curiosity
and drive.

All your rushing brought you to this invitation.
Now.
You are ready for it now.
No matter how out of breath you are from the climb
you must keep going,
you must keep growing.

The invitation is from life and the Mother-within-the-Earth,
the ones who know you without judgment.
You are being invited to take all that you have done
and grown it into an evolution of being.

Stand on the mountaintop,
declare who you truly are
(no need to list your possessions or your prizes).
In a single blink of life
all that you be
is invited to join with all other life,
to listen to a single heartbeat
and to follow it to home,
to home.

From the mountaintop of your beingness
(not your doingness)
listen.
Listen past the distractions of the chaos you used to create.
Listen to the whales surveying the consciousness of earthbeings
evolving,
growing,
stretching the more of what they are
into everything else.

You belong here.
Keep coming to your biggest, grandest picture of life.
Listen to its heartbeat
Every other plant, animal and stone follows it,
echoes it in their blossoms, their fur and their facets.
Just listen to the others,
now they will lead the way home.

Our Thanksgiving

One day, the Stonespirits said, "We want to write a reference book with you."

Of course we said, "Yes!" We felt utterly honored. And then nothing happened.

A year later, the Stonespirits spoke, "We are now ready for you to write our stories and our love into a reference book." They went on to tell us that they wanted this book written, edited, published, and printed in time for the Tucson Gem Show at the end of January. We blinked. After all, the Stones were politely asking us to produce a brand new book (by January) and it was already November.

Of course we said, "Yes."

"Stones Alive! A Reference Guide to Stones for the New Millennium, Volume 1" was written, edited and published in three weeks. We absolutely love sharing that story, because as we say it, we can see you blinking, too. When you hear that, you know that we couldn't possibly have done that in that amount of time…..alone. In your bones, you **know** we had help. You know in a place that defies explanation, that the Stonebeings must have helped us.

We participated in a miracle. While we were co-creating "Stones Alive! Volume 1," Tohmas (one half of Twintreess and one of the co-authors) was building a three dome with a pyramid home— a gigantic undertaking that demanded long hours and utter concentration (That's a great story, too: "House as Teacher" by Twintreess & Ursela Gurau.). That left Marilyn, the other half of Twintreess and the other co-author, to write some of the 322 page book, alone. Not once in that three weeks did we work all night; we simply worked regular hours, quietly focusing on the Stones' request.

It all came together easily, in one full breath, because we have been listening to stones forever. It's in our cells (and yours too); literally the Stonebeings are in our bones. They make up this earth, offering an endless foundation of matter and wisdom. Truly knowing this allowed us to listen to the Stones completely, letting go of judgment and even the need to understand.

This is not new. People who have lived close to the earth have been doing this for millennia. It only seems unbelievable to people who no longer pay attention to the earth, who no longer respect its perfect balance and generosity. For us to hear the Stones, we must focus on respecting all life, including ourselves, every moment. We live this way. We write this way. We build this way. And we listen to the Stones this way, trusting that when they want to co-create a book, it will be done … somehow, with perfect balance and generosity.

That's how "Stones Alive!, Volume 1" was born. That's how "Stones Alive!, Volume 2" is being birthed as well. It profoundly honors us to share that with you. For you to read what the Stonebeings have intended for you to listen to inspires our Hearts and fulfills our Spirits. We share this story of co-creation with you because in Volume 2, the Stonebeings are inviting all of us to go more deeply into listening <u>for</u> ourselves, into our core connection to everything and every being that we walk this earth with — into the very heart of the earth where we already know all of this, where listening to every wondrous lifeform IS the beat of our Hearts.

With all that we are, we thank the Stonebeings.
With all that we are, we thank the Earth, Spirit and Life.
With all that we are, we thank every one of you who contributed to this miracle.
With all that we are, we thank every reader who is now a listener.
With all that we are, we say, "**Yes!**" and we invite you to this celebration, a thanksgiving for us all.

How to Journey with this Book

Do you remember the first time (or the last time) you petted a brand new, wriggling puppy? You reveled in delight. The puppy's warm body caressed your skin and every one of your worries, too. You didn't *think* anything in particular. You were just there. You were so there with that puppy, that you knew what she was feeling. You and the puppy were a single, shared bliss.

That's how we invite you to enter "Stones Alive! Volume 2." Relax. Breathe. Okay. Now really *breathe,* from the roots of your toes to the tip of your head and into every, single, blessed part of you in between. When you truly breathe, ease enters your whole being and you can actually be present.

Be

present

with

this

book.

Let go of thinking in particular. Revel in the delight of the words. After all, each one has been prepared especially for you— no one else in the whole world will see them and touch them exactly like you. No one else will learn and grow from them like you can.

Let the book's warmth inspire you. Let it lift you to places where even imagination hasn't left its footprint. That's the territory of the

1

heart. You have to travel light to go there; all you can take (or offer) is **willingness.** Bring the full breath of your willing heart and see where it will take you. We know that it will be far beyond your mind, and even farther beyond imagination, right into pure magic. Just like a brand new puppy, pure magic cannot be known or understood in advance. If you jump ahead of the words, *thinking* what will be there, instead of truly waiting for willingness and your heart to offer their gifts, you will miss it. You will miss the magic, which is ever found gleefully wrapped inside of the unknown.

It's not just where you find magic that makes it so; it is how you find it and how it finds YOU. This book overflows with magic. We know this because it didn't come from just our heads and our hands, it came directly from the willingness of our hearts. That is where and how we found the Stonebeings and their simple, heart-filled stories. For you to actually **listen** to their magic you have to travel beyond the calculations of your mind and of your eye— you have to travel "light," with just your heart. When you read here, don't just look with your eyes, listen with your heart.

Where will you go then? Who knows? We feel that you will travel with the Stonebeings, yourself, into the unknown. Like us, maybe you will find your life gracefully and utterly interwoven with every other Earth being, with their wisdom awaiting you.

If you

relax,

breathe,

and read

with your heart.

Listening More Deeply to the Gifts of the Earth

Yes, we listen to stones. We always have. Once we focused on this communication, utterly, we realized that we had heard and felt the stone whispers all our lives. We just didn't know, exactly, that that's what they were.

Reading this book now is an open invitation to listening to the stones, <u>yourself</u>. Everyone listens to and hears life differently— but hear it they do! Somewhere in your cells, your body records every bit of information that ever has been (like the stones do). It's your own special library of life and we're going to offer some suggestions about how to check out the books and see what they have to say!!!

Accept that you can and do listen to stones already.
Perhaps the most difficult part of this kind of listening is simply allowing it to be possible. If you don't open up your heart to accept this miracle, then your mind will shut down all possibilities. It won't even let you consider any proof to the contrary. It'll just explain it away and call you crazy to boot. To live the impossible, you have to allow it to be possible first. Just ask Buckminster Fuller, Tesla, Henry Ford.......

The common language on this planet is not English, it's telepathy.
Faster than we can say "Yes," our bodies process billions of stimuli and record them in our beings. It recognizes every kind of energy on this planet, yet our conscious mind keeps us from recognizing all this because it's just too much! It would paralyze our decision-making almost immediately.

Still, if you **clearly** choose to receive communication from stones, and you tell every part of your being this repeatedly, then your mind will bring forth those stimuli so that you can review them.

This telepathy, this natural communication, is the birthright of every being on this planet. It connects us at the core. Accessing our innate, energetic language reminds us that we all belong here and that we belong to/with each other. Celebrate! You're not alone!

Offer respect.
You're walking in new territory here and you're asking the Stonebeings

to help you. It's important that you also give them something; that's how you establish a real conversation with anybody, anywhere. Offer the Stonebeings your respect. Thank them for their support and help.

Focus on listening.
Any time we learn something new, the first thing we had to do was simply to choose to learn. Otherwise any new information falls on deaf ears. Choose it. Want it. Focus.

Open up your whole being to listening in this new way. You're only risking that you'll think you're foolish (You're not. This is a grand adventure that can connect you to life!). The good news is that that foolishness is just a **thoughtform.** You can choose to base your following decisions on that thoughtform or not: You have choice! Your body already stores this listening/telepathy and your heart already accepts it. Just tell yourself, clearly (write a note where you can see it) *"I'm listening to stones."* Your body and your heart shout, "Yes!" And then they offer all their awareness to your conscious mind and you cannot help but receive it.

Everybody listens to stones in their own unique way.
Of course (Or as some friends of ours say, "Of quartz!").
You talk and listen to everyone around you in your own absolutely individual manner. This is no different. Remember that. Relax. It's a lot easier to learn and to receive *anything*, when you loosen your body and your control and **allow.** (Though you may not have considered it consciously, that's how you learn anything and everything, already.)

This is fun! Let go of the testing mentality (Hey, just do it for a while. If you really have to "test" yourself, that option will be waiting patiently for you later, anytime.). The words and ways of the stones will land upon your body in exactly the way you need to hear them. So realize the stone whispers can come in any form: a word; a phrase; a feeling; a sensation of hot/cold/tingling on your body; pictures; or just an inexplicable knowing, etc. Accept that the communication is being offered to you and then focus on it easily, but <u>continually</u>. When you offer that kind of willingness the telepathy will always come. Your focus will have to help you decipher what form that information is taking for you.

Be patient.
The first time I spoke Spanish on the phone to a Hispanic person, she

hung up. Guess we just weren't talking on the same wavelength. It may be like that with you and the stones. They may be talking and you may be talking and yet you haven't found the common language that you both clearly understand.

The first time you ask to listen to the stones, you may think you hear nothing (though I doubt they will hang up on you.). Be patient. They still may be trying to find exactly the ways to match their energy to yours. They may be learning about you and your unique way of listening and how to best support you. Just choose to be kind to yourself and wait patiently. The rewards are well worth the wait.

If you still don't hear anything, try doing the listening a little differently. After all, it can be pretty hard to hear **anything**, if your mind is ringing with TO DO lists the incoherent chatter. Meditate before you listen to the stones. Offer them your full attention. Most beings love to respond when they know we are truly offering our complete presence.

Or why not listen in a place that quiets your mind and inspires your spirit? Maybe you could listen to stones in nature, or when you're alone with them and a full, golden moon. Whatever you put into the experience, you will reap a hundredfold.

Trust what you hear.
Have you run out of the room screaming yet? Yes, it sounds crazy. Yet how can you build on any foundation of learning if you don't trust it? You have to allow it to prove itself and if you decide that it's not true even before you give it a chance, then that's what it will be— not true. Allow. Accept. Trust. These are the only building blocks from the impossible to the possible.

Speak with the stones.
Now that you are respectfully listening to the stones, realize it's a conversation. Even though you may not be consciously aware of it, your body already talks with the stones. They share their unique telepathy. That's why you immediately like some stones and not others. So make the conversation conscious.

What do you want to know? The world is opening wide! Ask if you understood what they told you. Ask if there's more they want to add to what they've said. Ask if there are stone energies that would particularly support you right now. Ask how you might connect with all other life respectfully, profoundly.

The conversation has begun.

If you have entered here with full willingness you can no longer pretend that you are "just reading" someone else's words.

The words and ways of the Stonebeings have offered themselves to your heart.

Open yourself, so that as you "read" these words,

you actually meet and know their energies at the same time.

Hear the stone voices.

They have been speaking to you all along.

How to Read/Listen to the Individual Stones

This book begins by featuring various, individual Stones because they offer gifts that humans specifically need right now. All of us upon the earth are evolving at lightning-speed. Integrating the vibrations of Stones allows us to evolve quickly AND compassionately because their energies come from the *whole matrix of life,* as opposed to human technologies which take apart Stones and Plants to create drugs with harmful side effects. Stones, instead, ever offer us holistic and natural vibrations that automatically support our most pressing needs. Being connected with Stones — listening to them — allows us to connect with the core of life and experience a union that ultimately heals and frees us.

In "Stones Alive! Volume 2," each of the Stones' unique energies is translated into the following categories (for the ease of human readers!):

Physical Description: Here you will find some of the basic geology of the Stone— how it is formed, along with some of its physical characteristics. If you allow yourself to feel the presence/presents of the Stones in your own body— instead of **just thinking** around/about the words (where the symbolism of the words are simply theory)— you will begin to truly listen to the Stones. You will start to know them and to understand what gifts they can specifically offer you. This part is not labeled, it simply speaks to you in the first person at the beginning of each Stone. We have consciously kept this section to a minimum because the geology of Stones has already been well written and written well and this information is readily and easily accessible through other books and the internet. As non-scientists, our intent in this book lies primarily elsewhere than in describing science. We utilize science and technology, we appreciate it, and then we act upon our own unique piece. Please join us here at the level of our intent as best you can and see if you can suspend judgment in this section to allow it to be a beginning that opens you to being more of a listener to what follows.

Elemental Earth Grid: Every part of the earth offers unique energies to the inhabitants of those areas, according to exactly what is needed. That means that the Stones (and the Plants and Animals) in one location will be imprinted with the vibrations of the Earth there and will possess qualities and gifts that they share in common with other Stones in the same area: Crystals in Arkansas will be somewhat related to each other, energetically, and simultaneously, they will differ from crystals from Nepal.

This is simply more of the earth's perfection and generosity. Arkansas crystals will uniquely serve the needs of the people, Plants and Animals in Arkansas, because they live in similar conditions and know how to complement the balance of life there. Wherever you live, consider the Plants, Animals and Stones there as family and your wisdom will understand the *"Elemental Earth Grid."* Also, see if you can then invite Crystals and Stones from other areas of the Earth Mother into your life in new respectful relationship, acknowledging their intricate and valuable holding of intent that is particular to their home region. Here we can learn more and more about respectful community and what that means in the big picture as planetary beings and what it means in our local picture as emotional participating individuals.

Physical, Emotional, Mental Integration: As you absorb the geology and the geography of the Stones, you also will be receiving their energetic gifts. Feel this for yourself. Your body certainly does, and like the Stonebeings, it even records the vastness of this in your cells. Your mind may not track all of this, but that doesn't matter. What matters is that your body stores unbelievable stimuli, each moment, and if you live in trust, your heart can access that in your own unique way.

The *Physical, Emotional, Mental Integration* will offer you possible clues to how you might be integrating that cellular wisdom with your day-to-day reality. Quietly, freely, observe the evidence of this in your body, your heart, your thoughts, your words, etc. It will slip out when you least expect it, if you allow it. And if you catch it, then you can use that cellular data to consciously, clearly form your life as you truly wish. This is the true gift of the Stonebeings in one sense. They are physically holding this space of cellular/data/truth unique to them. We can feel that if we choose and then we can choose to embody what we feel as a model to activate clear conscious movement in our life challenges.

Electrical Body Alignment: All around your body exists an invisible (to some) energy field. This field reflects your infinite consciousness. If you trust this, then you will access that awareness—maybe just a little bit, at first. Then as you get more practiced at allowing it you will align with more and more of your vast consciousness; you will change in every single part of your being. You will evolve. You will grow beyond your expectations.

Listening to the *Electrical Body Alignment* is the same as listening to your infinite consciousness, accepting it and merging that with your reality. The words you find here are clues that can take you to deeper parts of yourself in unknown ways, compassionately, yet powerfully. Here again, much like in the *Physical Descriptions*, the science of how you read the words may be less important than the PROCESS of HOW you choose to listen. As listeners, we are Heart-generated beings. We listen with our Hearts, and then our minds activate our Hearts' intent. This is a complete reorganization from listening with our minds and then being confused and struggling over why the physical manifestation of our desires does not seem to be compatible. See if you can read/listen to the words in this section from your Heart first, and then let that wisdom flow through what you think you know – and be ready and willing to change – all at the same time. This is the Spiral of Life in practice.

Affirmation of Support: Just listening to the Stones— to their *Physical Description*, their *Elemental Earth Grid* and the corresponding *Physical, Emotional, Mental Integration*— stretches you tremendously: You can *feel* yourself evolving. You're even **leaning** into it so that you can keep growing more life, more awareness and then even more possibilities, ad infinitum.

Yes! (Now you know why we are practiced at using that word.)

Evolving is a privilege and a joy and likely, a continual challenge, ever a larger responsibility. When we are challenged, all of our defenses rise to the surface to protect us— at least that's their obvious job. Yet when we are truly evolving (growing beyond expectation), defenses arise so that the vastness of who we are can view our protections, without judgment, to see if they truly still serve us. In all that growth, we will outgrow some of our defenses. Maybe our egos won't need to save us from getting our feelings hurt if that also "saves" us from stretching out into the universe and living in more compassion. Maybe some of our defenses will also need to evolve so that we can choose a focus <u>beyond just ourselves</u>.

The *Affirmation of Support* will help with this. When you say it and then repeat it throughout your day it will acknowledge your biggest potential. It will really support you, but you will have to turn your focus repeatedly towards it for it to become real in your life. It will affirm your electrical body and your vast cellular wisdom and it will merge it with all the rest of you in the kindest, most simple, efficient way possible. Whether you understand it or not, it will celebrate your growth, even when your old feelings and way of life struggle. The *Affirmation of Support* celebrates the you that you have always wanted to be, even as it is still forming. Yes!

Dreamtime Doorway: Here lies the magic. When you explore, you may fall off the edge of the Earth, or you may land upon a whole, new world!

If you take these words to heart, and then to action, you will be a true explorer, and no one can tell you where you are – only YOU can tell the rest of us when you return to share your adventure.

StoneStory: When we listen to the hearts of the Stonebeings, the *StoneStory* is what we hear. These words and ways of life come from their most profound core. Sometimes these precious words won't make sense to our minds (Remember we're growing beyond expectations, so how does "making sense" apply here?). You might read the *StoneStory* and think, '*These are just pretty sentences. It's too simple. If what they have to say is really that important, it would have to be more complicated.*' Maybe. Maybe not. Consider the brilliant, sudden epiphanies that you have had in your life. Weren't they **simple** once you realized them?

Most big truths are simple; it may only be our old, out-of-date defenses that pretend otherwise.

Listen to the *StoneStories*. Breathe with them. Maybe you will awaken to their simple truths and find that they helped you to change to be more true and simple, too.

Summary: When you just want a word or two about a Stone to take with you on your day, take this phrase. It's short enough that you can come back to it over and over again and keep coming up with new realizations and inspirations. It is also a cyclical reminder with the context of what is being presented on the page to take with you into the next relationship, the next turn of the page.

Personal Stories: It's one thing to hear truth from a Stonebeing. But to hear it from another *person*, well that is a horse of a different color. Sometimes we warm more quickly to big ideas when another person has gone before us and experienced them. When you listen to someone else like you tell you of how Stones touched them, it can be easier to imagine. And if you can imagine that, then what else in the whole world is suddenly possible for you?

Thank you to every person who wrote *Personal Stories* for this book and thank you to every person who reads them with an open Heart.

Yes.

Tools for Your Journey with this Book

Now that you're breathing and traveling through this book with your open, willing Heart, here are a few tools to help you to savor the full adventure:

- **Keep the big picture in mind**. Remember this book is a miracle. You're going to see unexpected things here and there could be things that you just can't explain yet. That's exactly what happens every time you *learn* something. Relax. Accept the uncomfortable, confusing part of meeting something new. That way you might just stick around long enough to learn something unimaginable! something incredible! something that would not have come to you any other way.

- **Trust yourself.** When you listen to the words here, take them into your own Heart and ask, "*What does this mean to/for me?*" Whatever answer you get will come from you. Okay, at first, those answers may be influenced by a lot of other things, but the more you trust yourself, the more your answers will clearly reflect your truth. And that's what you get to live with finally— your own truth.

- **Every single Stone is different.** Geologically, Stones possess certain traits in order to be classified as certain Stones. Yet, energetically, each and every Stone feels slightly different and perfectly unique (just like snowflakes). Life is like that. Every being on the Earth Mother shares so much in common and yet each of us turns out just a little bit differently, so that every one of us can contribute our own perfect gift to life, for the balance and the harmony of all.

- **Feel your own connection.** This book speaks of geology, geography, and energies. "*What does it really mean to you?*" These words exist here to catalyze your very own magic. If you let it, each word (and each Stone) will invite you to learn and then it will urge you to feel what that knowledge could add to your life. Knowledge for knowledge's sake is grand, but knowledge that matures gracefully into wisdom— well, that is something that's always worth the risks and the foolishness in the journey. Wisdom is borne of your own connection to everything/anything, and that's a companion that will keep you very kind company forever.

One more word ...

Someone once asked Einstein how many feet are in a mile. He responded that he did not know. He went on to say that he could look that information up in a second anywhere; why would he want to clutter his mind with this type of readily available information when he could be using his mind instead to create.

We are not scientists. We are **Listeners**. As such our energy/time/clarity investments are best spent listening. We live in such a changed, dramatic world these days where information is even more readily available than it was in Einstein's time. There are also so many talented beautiful humans out there who choose to do science with joy and passion. This information is easily and readily accessible in other books and through the internet. If you don't find what you need in our simple listener descriptions, please access the information you want through these other easily available sources.

Our stone descriptions are heartfelt, emotional, electrical/magnetic connections/links with the Stones and are our outreach, in the ways that the Stones themselves have asked to be represented. If you find seeming discrepancies here between what you consider hard science and what you are reading, we ask you to bridge these worlds with compassion and pause. See if you must choose hard science or the seeming "reality" of the proven world to make something else disappear, be "wrong", or just to deny it.

Most humans go into their mental bodies to determine their reality. That reality then can only be based on previous knowledge. This is not bad; it is just a choice and can create only a certain kind of reality – an important process **but not necessarily whole.** We choose as **Listeners** to utilize our emotional bodies as the core receivers of information and we choose to stay in them to identify and process our reality through our Hearts and then we use our mental body to actuate what our hearts have made real.

What the Stones are asking for here is to be treated as individuals. Yes, they seem to belong to families of origin and have genetic histories but they are so much more. So many of them (just like we humans) have veered off into unknown directions to co-create the enlivened world that we are now inhabiting. When we relate to them as co-creators we also enliven our reality as we are respecting theirs.

In these stone descriptions we are inviting you to create your relationship with the Stones from your own empowerment through your emotional body (which will honor and respect the Stones' own lifeforce the clearest, potentially) first, so that when you are asking what this Stone is about the reality of the response you get will be Heart and Listening generated. *Then* utilize the science and the knowledge. Trust in what you hear in your heart first. Trust in your trust. Then act. Can you see/feel what a different process/practice of life this is? Can you see how it relates to respect and compassion and engenders

Personal Story

One year at the Tucson Gem and Mineral Show, someone approached me (more like accosted me, actually) and asked me about a certain stone that was included in the first Stones Alive! Book, saying that it was NEVER found in one of the colors listed — that it could only be found the world over in one particular color that he then stated. I responded to his direct query affirmatively and looked at him questioningly. He proceeded to berate me for placing misinformation in the book and continued to tell me some of the reasons why he thought I had performed a "wrong" deed. I listened to him for a bit and then gently reminded him that maybe the information in the book was "correct" and he was "correct" and that maybe MORE things were possible. He was even more adamant then that he was "right" and the book was wrong. I thanked him and excused myself and moved on.

What I found so interesting about this encounter was that this man picked a stone to accost me about that was rather common

(con't on next page)

peace and harmonious relationship? Stones hold this space and model it for us, but it is up to us to step into the invitation.

Stones that come to us, as listeners, may not and quite often do not fit into regular categories and succinct boxes. They tend to be marriages of elements that have risen up out of the Earth Mother with a pur- pose– to be in relationship with humans and other life forms. If you find oddities in our descriptions it may well be because we are dealing with a specific stone energy from a specific part of the Earth Mother that needs to express in a certain way. It is our responsibility to listen to the Stone and respect its unique life force energy and then, having lived with that, pass it on to you. We don't fit the mold and we cer- tainly don't blend in with the "normal" humans (whatever that is) and so we don't have expectations of the Stones that come to us either and we do our best to not generalize and categorize them into boxes that they have already grown beyond.

The stone descriptions are like the rest of this humble book. They are an invitation to something that may be MORE. Is that not why we so passionately invite them into our lives and keep them with and around us so intentionally? As with all MORES in our world, we are the ones that have to choose to be responsible for going to the MORE and asking what is what, what is "real" and then our further respon- sibility is to trust that what we have heard or read is our truth, or not. We then go on to live/practice in our daily lives what we have trusted. In our lives, the practice of trust is not really in what we appear to place our trust in: We trust in our trust. Then the trust is our practice, not the mirror that brought it to the surface in the first place.

So trust, if you will, if you choose, in the information you find here and do with it what you will. Any trust you apply will only breed more trust and compassion and eventually even understanding of non- human life forms. You will become the living breathing embodiment of that trust as it is modeled for you from the Stonebeings. If you need other types of information, again we encourage you to access the many other great sources out there.

Finally, we want to let you know that we have a personal relationship with each of these Stones described within this book. They are in- cluded here (among other reasons) because we have lived with them and are living with them. They are a part of our daily lives, waking,

and could easily be found in sci- entific geological (and metaphysical) journals that all listed multiple colors including the one he listed and all the ones I had listed in Stones Alive!. (Not to mention that I had at home a whole bag of this stone in the color he said never appears.) I felt this encounter was of course as much for me as it was for him. I felt called to hold the space of open-heartedness and listen- ing with him. I remember feeling grateful that he had at least read some of Stones Alive! and had given it enough attention to re- member details and to pursue them. In our world (Marilyn & me) of freedom and respect it seemed apparent that he had ingested the feelings of the book to the limit that he was capable of and then, when overfilled, needed to make a choice. Would his life/reality be contained by what he thought was knowledge or could he move with the Stones beyond the known into more possibilities? Well, his choice seemed clear. His path appeared to be to do whatever he could to make the Stones Alive! reality unreal so he could maintain his status quo. It was important for

(con't on next page)

13

me to honor his reality, not attach to it, and move on. It is also very interesting to me that the stone in question is a stone that reminds us: "the loving guidance of Spirit gently whispering in your heart, every moment. Listen, it is with you now." It seems that stone was whispering in both our ears during that encounter so we each could continue to choose how we support ourselves in the face of a mystery. That stones' Affirmation of Support in Stones Alive! is "I am part of everything on the earth and that is how I fully honor myself." For us, the whole point of letting the stones tell their own stories in this requested book, is to allow for the unknown, for the mysterious possibilities, and for all the new relationships that continue to occur. For me, how I respond to my relationships (like this man's encounter) determines how I continue to form my cellular structure and how respectfully I maintain my walk on the Earth Mother. Thank you to this particular stone (and this particular man) for the opportunity, the lesson and the freedom.

~Tohmas T.

dreaming and walking. They are around us in every thing we do. We recognize them. Not from a place of linear knowledge per se, but mostly, and firstly for us, from a spiral of interaction that is respectful and ever growing and changing. This is why, for instance, you will find Green Kyanite here in this book instead of a listing for Kyanite which is very general and then may go into the color as an aside. This Green Kyanite listed here is the specific stone of the Kyanite family that has asked to come and give specific information from its respective uniqueness (that also does not deny its family).

Please remember, these descriptions are not here to "make" us into authorities; they are here as offerings of our personal experience with other life forms as individuals who may or may not happen to have histories. The more you may choose to delve into the expressions in this book, accepting their invitations, the more you may find yourself receiving the information that is between the words. That truly is where we reside – in the unknown between the words. We bless you on your journey. We are here. Who knows what will happen next!

A Word about the Pictures that are Not in this Book

When we originally put this book together, we felt it and the Stonebeings calling out to have color pictures included. We put up a fair amount of resistance to this, in a sense, at the same time agreeing to include them. However, as time/timelessness passed, it became more and more apparent that there was another "reasoning" behind the request. This seems to be the path of respectful listening as we experience it. First we have to invest – agree – to an original energy request. Then our deeper responsibility based on that original agreement is to be open to evolving change. This requires more of our open hearts — more trust, more courage on our parts. So goes life. It is never in the realm of right or wrong. We know, and have been shown continually by the Stonebeings, that our choices are never meant to be static and unchanging. They are always an open invitation to the more that we are calling to us.

So the "more" and the "reasoning" that we acknowledge we are being called to participate in as relationship with the Stonebeings and with you the reader, is to continue to invite you in ever deeper to the adventure of personal empowerment through recognizing and accepting your own awareness of your own truth in the clear naming of the Stonebeings in your life and in your encounters.

How to do this?

That is the question. In our lives, we have never, ever, identified a stone by matching it to a picture in a book. Every stone we have ever had come our way that we wanted to identify, never looked like the picture in the book. So we decided to leave pictures out of this book, as its whole Being is pointed towards listening and clarity based on your own declarations and affirmations of how you ingest energy as reality. Sure, it is helpful guidance to read and observe what has already been written and recorded, but we suggest that you do what you can to allow that information to flow from your already-affirmed-interior-reality, so that you can then use it as an acknowledgement of what you already know. You will need to trust. Not trust in us or any other acknowledged or unacknowledged "authority" but rather you will be trusting in trust and that can only reside within YOU, ultimately.

This book is a direct invitation to listening to the Stonebeings for yourself. The Stonebeings are the recorders and holders of all manifestation of life on this Earth Mother. If you can listen to them, you can listen to any form of life. This is about you stepping into your relationships with empowerment (instead of co-dependency, or giving away of any of your lifeforce) respectfully in order to graciously evolve right along with all the other life forms on this planet who do not have fear and separation as their focus. The Stonebeings are already, and always, holding the space of wholeness from their own unique individual aspects, and their hearts are open to us to join in that space no matter the time or the circumstance. And they never forget that holding of space regardless of how often the human may. So they are there when we need them. They are our support system. Jeffrey Maoussaieff Masson, in "Slipping into Paradise," (referring to the Maori tribe of New Zealand) writes, *"to have any kind of spiritual connection (i.e., to recognize a spirit in a rock, tree, plant, or animal) with your environment, as the Maori clearly did early on, is the beginning of ecological wisdom."* For the Stonebeings to continue to be our support system and our guides we need to choose continually to recognize their spirits — and to recognize them as they choose to be recognized, not as how we, as humans, would label them for our convenience.

So we ask you to identify the Stonebeings first through your own innate language of intuition and feelings. You can always go to any of the fine books out there that include pictures and other information if you so choose (and why not, we certainly do). This book's clear intent is to empower us all as respectful listeners. The pictures come later if need be, and if needed, you will find them. We bless us all in this adventure and hope that you find inspiration and encouragement in the following pages and in the personal stories of others like yourselves who have the trust and courage to base their lives upon their intuitions and inner wisdoms, first.

Jean Houston, in her book "Mystical Dogs," writes so profoundly that *"animals... require no priest, no interpreter, to put them back in touch with their power, their freedom, their strength, fleetness, beauty, endurance and capacities."* We would invite you to replace the word animal here with the word Stonebeings. We invite you, as she did in her book with animals, to allow the Stonebeings to be your guides, your family, your confidants *"...because they remember the original instructions given them by an ancient universe."*

You can trust in your relationship with the Stonebeings. You can trust in yourself in your relationship with the Stonebeings. If you discover seeming discrepancies in the blending of informations, try not to disavow your own awarenesses. Let the seeming discrepancies remain simply experience that can lead you down another path. Stay open. Remember gratitude. See if you can let your reality continue to be created through your heart first, not your mind or past knowledge.

Listen.

Totem Stories from Hawkseye Velvet Tourmaline

Isn't it glorious?

Isn't it amazing that we meet across time, space,
past logic
to know each other
seemingly stone
seemingly human
heart to heart
in words from the same.

Do you realize wonder when it is staring you in the soul?

Of course you do.

Your body recognizes all of this
it records each and every miracle faithfully
respectfully
while your mind ignores it
ignores it because it is too Large…too Special…too Much
because it specializes in comparison.
If the splendidness of our speaking together is too enormous
then it reasons that you must be too
small.

I compare nothing.
I accept everything.
I know nothing.

I am everything.

That is why I recognize you.

We are the same breath of lifespirit blown from star to star
shared amongst different bodies
for the sheer rainbowonder of it.

Wonder.

We speak together because we meet here in wonder.
Nothing will keep us apart now
not even your denial
not even total disbelief.
Your body still faithfully records it,
every moment of our incredible conversation and perfect realizations.
Even if you do not trust any of this miracle now,
one day
in a seamless reality
your wonder will open the recording of this meeting and
smile.
It will laugh, saying
"I remember that. I remember that I didn't believe a word of it. It was
all too crazy. Yeah, I didn't believe that all life came from the same
love— that I could be the same as anything else on the earth and still be
me, too. I was too scared to trust any of it and I almost missed the awe of
it all.........."

How do I know this?

I see across your boxes of times and I open them all at once!
Like the simultaneous, sweet presents they are
they tell me everything
anything
right now.

You will remember the power- in- everything in a single moment.
That could never be kept from you too long.........
And when you absorb it all

I will be there stretching you across stars
to remember more and more
and MORE.
The miracles will land upon us
until we must talk with every other life form
smiling.

I am the spirit that lives in Hawkseye Velvet Tourmaline.

I am the totem Stonebeing, guide, of this bookmiracle.

My heart is here traveling with yours, endlessly remembering.

I am honored to recognize you.

Our
   conversation
      is
       forever...............

Stones A-3

Actinolite

I am Ca2(Mg, Fe)5Si8O22(OH)2, Calcium Magnesium Iron Silicate Hydroxide, with a hardness of 5 and 1/2 - 6, a specific gravity of 2.9 - 3.3 and I can be found in Germany/Austria/Switzerland/Italy, USSR, USA, New Zealand, Canada and China. My color is usually green, gray or white to colorless although I am usually green. When you hold me you may feel a tough directness and a calling to speak of things of which you may be afraid.

Elemental Earth Grid:
Europe: I emphasize directness.
USSR: I emphasize the depth of explorations.
USA: I emphasize the integration of head and heart.
New Zealand: I emphasize the glory of adventure!
Canada: I emphasize calm...peace...
China: I emphasize regeneration.

Physical, Emotional, Mental Integration: Your heart links you to your spirit. When it's not easy to hear your heart, I make a pathway of quiet that you can travel to it. I remind you of simplicity during stress, focus during distraction, and strength during dis-ease.

Electrical Body Alignment: I can help you find your awareness.

Affirmation of Support: *"I know the truth and I act upon it."*

Dreamtime Doorway: I reveal the truth of union, even when your challenges and your learning insist upon separation.

Stone Story:

The world opens its banquet to you.

Feast upon forest

skies

& roses unfurling.

While you feed your soul

the earth and all her beings will know you

they will understand you beyond the reach of secrets

~they will accept you.

They will nod at your scars

and your fears.

They will not turn away their eyes.

Look upon their acceptance and nod.

Your allowability fuels all of life.

Summary: Actinolite helps you to bring your awareness and acceptance to every choice and moment.

Allanite

I am (Ca, Ce, La, Y)2(Al, Fe)3(SiO4)3(OH), Calcium Cerium Lanthanum Yttrium Aluminum Iron Silicate Hydroxide. I am one of the minerals where you can most commonly find Rare Earth Elements. I have also been called Orthite. My hardness is 6 to 6.5 and my specific gravity is 3.1 to 4.2. I tend to attract Elements that other minerals do not want or are throwing off. I can also be slightly radioactive when I contain a higher percentage of the Rare Earth Element, Thorium. I am usually black to brown and can be found in Europe, USSR, USA, Canada and Australia. (We, Twintreess, have a specific form of Allanite found with the Desert Snow Quartz.)

Elemental Earth Grid:
Europe: I emphasize integration.
USSR: I emphasize earthiness.
USA: I emphasize presence.
Canada: I emphasize the expansiveness of anything, everything.
Australia: I emphasize supporting uniqueness.

Physical, Emotional, Mental Integration: I am with you. When you speak to me, I gently insist that you be in your body and completely present. How else will you receive all the wisdom that is awaiting you each moment?

I firm your body. I point out all the resources you have. You **know** your strengths when you are with me, and all the while, I'm urging all the unloved emotions within you to come out into safety and freedom forever.

Electrical Body Alignment: I unite you with your own healing powers.

Affirmation of Support: *"I am well and I am whole."*

Dreamtime Doorway: Even in separation, you are union.

Stone Story:

>   *Peace.*

>   *This moment decorates us in peace.*

Every moment showers us with it and if we are

quiet

whole,

we know it.

We know it forever

and we simply get reminded

a

minute

at

a

time.

You overflow with so much

that you cannot see it all...............

You shower the world with your unique power and special voice

while it smoothes you over with calm.

It gentles you

so that all that you are can come out

and play in the sunshine

even every unwelcome emotion.

You are free.

I am the witness to your completeness.

Summary: Allantine grounds us and reminds us to integrate all parts of our being.

Amblygonite

I am (Li, Na)AlPO4(F, OH), Lithium Sodium Aluminum Phosphate Fluoride Hydroxide with a Hardness of 5.5 - 6; a Specific Gravity of 3.05 and my color ranges from colorless, to white or pale yellow, green, blue, beige, gray or pink (The ones we continually have in our life are a nice pale but strong yellow from Brazil.) My name comes from Greek words that translate to "blunt angles" which is a reference to my unusal ability to cleave in 4 directions. Some of the places I am found are Brazil, France, Germany, Sweden, Burma, Northwest Territories, Canada and in the United States I have been found in California, Maine, New Mexico, Arizona and the Black Hills in South Dakota. When you hold me in your hand or put me close to your body or in your energy field you may notice an inner calm, a soothing, but one with an extra tingle that is not complacent. I can be insistent about the co-creation of inner calm, not based on learned programming that results in comfort, but based on the freedom that comes with release and integration.

Elemental Earth Grid:
South America: I emphasize emotions.
Europe: I emphasize logic.
Sweden: I emphasize freedom.
Burma: I emphasize alignment.
Canada: I emphasize intuition.
USA: I emphasize the unpredictable nature of my gifts.

Physical, Emotional, Mental Integration: I invite you to this moment. Just this one. Right now. If you join me there, you will find all the support that you have ever needed and more than you can imagine. It will help you to straighten up and live in your body, to be clear in your choices, and to be full in your power.

Electrical Body Alignment: I help you to connect with the perfect you.

Affirmation of Support: *"I imagine who I would like to be and that is who I am."*

Dreamtime Doorway: Yes, you simply know more than you can think.

Stone Story:

Sit down beside me.

I know you.

You know me too, though maybe you will say you don't quite remember.

I understand, but we know each other.

How could it be any other way?

We are earthbeings together and there is nothing about us that is unconnected.

I know everything about you.

I see how you surround yourself with endless thoughts, explanations, apologies, hopes.

I hear them all. I hear them more than you do.

I see how you glow with divinity— your love shines like me –

an infinite crystal.

What else is there to know about you?

Everything and no-thing.

Do you wonder how I know this?

If I had an answer to that, it would be, "How could I NOT know this?

I am a being of the Earthstar. I breathe the air. I warm in the sun.

I feel the mountains tremble with change."

*The answer I have for you is, "**How do you know these things?**"*

Summary: Amblygonite insists that we be our true selves.

Amethyst Cathedrals

I am SiO2, a variety of Quartz, in various hues of purple. My name comes from a Greek word that means, "not drunken," possibly connected, for them, to a belief that I will ward off the effects of alcohol. I have a hardness of 7 and am found in many, many locales around the world, however most of the Cathedrals so prevalently exposed are from Brazil. We are drawn to each other through beauty, royalty and the distinct elemental influences of my birthplaces and quite possibly as a way to dissipate the huge violent influence that alcohol has on our society and on our personal relationships. (Look to the Amethyst section of **"Families"** to realize more information about me as I appear in different forms, places and relationships.)

Elemental Earth Grid:
Africa: I emphasize bringing the ethers to the earth.
Brazil: I emphasize all the senses.
Bolivia: I emphasize the quiet link to spirit.
Mexico: I emphasize appreciating beauty.
Nevada: I emphasize focus.
New Mexico: I emphasize humbleness.

Physical, Emotional, Mental Integration: If you touch me on the outside, you will feel my rough protection. If you touch me on the inside, you will know my smooth beauty. If you let me touch you, you will know that your defenses are not all that you are.

Electrical Body Alignment: I will help you to remember the creativity of the child-you.

Affirmation of Support: *"Inside of me is limitless magic!"*

Dreamtime Doorway: Many meetings with spirit open before you. How will you choose the one that most honors you?

Stone Story:

Welcome. To find me you must come inside the earth. To talk to me, you must come deep inside of me. To grow all that I am, I protect myself from distractions. I take in all the fires, the rivers and the

---

Personal Story

Can you see?

Can you see

my cave of mysterious beauty

which fulfills dreams…

Come,

come and get in touch with your spirituality…

Don't be afraid.

Peace, strength and stability

will help you maintain the state of meditation.

~Charlotte L.

winds of the earth to sculpt a garden of unbelievable crystal flowers. No one can see inside of my shell, but I know what I am forming. No matter what it looks like from the outside, I am an artist. I shape points of regal purple with rainbows inside. To know what I know, all you have to do is to open me up and look at me in the possibilities of the sun's bright light.

This is why I know who you are. I see that you are rough on the outside and I feel that you are polished and colorful on the inside. Just like me, you take everything that happens around you and you make your own art with it. Your art is inside of you where it is safe from distractions and harm. I understand. We are fine artists, you and me. We appreciate inner colors that are always growing.

If you understand this, too, then come into the earth. Visit me in the peaceful dark where we can grow purple that the world cannot yet imagine.

Summary: Amethyst Cathedrals receive the pressures inside the earth to carve elegant purple cathedrals that revere the perfection of all things.

Anatase

I am TiO2, Titanium Oxide, and have the same chemistry as Rutile and Brookite. At a very high temperature, I will again become Rutile. I can be brown to black as well as yellow and blue. I can often be found with quartz. My hardness is 5.5 to 6 and my specific gravity is 3.8 to 3.9. I can be found in Germany/Austria/Switzerland, USSR, USA, and Brazil. When you hold me, feel my strength and power, compassionately.

Elemental Earth Grid:
Europe: I emphasize receptivity.
USSR: I emphasize looking at things from all angles.
USA: I emphasize wonder.
Brazil: I emphasize fierceness.

Physical, Emotional, Mental Integration: If you know what you want, I fill you with such resolve that you cannot help but attract it. I align your body with integrating it and I help your heart to let go of any contradictory beliefs.

Electrical Body Alignment: I align you with your ability to create your choices.

Affirmation of Support: *"I bring my fortune to me."*

Dreamtime Doorway: Look for shamans and beings of magic for they come to all, no matter what you might believe.....

Stone Story:

> *Nurturing.*
>
> *You recognize it in gentle strokes and smiles.*
>
> *I give nurturing*
>
> *that comes on*
>
> *powerfully*
>
> *for its care grows your strength*
>
> *in the most amazing challenges and possibilities.*
>
>
> *I nurture the parts of you*
>
> *you may not even know yet—*
>
> *the incredible powers that arise*
>
> *only when fully tested.*
>
>
> *Bring your determination*
>
> *and you will reward it a thousandfold.*

Summary: Anatase presents us with unbending intent.

Andalusite

I am AL2(OlSiO4), Aluminum Silicate. I have a hardness of 7.5 and a specific gravity of 3.1 to 3.2. My color can vary widely from grey, yellow, brown, red, green to occasionally colorless. I am a polymorph with Kyanite and Sillimanite and my Chiastolite form is less hard (5.5) and contains inclusions in the form of an "X". I can be found in Germany/Austria/France/Italy, USA, Brazil, China and Andalusia, Spain.

Elemental Earth Grid:
Germany: I emphasize meditation.
Austria: I emphasize creativity.
France: I emphasize YES!
Italy: I emphasize warmth.
USA: I emphasize innocence.
Brazil: I emphasize peace-within-wonder.
China: I emphasize balance.
Spain: I emphasize full-out excitement!

Physical, Emotional, Mental Integration: Yes. Delight is all around us and when we speak it enters our hearts. All is warm. The ease that we have dreamed of is now US!

Electrical Body Alignment: When you join hands with me, you join hands with the hidden, secret pleasures stored in your heart, that your mind had all but forgotten...

Affirmation of Support: "I AM joy!"

Dreamtime Doorway: Watch for life. It will not make you find it. It will ask you to run with it, instead of away from it.

Stone Story:

An unexpected waterfall

a child staring at you with open curiosity and a full-body-grin!

a deliciously colored balloon

one tree tall— taller than all the rest— stretching a hole in the sky

just for dreams to dance in.

All these moments have visited you.

They leave an almost wistful mark—

the opposite of a scar—

they leave you the forever-hint

of pleasure

living within you

just beneath the surface.

It waits timelessly

though you seem to ignore it

or pretend to have bigger and better things to do

than

watch and dance the parade of wonders.

Summary: Andalusite never forgets the simple, constant pleasures.

Apatite

I am $Ca_5(PO_4)_3(OH,F,Cl)$, Calcium (Fluoro, Chloro, Hydroxyl) Phosphate. My name comes from a Greek word meaning to "deccive" and I am actually three different minerals: fluorine, chlorine or the hydroxyl group. I am also the mineral that makes up the teeth in all vertebrates. I have a hardness of 5 and an average specific gravity. I can be yellow, blue, green, brown, reddish brown, purple and colorless. I can be found in Western Europe, USSR, Mexico, USA and Ontario/Canada. You will feel differently depending on which color and locality of me that you pick up. What may be the constant is the movement of your breath to your heart with compassion. Alertness is key here.

Elemental Earth Grid:
Western Europe: I emphasize pure relaxation.

USSR: I emphasize potential.
Mexico: I emphasize agreement.
USA: I emphasize joining joy.
Ontario, Canada: I emphasize releasing suspicion.

Physical, Emotional, Mental Integration: Stop. Listen. All around you wonder is happening. Listen with my heart and you might find wonder everywhere, even within you.

Electrical Body Alignment: I link you to the eternal-child-you.

Affirmation of Support: *"My heart overflows with awe."*

Dreamtime Doorway: Where are you? Where can you be found? If you do not know, how can joy find you?

Stone Story:

To you I am an ancient one.

In me and all around me, no time exists.

There is no measurement equal

to the glory of

what is.

Right now.

Everything, everyone, is right now

except the masks of fear.

I am here right now.

Where else would I be?

How else would you find me?

I am ever right here

right now

with you

Smiling.

Summary: Apatite fills us with wonder so that we might integrate true joy.

Astrophyllite

I am Potassium Iron Titanium Silicate Hydroxide, $(K,Na)3(Fe,Mn)7Ti2(SiO3)8(O,OH)7$, with a hardness of 3 and a specific gravity of 3.3-3.4. My color is usually brownish yellow, golden yellow and sometimes even greenish brown. I can be found in Norway, Quebec/Canada, Colorado/USA, and the USSR. My presence can be obvious, yet my softness can deceive you. If you pick me up you may feel parts of you related to softness that you don't want to feel, so what you may really think you are feeling is confused. Ask yourself if you want to think about your feelings, or *feel* them? This well may be where the treasure lies.

Elemental Earth Grid:
Norway: I emphasize solitude.
Quebec, Canada: I emphasize calm.
Colorado, USA: I emphasize expansion.
USSR: I emphasize the wonder of every possibility.

Physical, Emotional, Mental Integration: I enter softly because you have so many, many defenses. If you knew that I was here to look truthfully at everything you are and everything you say, think, and do, and then respond, "You are a treasure," you would run away. You would run away so that you could pretend that you didn't hear and therefore you don't have to face this. If you stay here with me, I will point out every time you escape every abundance.

Electrical Body Alignment: I support you finding your own spiral of abundance.

Affirmation of Support: *"Every time I face myself, I find an unlimited universe."*

Dreamtime Doorway: I wonder if treasure will find you today. I wonder if you are looking for it, or if it will be looking for you.........

Stone Story:

> *Once upon a time*
>
> *(I know you like to begin that way)*
>
> *I lived deep in the earth.*
>
> *Everything around me stretched and grew.*
>
> *I gathered minerals to my heart*
>
> *and I grew, too, in whatever directions allowed me.*
>
> *Can you see me?*
>
> *I was very strong.*
>
> *I helped hold up the earth.*
>
> *Then people came and pulled me out of my home.*
>
> *I didn't know how the earth would stand up straight without me.*
>
> *The people looked closely at me and they smiled,*
>
> *"It's beautiful."*
>
> *I remembered that I could be strong and supportive wherever I was.*
>
> *This is one page of a story.*
>
> *If you hear it from someone else, you might truly listen to it—*
>
> *you really can see how rich and powerful my life is.*
>
> *Yet the story won't have any meaning*
>
> *unless you put yourself in it*
>
> *and let your heart travel it one beautiful step at a time.*

Summary: Astrophyllite points the way to the source of our own abundance.

Barite

I am BaSO4, Barium Sulfate. I am very common and therefore easily confused by not looking and feeling clearly. I am commonly colorless or white but can be blue, green, yellow or red, to black. I have a hardness of 3 to 3.5 and a specific gravity of 4.48. I can be found notably in the USA, Germany and England, as well as the USSR, Australia and Africa. I like to form bladed or tabular crystals. When you touch me you may go right past who I am to who knows where. Stop. Come back. Consider me.

Elemental Earth Grid:
USA: I emphasize profound truth and freedom.
Germany: I emphasize sheer clarity.
England: I emphasize the grace of challenges.
USSR: I emphasize focusing upon priorities.
Australia: I emphasize my sacred geometries.
Africa: I emphasize the pause for awareness.

Physical, Emotional, Mental Integration: My gifts are many, yet you may not be aware of me, almost all of the time. I communicate more with your body, than with your mind. Quietly, I remind you of the needs you have to fulfill and remind you that you have all the responsibilities and resources necessary for them. If you pretend to have forgotten this, I hint at where you can find whatever you need.

Electrical Body Alignment: I invite you to the core of all moments and things.

Affirmation of Support: *"I practice responsibility for my life."*

Dreamtime Doorway: You have the gift of speech and unique consciousness. Where does it travel you? Choose. Know. Act.

Stone Story:

I am honored to be here

to speak and listen and feel with you.

So often what I talk about with you

is not always immediately welcomed.

It's not that you don't want to know about your unfulfilled wishes—

you do—

but you often don't want to talk about them

unless you already know how you will satisfy them.

If you are judging yourself

(and I feel parts of you doing this already

even though your mind seems not to know what I will say next)

then you may be indulging your fears

and seeing yourself as pitiful and powerless—

unable to satisfy even one dream.

Then you do not want to talk about your needs.

All you feel around them is pain

the pain of inadequacy that you are pretending.

Do you see what I am showing you?

The mirror is clear (if unappreciated at times).

Look at all your desires and dreams

and if they are not yet walking in the world,

then do not let fear paralyze you—

and keep you from seeing why and from making your dreams truth.

There is no dream

for which you do not have the power

and the creativity.

It is so.

If you hear me now

then you have silenced your judgments.

Summary: Barite calls forth the deepest truths.

Calcite with Realgar

I am a marriage of mostly Calcite, with Realgar deeply embedded in my heart. (Look to the individual descriptions of Calcite and Realgar in "Stones Alive!" for more information about each.) I come from China. I am mostly light green, grayish to yellow and my Realgar heart is, of course, deep red. When you pick me up you will probably be attracted to me or repulsed by me, just like your relationship with certain parts of yourself. See if you can hold me, and at the same time, allow your breath to flow completely through your body opening and activating your root chakra. Can you go beyond what you like and don't like to really see me as I am?

Elemental Earth Grid:
China: I emphasize whatever you choose.

Physical, Emotional, Mental Integration: Certain combinations of stones and minerals are rare — I am one of these. When you bring your open heart to me, I smile. I show you the way to find the most rare, unusual parts of **you**. You are a unique combination. Together we can listen to you and find those special places within that want to come out now and be heard and enjoyed for their unique talents.

Electrical Body Alignment: I support you aligning with strength, courage and vitality that you never knew existed.......and the immediate ways to use them.

Affirmation of Support: *"I am a unique, perfect expression of life."*

Dreamtime Doorway: There is mystery here that only you can explain.

Stone Story:

I am so glad, so honored to be listened to, by you, here. Most of the other stones who have asked to be a part of this book are more easily found. I know that I am quite unusual and perhaps many of you will never see or touch my Stonebody.

That is why I am here.

I am here so that you can *feel* me. Stretch your heart out to mine; it already awaits you freely and so openly! *You do not need to see me to know the wonders of the gifts that I give to life and to you.* That is the wisdom I leave with you. If you absorb that with your unlimitedness, then you will remember all of us on the earth are connected, and connected beyond any calculation, thought or maybe even imagining. Though you may not always believe that we can talk, it does not matter. Our hearts are joined. We know each other at a core where you do not always visit life. Go there again. I live there and I offer you the gifts of my being always.

Feel how we are joined. Talk with me and show the doubts in you what is true.

Q: How can we integrate your gifts to us right now?

I live in acceptance of all things. Do you? When you listen to me, listen to all the rest of you, for you have many, many facets. Talk with them all. What do you believe in every part of you? Invite even the most unusual part of yourself to speak to your heart, to tell its story no matter what. Then breathe acceptance. You'll be breathing in my smile as well.

Q: What will happen when we listen to all parts of ourselves?

The parts of you that have not been accepted fully are the ones who will need to talk the most. They may be afraid at first. Please encourage them. Truly be the acceptance that you know is possible. Then the selves that have been called weaknesses and faults will come forth. They will tell you their stories and every one of them holds unexpected magic that all of you can use to love more, to be more whole right now. Listen. See for yourself.

Summary: Calcite with Realgar insists upon connection.

That was exactly the feeling that had come over while I was lifting stones, and standing right next to the Calcite with Realgar at the same time.

I put a big one on my desk and it still sits there now.

~from Marilyn T.

Carrolite

I am Cu(Co,Ni)2S4, Copper Cobalt Nickel Sulfide. I am a gray metallic mineral, recently found in Africa, that froms crystals in hydrothermal veins. I have a hardness of 4.5 to 5.5 and am named after my place of discovery in Carroll County, Maryland, USA. I am most often found now in Africa. When you pick me up you will feel the need to be clear of your intent. If you are not, keep holding me until you can find that clarity in your body.

Elemental Earth Grid:
Maryland, USA: I emphasize timeless wisdom.
Africa: I emphasize interconnectedness.

Physical, Emotional, Mental Integration: Hold me; I love being touched and I share that love with your hands. However I can help you with what I am, I offer it. I show a different face to every being. That is my gift and my honor.

Electrical Body Alignment: I will point you to whatever support will touch you and affirm your whole lifeforce.

Affirmation of Support: *"I am here to give and receive endless, perfect gifts."*

Dreamtime Doorway: Will you accept the support that will set you free?

Stone Story:

Breathe.

Breathe while every part of your body awakens
and turns to your heart and bows sweetly.

Stretch your possibilities.
Watch them root farther into the earth than you can see.

Toss your dreams into the skies;

listen as they land upon the fires of stars

and spark.

Breathe.

You possess sparks of dreams and roots of possibilities

within you each moment

though I know you sometimes guard them jealously

thinking that once you set them free

you may never have another possibility or dream again.

How could you live like that?

*This is exactly how to **live**.*

Set everything within you free.

When you wear your invisibility

Every color freely comes to you.

Summary: Carrolite offers unconditional support.

Cassiterite

I am SnO2, Tin Oxide, with a high luster and a propensity for twinning like my cousin, Rutile. I have a hardness of 6-7 and a specific gravity of 6.6-7-- very heavy. This may be the first thing you notice about me when you pick me up: my weight in your hand. My color is usually blackish to brownish, reddish brown or yellowish. I have been an important source of Tin for decades. Here, I would ask you to go beyond that sourcing to the strength and purpose inherent in the feel of my weight in your hand. I can be found in Czechoslovakia, England, Africa, Indonesia, Bolivia, Alaska. My forms in Bolivia and Cornwall, England are mysterious and not fully understood.

Elemental Earth Grid:
Czechoslovakia: I emphasize specific concentration.
England: I emphasize multi-dimensionality.
Africa: I emphasize the sound within me.
Indonesia: I emphasize the movement within my energy.
Bolivia: I emphasize everything.
Alaska: I emphasize my pristine beauty.

Physical, Emotional, Mental Integration: Peace I offer you. When you allow yourself to fully receive it, you will recognize the peace that you already are. Then you will find all the other parts of your body and being that support and reflect peace and that will give you Life.

Electrical Body Alignment: I align you with the center stillness.

Affirmation of Support: *"I AM peace."*

Dreamtime Doorway: You speak of the life that you so desperately want. You complain, you exalt, you wonder so much I do not know what you intend. **Do you?**

Stone Story:

I am so honored to speak with you. Sit beside me.

When you are next to me, you feel your body loosen,

your mind soften, and your heart soar!

I am a being of peace.

I know this. I accept this. It simply is.

Unlike you, I do not ever forget this.

I focus every cell upon peace

until each one lights up and they radiate

Calm

Love

endlessly.

They know no other way. They need nothing else.

Listen to me now.

You are a being of peace also. It's true you travel a different journey with it,

yet that does not make your path or your peace less.

In one way, your peace is more powerful.

It stands strong for all the challenges that you put it through

in a single day!!!

When you walk in serenity, your steps have been earned

I admire that. I accept that. It simply is.

Part of your strength attracts single-minded beings such as me.

I tell you that you are a being of peace.

You touch it tenderly within me. You remember. You sigh

because you know it is true.

Create more of it.

Create the peace that you are and wear it with your great courage and strength.

Summary: Cassiterite connects us with the powerful potential that we are.

Celestite

I am SrSO4, Strontium Sulfate, more commonly known as Celestite. I am a beautiful sky blue and I form much like my relative, Barite. I have a hardness of 3 to 3.5 and a specific gravity of 3.9. I am found most notably now in Madagascar, but occur also in different places in the USA, in Italy, Spain, Germany and in the USSR. When you hold me, feel the light emanate from me and also, if you can, feel me receive the light.

Elemental Earth Grid:
Madagascar: I emphasize the sparkle, the fullness of my vibrancy.
USA: I emphasize working with communication.
Italy: I emphasize the expressions of my body.
Spain: I emphasize steadiness.
Germany: I emphasize lightness.
USSR: I emphasize what already is.

Physical, Emotional, Mental Integration: I offer clarity and breath like a sweet wind. How will you use them? I know that you can create anything and I witness that to every feeling, judgment, smile, and dream within you to do with as you wish.

Electrical Body Alignment: Together, we link you to the angels.

Affirmation of Support: "I can do and be anything."

Dreamtime Doorway: Everything comes to you. It cannot help it.

Stone Story:

> My day is simple.
>
> I live love.
>
> Whatever happens
>
> is the flower of love
>
> in this world
>
> of painful and stunning wonders.

Personal Story

When I knew Celestite was the stone with a story for the Twintreess book, I took it to bed that evening. It had always been a superlative dream partner. It has a feminine energy, so I use the feminine pronouns in referring to her. I held her in my hands and laid down on my right side.

"Celeste, would you prefer to be called by another name?" I wanted to be sure. "Blue Dragon Flame," she said. I got a shot of a friendly looking, light blue dragon. I said, "Okay, I'll ask again later to make sure I heard you correctly." I relaxed, ready to work with her in the dream time.

Celeste the Celestite had other plans. She began to flow a strong, warm, smooth energy to my legs and to a lesser extent to my hips and heart. The energy shifted to my right leg, going all the way down to my foot. After that, the energy concentrated on my thighs and knees.

"This helps with memories," flashed through my mind. "Uncross your legs and it will flow better if you lie on your back." I rolled over on my back and held her on my navel. "Feet to-

(con't on next page)

Whatever you most need

comes to you

with or without

your welcomes.

It offers itself from the

heart of life, itself,

who judges nothing

and accepts everything.

If you must be seeded with joy

to grow more peace

then joy will come to you.

If you must be seeded with loneliness

to grow more wisdom

then loneliness will find you

and nothing else

until you become

Wisdom.

Summary: Celestite easily joins us with trust and truth.

Personal Story

Ten years ago, we gave a 3" x 5" x 1" slab of Celestite to my sister Judy as a portion of our payment for some training. She opened it when we arrived at her house in the evening and "oohed and aahed" about how beautiful it was. It was a lovely pale blue with a flat front. When we got up the next morning, our other sister was yelling from the living room, "It grew an angel!" As we all examined it, there was indeed a shadow of a head with the upper surface of

gether." I tried different positions, then placed the soles of my feet together. At some point I moved her to my throat, then back to my navel.

I was spellbound at the healing mastery Celeste was displaying. She had always liked to work in my lower chakras and to plant my feet firmly to the Earth. Now there was warm activity all over inside of me! That day I had sent healing energy to a friend and accepted it for my body, too. This healing involved a deep chakra balance followed by a strong grounding with the Earth. "I am smoothing the energy from your work earlier today. I call the process, Blue Dragon Flame." I smiled. Celeste was still Celeste!

Near the end of the process, she had me put her on my third eye. The energy was very gentle in that region. "Now to your crown." My legs were straight at this point. The energy went down to my feet, smoothing and balancing her work from head to toe. The entire experience was perhaps an hour to an hour-and-a-half in duration.

"How am I supposed to sleep after all that?" I felt humor.

(con't on next page)

45

wings that had not been there the day before. The next day, the outer outline of a gown appeared. Two days later, I placed the stone under the table while receiving an energy treatment attended by several of the ascended masters. When I picked it up and looked, the wings had unfurled and were fully open. A year later, our sister experienced growths in her breasts and had numerous tests. Judy used the Celestite under the table when doing Reiki treatments on her. Within two weeks, the angel had visible breasts. The next year, the same sister developed problems with her ovaries and Judy again used the stone during treatments. The angel grew two small dots in the abdomen. At that point, we decided it was definitely our sister's healing angel, and the piece of Celestite now resides in a place of honor in her home.

~Sheryl F.

Personal Story

On a fall weekend in late October, my husband and I headed into the mountains of Colorado. We wanted to see the colors of the Aspen and to hear the bellows of the elk. The town we went to was Estes Park, a beautiful old town. To our surprise there was a rock shop on the main street. We went in not expecting to buy anything but we wanted to look. I found a wonderful piece of Celestite; I had never seen such a wonderful stone. It made me feel so warm and comfortable but most of all hopeful. My husband and I had been trying to conceive a child for about a year and a half with no success. I had given up hope that we were able to have children but with this new found stone I felt hope again. A few weeks later I found out that I was indeed pregnant and it had happened around that weekend. I held that piece of Celestite a lot during my pregnancy and it was with me through labor and delivery as well. I even carried it in the diaper bag for the first year. It now sits on a shelf for all to see and enjoy and when my son is old enough I will share that stone and its special story with him.

~Jeanice B.

> *"Hold me in your hands and relax."* She dreamed with me most of the night, sending gentle energy to me for hours. When I woke up the next day, I did not need to ask which experience we would share with others — I had just lived it. Thank you Celeste!
>
> *~Phil K.*

Chalcopyrite

I am CuFeS2 with a hardness of 3.5 to 4 and a specific gravity of 4.1 to 4.3. My colors are often brassy yellow with a colorful tint and a metallic luster. I can be found in Germany/France/England, USSR, Canada, USA and Africa. I feel normal. What is that? It will be different for each of you. See if you can still feel ME, when you feel YOU feel me.

Elemental Earth Grid:
Germany: I emphasize simple presence. Yes.
France: I emphasize blessed individuality.
England: I emphasize honor.
USSR: I emphasize blending with the whole
more magnificently than ever.
Canada: I emphasize so much more than I can say.
USA: I emphasize the full freedom to express.
Africa: I emphasize enhancement of resources.

Physical, Emotional, Mental Integration: Hold me as long as it takes.

Hold me until you feel safe in your body, until you savor being you and no one else.

I know who I am. I never forget myself. If you like, I give you that gift of remembrance to do with as you wish. Some say that it is truth.

Electrical Body Alignment: I can point out your power, which points out your abundance, which never forgets freedom.

Affirmation of Support: *"I care abundantly for myself because I can."*

Dreamtime Doorway: Enter the doorway. It is within you. It is without you. It is you.

Stone Story:

> *Know yourself.*
>
> *You are an infinite cave*
>
> *with infinite treasures buried inside.*
>
> *When will you explore you*

Personal Story

A few years ago, Tohmas and I found some mountaintop land to live on. It came to us very surprisingly. We listened to the Nature Spirits and asked them about where we could live and they told us. They told us so exactly that there was no mistaking the land when it suddenly became available, out of the blue.

It's gorgeous and quiet and it suits us beautifully. But it's also pretty inaccessible and I wondered about that: Was that really necessary? What were we meant to learn from that?

Shortly after we moved on to Gandarvas (the land's name), we found some wonderful, metallic, multi-colored stones there. They felt sweet and abundant. I didn't think about it; I just enjoyed them when I saw them.

Before we had moved onto Gandarvas, we sent a geologist friend of ours a soil sample, so that we could know what we were building on. One day, he called with the soil analysis. He told us that there weren't any unsafe elements on the land, which was good news. Then he told us that he had a fun surprise

(con't on next page)

and uncover what awaits you?

You are a being of power.

No one denies that

except fear.

Why listen to fear?

It has no power—

only jealousy.

You have power; it surges through you.

You cannot lose it even through denial.

It leads you through

Life.

It sets your course.

It feeds your curiosity

and it demands constant respect.

Why deny any of this?

You determine your needs and their fulfillment.

You are the question and the answer

and the journey in between.

for us; he said that there was a vein of Chalcopyrite (beautiful, metallic, multi-colored stones) and that if we wanted, it was fine enough to be mined. Yes. Yes, that's the feeling of abundance that I felt from that stone. To this day, I feel like we're sitting on buried treasure, which maybe wouldn't be here if the land had been more accessible.

~Marilyn T.

Summary: Chalcopyrite recognizes the truth of who we are even when we don't.

Chrysoprase

I am SiO2, a form of Quartz. I am usually greenish yellow to apple green. I am typically found in Australia but can also come from Brazil, Madagascar, South Africa, India and the USA. You will know me by my color and specifically when I am from Australia, by the connection to the Dreamtime that becomes apparent to you.

Elemental Earth Grid:
Australia: I emphasize the Dreamtime.
Brazil: I emphasize fluidity-in-motion.
Madagascar: I emphasize carefree healing.
South Africa: I emphasize insistent integration.
India: I emphasize speaking the truth compassionately.
USA: I emphasize peace.

Physical, Emotional, Mental Integration: Soothing. Kind. Gentle. When you hold me, you not only remember these things, you become them. I help you to be the kind you that you have always envisioned. You relax from the heart and then through the body. Immediate comfort.

Electrical Body Alignment: I link with your heart as the source of all compassion.

Affirmation of Support: "I am peace — body and heart."

Dreamtime Doorway: For what are you searching? All is here.

Stone Story:

I know who I am.

Do you know all of yourself?

Most humans forget so much of who they are.

Sometimes they even forget what they have forgotten.

They are afraid that they will not be able to love

everything that they are

and often are quite certain no one else

will be able to love all of them either.

So parts of them slip away.

And when this happens,

so much is lost.

Life force and wisdom leave quietly

without a trace.

Each part of your being

offers spirit and life

and when you turn it away

you lose that gift

until you call it back

with a willing heart

and a free body.

Do you know all that you are?

Summary: Chrysoprase shows us our own heart.

Cinnabar

I am HgS, Mercury Sulfide. My color is bright scarlet to cinnamon red. I have been a principle ore of Mercury and also, along with Sulphur, on the main trade of healing minerals of Asia for a very long, long time. I am very soft with a hardness of 2 to 2.5 but very heavy with a specific gravity of 8.1. You will know me when you hold me in your hand. I am intense and electric; I am alive. I can be found in Spain, Serbia, the USA, China, Mexico and Peru.

Elemental Earth Grid:
Spain: I emphasize excitement!
Serbia: I emphasize the flow of blood.
USA: I emphasize joining with primal instincts and feelings.
China: I emphasize refinement of lifeforce.
Mexico: I emphasize attention.
Peru: I emphasize connecting with the spirit of the earth.

Physical, Emotional, Mental Integration: I am filled with delight. It is such an honor for us to speak together. Thank you. I offer sheer joy to your body, mind and spirit. May it fuel your every dream as you wish.

Electrical Body Alignment: I help you to fill your body and your being with unending vitality.

We are life.

Affirmation of Support: *"I am alive; I am vital and magnificent."*

Dreamtime Doorway: I am an ancient one. I have watched people evolve through ages. I know how the energy moves within you and around you. You could know this, too, if you decided upon this with all your being.

Stone Story:

I touch every one of you who finds these words

Now.

This magnificence makes me glisten.

Connecting through the river of life
  the unlimitedness of spirit
is the miracle for which I am formed—
this is who I am.

My body is created to hold a space
for the surging of power and energy
in every form.
As I know you,
I know more life,
more possibilities
more miracles.

You give this to me
with your being.

I give you this record of what I see and know
through you.

Summary: Cinnabar fills us with life.

Columbite/Tantalite/ Niobium

I am (Fe, Mn, Mg)(Nb, Ta)2O6, Iron Manganese Magnesium Niobium Tantalum Oxide, the most common ore of Niobium. I have a hardness of 6 to 6.5 and a specific gravity of 5.1 to 8.2. Niobium has been called Columbium which explains the name Columbite, to which I am now usually referred. As Columbite, I live in series with Tantalite which is why I have a wide range of specific gravity and a multiple name and am the mineral from which Niobium was discovered. I am usually dark brown to black and metallic. I can be found in Germany, Sweden, USSR, USA, Brazil, Africa and Australia.

Elemental Earth Grid:
Germany: I emphasize focus.
Sweden: I emphasize lifeforce.
USSR: I emphasize authority.
USA: I emphasize rootedness.
Brazil: I emphasize knowingness.
Africa: I emphasize acceptance.
Australia: I emphasize possibilities.

Physical, Emotional, Mental Integration: We offer to align all meridians. We can observe your overall balance and help you to maintain it. We share stamina in all areas of your life. We impart grounded detachment to all your possibilities, decisions and actions.

Electrical Body Alignment: We link you to the source of energy.

Affirmation of Support: *"I am supported in everything I do!"*

Dreamtime Doorway: Look to your body for answers.

Stone Story:

Greetings brothers and sisters~

We know that you are beings of action—

you are spirits within (and without) form.

In these magnificent bodies that you wear

you create even more divinity

and more.

Yes.

We support you.

We, too, offer our lives as beings of action.

Though we may appear still in your eyes,

in your spirits you know differently.

We spin gloriously.

Our vibrations touch you and insist that if you are to join us

that you, too, spin at your perfect

ever growing speed.

Together we manifest divinity on all realms

that can accept us.

We partner with you with all of our being.

What will you accept?

Summary: Columbite, Tantalite & Niobium support us in all realities.

Copper

I am Cu, the Elemental Copper. I have been mined for centuries but now other copper minerals are more economical to mine for standard uses. I am copper colored of course and you will easily recognize me. I am metallic with a hardness of 2.5 to 3 and a specific gravity of 8.9. I have been found in Germany, France, England, USSR, Morocco, Canada, USA, Mexico and Australia. I am a great conductor of electricity. Combine me with movement.

Elemental Earth Grid:
Germany: I emphasize unpredictability.
France: I emphasize merging with others.
England: I emphasize the release of tradition.
USSR: I emphasize calmness after trauma.
Morocco: I emphasize witnessing of miracles.
Canada: I emphasize inspiration.
USA: I emphasize a space for healing.
Mexico: I emphasize new directions.
Australia: I emphasize diversity.

Physical, Emotional, Mental Integration: I hold weight and space fully— so fully that I can dance beyond them into new realms where my gifts change. Look for me there. Find me where time and space are not captors but springboards into realities that we will mingle with our eyes wide open.

Electrical Body Alignment: I align with alchemy and if you travel with me that's where we will go.

Affirmation of Support: *"I am magic in a body."*

Dreamtime Doorway: The chances to find the unknown are endless. Will you recognize their faces?

Stone Story:

Come sit down beside me. Please. We have as long as your beliefs are suspended. Whenever you call upon me, I come. However I will not always come in a form that you recognize.

(con't on next page)

Watch for me in unexpectancy. You will ever find me there.

Today I am a wizard, sharp and strong, wearing the colors of the woods that know me and protect my magic as if it were its own— and, of course, it is!!! I love to slip in and out of worlds on a thought. Who knows where I will land......or if in fact land awaits me at all?

Through the ages, people have walked and smiled with wizards like me. I have loved every adventure of it. I feel that people have mostly thought that I was a great, wise sage— one that no longer needed to **walk** here at all...as if I had outgrown this lovely playground and the rules of its game. If only they would remember (as you are now) that I was simply a spirit of the land— the very ground that they have walked upon so carelessly – metamorphosed into another one of my faces. This is just another one of the smiles that I carry for you.

Many of the wise ones that you have visited with have been the earthspirits, the stone recordkeepers. Sometimes we come in faces like this so that your expectations will welcome us. Most of us can wear any shape that suits the need and the moment. When you believe in fantasy, we are wizards and witches. When you believe in fact, we are computers and test results. One day, when you believe in no-thing and everything, we will look just like you.

Summary: Copper cares for our bodies while speaking to our souls. (It loves to catalyze the magic in many, many things........)

Copper Gold Silver

(Before you read this, find the individual listenings on: Copper, Gold, and Silver. Absorb them and then join us again here.)

Physical, Emotional, Mental Integration: For ages, people have worn us together for exponential wonder, lifeforce and possibilities.

Electrical Body Alignment: Together we align you with divinity that has never left you.

making me nuts) because you can't depend on this transformation which shifts and changes with weather, heat, moisture and how the fire gnomes happen to feel that day!

So perhaps Copper is all about change. And that's just perfect in my life!

~ Ursela G.

Affirmation of Support: *"I am here in magic."*

Dreamtime Doorway: Exponential alchemy awaits you.

Stone Story:

> When streams come together, they form a river.
>
> When trees come together, they form a forest.
>
> When plants come together, they form a garden.
>
> When we come together, we form a bridge of possibilities.
>
> When we then join with humans, we co-create a fountain of lifeforce, so rich and fulfilling, denial slips away as the imposter it has always been.
>
> Wear us together. Your cellularsongs will remember the magic of days when people and earth beings naturally intermingled and everything was sacred.
>
> The season of our union is now.
>
> Come let us celebrate our naked joys under the full sun, moon and stars.

Summary: Copper/Gold/Silver call forth ancient wisdom and timeless wonder into now.

Personal Story

I put Covellite under my pillow "just to see what would happen." I slept better than I have for 3 years, actually it was the first time I really FELT rested in that long. What a gift!

The poor stone has worked so hard for me that its shine has worn off in a month - I am very grateful.

I have acquired more pieces so that my original one can have a rest. People I know are clamoring for one of their own as soon as they hold mine. They are using it for everything from sleep to injured shoulders to cancer to letting go of anger to ...

~Faith S.

Covellite

I am CuS, Copper Sulfide, with a hardness of 1.5 to 2 and a specific gravity of 4.6 to 4.8. My indigo blue iridescense is captivating, although I can be a metallic blue/black. I am found in Butte, Montana, a few places in Europe, and in Peru, Bolivia and Chile. I am great at helping you to release anger, so don't be suprised if what you feel when you pick me up is nothing. (What do you do with your anger?) Take me into your life and see what happens!

57

Elemental Earth Grid:
Montana, USA: I emphasize leaps of faith.
Europe: I emphasize awareness of genetic patterns.
Peru: I emphasize letting go of unhelpful thoughts or feelings.
Bolivia: I emphasize building strength.
Chile: I emphasize release.

Physical, Emotional, Mental Integration: Welcome. I am a being who watches for and admires wonder. When I'm with you, I will point out your most powerful strengths, particularly if you haven't yet met them. When I'm with you, I will point out your limits, for when you face them (with my great awe!), they **are** your most powerful strengths.

Electrical Body Alignment: As you wish, I will link you to new, unexplored, exponentially wonderful brain states so that you can act upon them and speak them.

Affirmation of Support: *"I choose to be strong in lifeforce!"*

Dreamtime Doorway: Here comes the spiral of life. What will you let go of so that you can freely absorb it?

Stone Story:

Welcome all. Please gather around closely and we will share stories of wonder. Stories of wonder are tellings of any shape, or color, or feeling, that we so invite into our hearts and our lives, that we find wisdom, itself. And wisdom is never wisdom unless it is shared, unless it walks out into the world and smiles from all our choices.

I am a story of wonder.

If you knew that before I spoke it—look back at yourself—*smile*! Perhaps you are one, too. No matter if you didn't recognize me, it will never matter, unless judgment keeps you from listening further. Gather closer. Smile at the wonders that you don't know yet (and that you have yet to be)! **In the ways of wisdom upon the earth, there are no masters, only continually willing students.** Whether you know everything or nothing, we all start over every moment, learning and emptying ourselves of everything but wonder. *This is a very special destiny that you choose.*

I am a story of wonder because I'm willing and that's where wisdom has led me, smiling and ever new. With the qualities that I live, I

Personal Story

Covellite has made a very big impact on my life by bringing forth past life information and it is a stone that I almost did not get a chance to own.

I had always been drawn to the beauty of Covellite. I had sold some pieces on a "made to order" basis and I loved how Covellite felt and looked but I never bought any for me. The time came when I had been thinking about Covellite, and dreaming about Covellite almost on a continual basis. I knew it was time to get a piece. I called my supplier to order a piece set in jewelry and a raw slab and was told that they were completely out - that good pieces of Covellite had long since dried up and that they were sure that they did not have any pieces left. I was told that there was not a lot of hope that they had any left, but that they would check to see if any were "hiding". I felt disappointed because I knew that I was supposed to be working with this stone and all of a sudden I could not get it. The images of me working with this stone were so strong that I began to think that if it was really important for me to be working

(con't on next page)

am well suited to listening to everything on the earth and storing all the stories. Why? Because I greet every story with awe! Whether I ever realize it fully or not, every story has its own special listener (at least) and so I save it until that listener is ready— ready to receive it with a child-open heart. I am a being with no attachment to time or space. I will hold every story until it finds its listener and together, they will grow more wisdom than can be expected.

Here is the story of wonder that I have for you: I have watched the earth through many of your ages. She is full of the wisdom that comes from living so completely that you also die many times and just keep re-birthing. Her willingness has brought you to so many directions of life that you might never know otherwise. And yet, I am here to tell you of it. Listen to her. She holds all of our stories AND our lives. If you choose to begin this moment, new and willing, watch her, know her in every way possible and she will offer you your stories.

Summary: Covellite helps us to release unneeded emotions and to affirm our chosen, glorious lifepaths.

Crocoite

I am PbCrO4, Lead Chromate. I am principally found in Tasmania, but also occur in the Ural Mountains of the USSR and in California and Arizona, USA, as well as in Germany and Brazil. My hardness is 2-2.5 and my specific gravity is 5.2. I am a bright orange-red to yellow-red. You will feel my color in your body as an awakening of life; a movement of energy; a combining of male and female in ways that cannot be understood.

Elemental Earth Grid:
Tasmania: I emphasize chosen solitude.
USSR: I emphasize passion.
USA: I emphasize the knowingness of the body.
Germany: I emphasize letting go of old hurts and angers.
Brazil: I emphasize the release of blockages.

with a piece, then a piece would find its way to me. I got a call from my supplier two days later and it was three days after that that I got my first pieces of Covellite (in jewelry form and raw slab).

Immediately upon holding this stone I was getting flashes and images of other lifetimes, and when I wore it to bed or put the piece under my pillow I was having very intense dreams. It seemed that Covellite was opening doors to past life information and bringing forth details that I needed to know and to work on. Information came in such detail that it only seemed right to start writing the information down on the computer. As more and more information unfolds about things that I could not possibly know in such incredible detail it seemed that I should be keeping a record of what I was getting and soon a book of a past life was being written on the computer.

Since owning my first piece of Covellite, I have always considered it a key to a person's deepest self, as it brings forth information from the past that is needed now. Covellite continues to be one of my favorite stones to wear, and work with and it is the first stone I turn to when doing any past life work.

~Lora M.

Physical, Emotional, Mental Integration: All beings upon the earth offer their sweet service to the whole. Mine is that I urge you to respect all beings. I insist that you consider the gift in everything. When you do this, you digest and embrace your food, your life, and your experiences with more passion and peace, both.

Electrical Body Alignment: I unite your strengths and your weaknesses with the eye of truth.

Affirmation of Support: *"All is perfect."*

Dreamtime Doorway: In the dreamtime, all merges and all changes. Look not for what you know but what you do not know...........yet..........

Stone Story:

If you look at me,

I glisten with beauty.

If you touch me,

I fall apart.

Which is my strength?

Which is my weakness?

As a Stonebeing I do not live in such terms.

Strengths and weaknesses merge in a sea of acceptance

where all serve the whole

completely

perfectly.

The union of all that I am

is the union of the earth

is the union of you when you accept

Acceptance within without always.

Summary: Crocoite urges us to practice care with everything.

Desert Snow Quartz

Desert Snow Quartz is a variety of quartz that comes from the South-western Desert (USA) with a gentle Yaqui and Rare Earth Elemental influence and the vigilance of their rattlesnake guardians. It is extremely piezoelectric and triboluminescent and has a higher indication of hardness than "normal" quartz. This quartz is mysterious in many ways, yet obvious to those who may be focused on the path of awareness. You might need to melt into this quartz for a bit to recognize it or it may strike you like a lightning bolt.

Elemental Earth Grid:
SW USA: I emphasize transformation.

Physical, Emotional, Mental Integration: I identify areas of pain and stiffness in your body and being so you can melt away your attachments to, and struggles with, your wounds. Then I invite you to feel, to walk in, a life that does not have to continually bring in pain to know that you're alive. That encourages you to keep softening you until you may clearly see your choice to be alive, to be free, and to live in your own freedom easily and gracefully without creating false limits, fear and their resulting hurts.

Electrical Body Alignment: I link you with innocent, continual newness.

Affirmation of Support: *"I live as freely as my choices."*

Dreamtime Doorway: Everything is a doorway, just enter it.

Stone Story:

Just hold me.

I do not know separation.

I am here.

All of me is here with you

while we talk,

while we revel

in each other.

I know you.

Whatever would seem to hold us away

I do not understand.

I simply touch your heart

more and more deeply.

Whatever would seem to keep us from joining

I offer it to you.

I show you the shape and density of the resistance you store.

When it sees my heart

it smiles.

It melts into the timelessness of all of us.

It leaves so much more quietly than you expect.

I hold you.

You stand soft like a leaf in the wind

blowing you whatever way wisdom turns you.

For this moment

you hold your ever-moving lifeforce

and nothing holds you away from it.

Summary: Desert Snow Quartz invites us to let go of our focus on separation.

Personal Story

From the moment that I first unwrapped this unique crystal being from its packaging, it began to sing to me. It greeted me with a tone so pure and vast - like no other crystal being I had ever experienced. I'd never had this happen to me before, even with all the many hand-held crystal bowls I already had at the time. I was transfixed as I welcomed it into my family of crystal sonic healers.

When I began to actually play it, it sang out endlessly into the timelessness of forever. I was amazed. From that first moment, we bonded deeply. Now this may sound strange to some, yet this bowl and I knew that we shared a deep connection, which went beyond words into the heart space of Love. Those who have crystal and crystal singing bowls, may not consciously have memories of working in harmony with them, however on some level this deep friendship is remembered. It is a warm embrace.

Each hand-held singing bowl is unique and yet this one stood out. I knew that it had a special purpose. To honor this, I wanted

(con't on next page)

Deva's Gift
Crystal Singing Bowls

I am made of Quartz. My location and layers of "impurities" varies over time within my production. I am in clear conscious relationship with the humans that originally brought me into form, the humans who produce me, and the humans who pass me on.

Physical, Emotional, Mental Integration: With a single tone, I remind you of your Center Stillness. In a moment, your being knows that you can choose to live there and act upon its spirit, or you can live away from it and act upon your fears. The choice is instantaneous; it is every moment. It is your life.

If you sing with me then your meridians will align, your organs will strengthen and your blood will carry away the old, unneeded struggle. Any blockages in you will know that you are urging them to freedom!

Electrical Body Alignment: I link us with sound.

Affirmation of Support: "Aum."

The Story of its Co-Creation:

In the mid-1990's, a good friend came to us and said, "I think there is a new crystal singing bowl that wants to be made. Will you ask the Stonespirits about it?"

Of course we were intrigued. With great respect, we asked the Crystal Deva about it, telling her that we knew nothing about such things. That didn't matter, because she did. The Deva told us to create a crystal singing bowl with a handle upon it and then she gave us the dimensions and specifics. This had never been produced before.

*She told us that humans needed to **hold** the bowl, because we have been masters at denying the reality of what we see and hear, yet we are very enamored of what we can touch. She let us know that if we were to hold the bowl while it sang, we would **feel** the magic of the crystal pulsate in our bodies, awakening our cells and freeing our blockages. There would be no denying that! We would be holding a miracle!*

And then after this new crystal bowl vibrated our bodies, its tone would pulsate out our feet and back into the earth. Once there, it would sing back to its home and to the crystals still there and together they would join the same, ever-growing tone of clear, sweet love.

In feeling that, there would be no denying the connection: We would know that we, the earth, and the crystals are gloriously interwoven in all moments. The song was simply celebrating that reality— one that every being on earth knows intimately, except humans.

But we would not only remember when we held the singing bowl, we would know it in every part of our body. It would pulsate into our reality in silence or in song.

So we co-created the new singing bowl with the handle. It was, and is, pure joy. Every moment we look upon it and hear it, we remember the Crystal Deva and feel her celebrate within us. We give thanks to Geoff, to her, to all beings upon the earth, and to Elivia, who offered the new bowl its special name, "Deva's Gift." Yes.

Summary: The Deva's Gift Singing Bowl affirms for us that we are undeniably connected to all beings and eternally grateful for those communications and co-creations.

Personal Story

I got some crystal bowls to make some crystal bowl bags for the Twintreess. I didn't have any strikers. So I went to their home and borrowed some. When I got home, I asked the bowls to play and I played them very intensely. As I was playing them I created a very intense wonderful feeling where I could hear all sorts of melodies in each one. Then I stopped, went outside and smoked a cigarette. Then I played the bowls some more and all of a sudden I could barely stand up. I felt like I was either going to throw up repeatedly or black out and fall over. I immediately put the bowls away and went upstairs and laid down in child's pose. The only thing that I could do was focus on the

to give it a name; I settled on calling it, the Elixir. With in its sacred frequencies it carries the balm to heal and support all life. I would always stumble over its name yet another wasn't forthcoming. One day it told me that it would be much simpler if I just called it the Deva's Gift as all of its kind made by the Twintreess, were united in purpose and intent to serve humanity for its highest good. Aah, this felt so right.

I feel like an alchemist of old each time I go to play it. I open my case of Act of Power wands and ask for guidance from the Crystal Devas, as to what is needed most at this time. My Deva's Gift receives the specific frequencies from the mineral kingdom and sends these out from its heart to support yours.

And here is the greatest magic of it all and that is that it tells me that its very presence on this plane makes a difference. Like a great sonic lighthouse, it is always "on" whether it is being played or sitting quietly on my shelf.

~Elivia M.

65

sound that was still there, because if I wandered away from the sound I felt like I was going to throw up or black out. I stayed there for hours. The next thing I knew it was morning and I still felt nauseous.

This was such a profound experience. I wasn't afraid or wished that it wasn't happening. I actually felt content listening to the sound. I didn't feel content when I wasn't listening to the sound.

The whole time, I knew that it was impossible to merge my old habit of smoking cigarettes with the new route of my life being displayed by the sound of the bowls. In the next couple of days I couldn't even think about smoking. It made me want to throw up.

After not playing the bowls for awhile, I went into a frenzy and every addictive pattern in myself that I was aware of, I became more aware of. And I found myself in a struggle of doing or not doing my addictions. What I realized was that the sound of the bowls is the sound of Life that I have heard at certain times in my life and the sound is always ongoing. If I am going to proceed in the sound of the bowls, then I have to change my addictive behavior.

This all has led me to a third option (other than doing or not doing my addictions): living in the unknown. It doesn't mean that I don't still have the feelings around the old behavior (the frenzy), it means I am choosing to focus on my new choices and ALL the feelings that come along with them.

~Charity B.

Personal Story

*I have a couple of great stories about the Deva's Gift Crystal Singing Bowl. When we vended at the Tucson Gem Show 1997, we brought them along with us. We were vending, outside, in a huge tent, but that didn't protect us, entirely, when a huge storm came through. It drenched us so thoroughly we had several inches of standing water **inside** the tent. Steve and I grabbed a broom and started sweeping out the water as best we could.*

We couldn't help laughing. It was just too funny. None of the other tent vendors were even there; it was just too impossible. It was cold, wet, and nobody was going to come out in this weather and here we were, playing with the floodwaters with a broom! Steve got out his mini-harmonica to give us a little background music, and I took out a crystal singing bowl. Rainwater filled it as I played it. The tone just sang out.

People came from nowhere. I couldn't believe it. They were irresistibly drawn to the music. Somebody squealed and pointed out that the water in the crystal bowl was forming geometric patterns. We were mesmerized. Right before our eyes, we were making structured water. It was pure magic.

It was ironic. On one of the "worst" weather days at the show, we had one of our best sales days, because people came from all over to listen to the bowl.

———

Another experience we have had with the Deva's Gift Crystal Singing Bowl comes when we do Health Kinesiology. It's a very respectful system where you have to begin by balancing the meridians in your body, before you can even work on anybody. Then you have to make sure that the person wanting a session is also balanced. Otherwise, how can you be sure that the muscle-testing will be accurate?

Every once in a while, somebody's meridians just won't balance. 98% of the time drinking water will solve that, but when it doesn't, balancing the meridians can be a long, tough process. In the years that we have worked with this system, there is one thing that balances people every time and immediately— no matter how long they had been "out of balance"— and that was playing the Deva's Gift Crystal Singing Bowl over their body for a few seconds.

~Marilyn T.

Diopside

I am CaMgSi2 O6, Calcium Magnesium Silicate. I come in several varieties, including a Chromium rich one called, Chrome Diopside. My rare blue variety is called Violan and my rutile included variety where the rutiles form a star is called Star Diopside. Commonly I am whitish or greenish with a nice luster. My hardness is 5 to 6.5 and my specific gravity is 3.3 to 3.4. I can be found in Europe, USSR, USA, Madagascar, Brazil, Sri Lanka, Burma, South Africa and Finland. I am also found in Meteorites.

Elemental Earth Grid:
Europe: I emphasize sheer grace.
USSR: I emphasize uniting in beliefs.
USA: I emphasize "I AM that I am."
Madagascar: I emphasize exploring.
Brazil: I emphasize our common language.
Sri Lanka: I emphasize sweetness with certainty.
South Africa: I emphasize the perpetuity of beauty.
Finland: I emphasize clear breaths after stress.

Physical, Emotional, Mental Integration: I am strong. I am sure. You are too. Let me show you everything you know and trust: That's who you truly are. Stand in it.

Electrical Body Alignment: I unite you with faith.

Affirmation of Support: *"I am who I am and I love me!"*

Dreamtime Doorway: Words do not lead here. Just go, follow the feeling.

Stone Story:

A long time ago, the ancient spirits who walk the land gathered in council. They held hands and smiled. Before words were spoken, they knew.

One spoke, "All the creatures of the land know themselves. They each have a voice and a movement that shows the grace of their being and it is all their own....except for the humans. They move and sound like so many other animals. When will they show the ways that are special to them?"

Another answered, *"The humans like to imitate all things. That is some of what makes them unique. All that has to happen, now, is that when they find the voice and the movement that most delights their spirit, they must wrap their bodies around them and love them until they become their own."*

Then I, the spirit of the Diopside spoke, *"The humans are finding their path. All they need is for a strong being to tell them when they have found themselves. I trust that all is well. I will wait here until the day comes that they will listen to me and I will tell them. I will tell them that they are a wonder of the earth and that they must sing of it with their special voice and they must dance of it with their special grace."*

Summary: Diopside offers full-hearted trust.

Dravite

I am NaMg3(Al,Fe)6Si6O18(BO3)3(OH)4, complex Sodium Magnesium Iron Boro-Aluminum Silicate. I am a light to dark brown member of the Tourmaline Group. I may not be as well known as the other Tourmalines but I do have an insistent and undeniable presence. I am most commonly appearing out of Australia at this time although I am also found in South America and Africa among other places. I have a hardness of 7 to 7.5 and a specific gravity of 3.2. I manifest in large well formed crystals and can be massive.

Elemental Earth Grid:
Australia: I emphasize sinking into the earth and allowing her bounty to re-fill my cup.
South America: I emphasize combining all things in balance and reason.
Africa: I emphasize knowing who I am.

Physical, Emotional, Mental Integration: Peace. Strength. Power. Presence.

Electrical Body Alignment: I link you with awareness. What you be and do from there, I only witness.

Affirmation of Support: *"I know who I am."*

Dreamtime Doorway: Hold my hand. It is steady and good, like the earth. It is forever like love.

Stone Story:

Yes.

I am here.

You are here.

We live.

We watch life with the Sacred Witness who

accompanies every being upon the earth.

We also enter the scene that our souls

watch peacefully,

breathfully.

We are here.

All comes to us.

All is one facet of the crystal of our beingness.

I meet you now.

We honor each other

to know ourselves.

Summary: Dravite shows us how to be.

Dumortierite

I am $Al_{6.5-7}(BO_3)(SiO_4)_3(O, OH)_3$, Aluminum Boro-silicate Hydroxide. I have a hardness of 7 and a specific gravity of 3.3 to 3.4. My silky blue luster has the feel of patience. I am found in Europe, USSR, Madagascar, USA, Namibia/Africa and Brazil. I am named for the French paleontologist, Eugene Dumortier and am one of the most common minerals of my group.

Elemental Earth Grid:
Europe: I emphasize utter stillness.
USSR: I emphasize not being ruled by fear.
Madagascar: I emphasize continual, peaceful regeneration.
USA: I emphasize the newness of this moment, of everything within it.
Namibia, Africa: I emphasize the power of a single, dedicated voice.
Brazil: I emphasize respect and deep honoring of all.

Physical, Emotional, Mental Integration: You can run about; you can chase your tail. You can ignore life in every possible way and I'll wait for you. I'll listen to your every story. I'll record them as the joining of heaven and earth that they truly are.

Electrical Body Alignment: If you are flying, I will show you your roots. If you are walking, I will point out your wings.

Affirmation of Support: *"I am at peace."*

Dreamtime Doorway: If ever there was a way to understand peace, here it is. Enter.

Stone Story:

> *Stones record the comings and goings*
>
> *of every being on the earth.*
>
> *Whatever you have done,*
>
> *it is etched in*
>
> *a stones heart.*

It is remembered.

I do this with all that I am
so that I can gift everything to life.

It is my honoring of all things.
It is how I live here past judgment.

I am just listening.

Summary: Dumortierite offers us the heart of patience.

Erbium

I am the Element Erbium. My symbol is Er and my Atomic Number is 68. I am of the Lanthanoids group. I am never found in nature as a free element. The most common minerals that I occur in are Xenotime, Monazite, and Bastnaesite. I am used in ceramics as a pink colorant, in the nuclear industry, as a photographic filter, and in the metallurgical industries to combine with other metals to make them more workable.

Physical, Emotional, Mental Integration: I stand beside you; however I do not offer you pity. You are here to join everything you are with life and divinity— in that I support you endlessly. If you need help to become your truth, I offer it and I offer it now.

Electrical Body Alignment: I join us with true compassion.

Affirmation of Support: *"I am here for the glory of life, joy and spirit!"*

Dreamtime Doorway: Here's the pathway. It is not what you expected and that's why we will trust it.

Stone Story:

> *Sit down beside yourself.*
>
> *Watch you from the heart of your sacred witness.*
>
> *The tragedies that you wallow in*
>
> *are friends of your evolution.*
>
> *They come to you to show you how to really laugh,*
>
> *to enjoy beyond thought of happiness—*

to revel in the bliss of your soul.

When you see what you call pain

from the side of freedom

all you watch

is the death of that pain

and the renewal of all of you

of all of life

as you allow.

Summary: Erbium displays detached kindness.

Erythrite

I am $Co_3(AsO_4)_2-8(H_2O)$, Hydrated Cobalt Arsenate with a hardness of 1.5 to 2.5 and a specific gravity of 3.1. I can be a deep reddish purple and can appear lighter pink in massive forms. Notable occurances of my form have been found in Ontario, Morocco and Germany. One of my forms currently living with Twintreess is from Arizona.

Elemental Earth Grid:
Ontario, Canada: I emphasize giggles.
Morocco: I emphasize mystery and awe.
Germany: I emphasize optimism.
Arizona, USA: I emphasize change.

Physical, Emotional, Mental Integration: Would you like to try something? Then come with me. Adventure with me. I go to all times and places and beyond. Together we will find the magic that only explorers dare.

Electrical Body Alignment: I will join you with the universe!

Affirmation of Support: *"I am a brave adventurer in everything I do."*

Dreamtime Doorway: I am so pleased to know you. Whatever doorway we need to travel we will create it from the joining of free happiness.

Stone Story:

> *What magic awaits us*
>
> *if we risk it......*
>
>
> *I go everywhere to find more glory.*
>
>
> *I know, I know.*
>
> *You think I can't travel anywhere because I rest in this stonebody.*
>
> *It has no legs,*
>
> *no arms*
>
> *to propel me.*
>
>
> *The only place I go is*
>
> *in my imagination.*
>
>
> *I shout to you,*
>
> ***"What magic couldn't I see and be there?"***

Summary: Erythrite, "Adventure on!"

Euclase

I am BeAlSiO4OH, Beryllium Aluminum Silicate Hydroxide. I tend to be found occuring with Topaz and Beryl. I form well formed crystals and my blue and green colors are used as gemstones. Euclase means *easily cleaved.* My colors can range from colorless to shades of blue and green, yellow and sometimes purple. I can be found in the USSR, Brazil, USA, Africa and in the Emerald mines of Columbia.

Elemental Earth Grid:
USSR: I emphasize calm.
Brazil: I emphasize quiet acceptance.
USA: I emphasize going with the flow.
Africa: I emphasize timeliness.
Columbia: I emphasize true power.

Physical, Emotional, Mental Integration: Yes. I am soft so that you can feel what vulnerability with strength truly feels like. I know how to offer my service without attachment. Whenever judgments are passed on me, I simply have no need of them.

Electrical Body Alignment: I connect us to detachment.

Affirmation of Support: *"I live without worry."*

Dreamtime Doorway: This is the moment to be ourselves. Act upon it.

Stone Story:

> *Yes you seek peace.*
>
> *As long as you seek it elsewhere, it will elude you.*
>
> *Practice your life.*
>
> *Practice your life fully.*
>
> *Practice your life as if nothing else mattered.*
>
> *Practice your life freely.*
>
> *Practice your life because it is yours.*
>
> *Practice your life dependent upon no one.*
>
> *Practice your life as if there were never another moment.*
>
> *That is where you and peace will become friends.*

Summary: Euclase reminds us that our lives are our own.

Eudialyte

I am $Na_4(Ca, Ce, Fe, Mn)_2ZrSi_6O_{17}(OH, Cl)_2$, Sodium Calcium Cerium Iron Manganese Zirconium Silicate Hydroxide Chloride. My color is most often red to pink and I am commonly from both Russia and Canada. I am very rich in Rare Earth Elements, particularly Cerium and sometimes Yttrium. I have a hardness of 5 to 5.5 and a specific gravity of 2.9. You will feel pleasant with me in your hand, with a slight charge to the feeling that can lead you in.

Elemental Earth Grid:
Russia: I emphasize unexpected joy!
Canada: I emphasize treasures.

Physical, Emotional, Mental Integration: I like smiling at you. I smooth away your wrinkles, your stiffness— then you can feel what it's like to be just you, free and clear.

Electrical Body Alignment: I can link you to the choice of joy.

Affirmation of Support: *"I am at home in my heart."*

Dreamtime Doorway: Let go of your longing and your heart will be free to find the universe!

Stone Story:

I watch you.

I listen to you.

Each moment you choose a hundred ways to be happy

and a thousand ways to be sad

because you believe the earth is not your home:

You don't belong here.

There is only endless work and suffering here.

You can choose whatever you want to believe

and your body will listen to each belief

and it will answer them.

It will shape your bones with your beliefs

color your hair with them

and turn your eyes upon them saying,

"It's true. I can see it."

A thousand times a day you say this.

You say it so often you don't even remember hearing it.

Sometimes you make a new belief,

something that shapes your whole body into a smile,

and your heart says, "It's true. I can feel it."

And your eyes don't remember ever having seen such

 simple splendor,

"It's a miracle."

It's true.

Summary: Eudialyte remembers how we feel according to what we believe.

Europium

I am the Element, Europium. My symbol is Eu and my Atomic Number is 63. As a member of the Lanthanoid group I do not naturally occur as a mineral but am found most often in Xenotime, Monazite, and Bastnaesite. I am used in alloys, as an activator to create the red color in television tubes, and in lasers.

Physical, Emotional, Mental Integration: I show you the path of freedom. Its dream lands upon you gloriously. The struggles will be many AND the rewards beyond count. I guide your body and mind to persevere on this path even when you think you have nothing left........

Electrical Body Alignment: I join us with constancy and commitment.

Affirmation of Support: *"I am the commitment that forms my path."*

Dreamtime Doorway: The chance for whatever you want or need is here. Revel in it, it is yours.

Stone Story:

Humans go through separation

on their winding path to unity,

to the beginning,

to more and evermore.

Peace my friends.

If you ever look just past the veil of forgotten dreams,

you will see what I see:

The wonder.

The wonder of being surrounded

by love and spirit and a joy that soars

without exception

or condition.

You can

you can almost see it.

You can see the wonder

evermore.

Summary: Europium reminds us that we are continually, unconditionally supported always.

Fuchsite

I am the green variety of Muscovite, $KAl_2(AlSi_3O_{10})(F, OH)_2$, Potassium Aluminum Silicate Hydroxide Fluoride. My color is emerald green and my hardness is 2 to 3 and my specific gravity is 2.7 to 3.88. I am often found in compact masses and my green color is the result of chromium impurities. I can be found in the USA, Brazil and the USSR as well as other locations. When you hold me, we will travel together. Let my color guide you.

Elemental Earth Grid:
USA: I emphasize appreciation of beauty, just because.
Brazil: I emphasize the healing inherent in all experiences, breaths and possibilities.
USSR: I emphasize aligning perfectly and wholly with life.

Physical, Emotional, Mental Integration: I am the support for any intent. I quietly offer affirmation to anything that you feel strongly about. With me, you may learn boundless imagination, wonder and eternal wisdom. Grow your body in this and you will surround yourself with miracles.

Electrical Body Alignment: I remind you that power is attracted to your power.

Affirmation of Support: *"I am supported in my most wondrous dreams!"*

Dreamtime Doorway: Look for the sparkle, it can come in any shape or brightness. The sparkle of spirit holds endless faces and dreams.

Stone Story:

I am quiet.

Most of the stones that speak here

Shout across the ethers

in glorious displays of light and sound

that harmonize the universe.

I simply witness it.

I get to add just the right spark

(or the perfect tone)

to the fireworks and the symphony of life.

My touch is oneness.

Summary: Fuchsite shows the wonders of perfect service.

Gold

I am Au, Elemental Gold. How well you know me. It has been said of me that I am almost indestructible. It has also been claimed that of all the Gold known to have been mincd almost equals all the Gold now in known existence. My hardness is 2.5 to 3 and my specific gravity is 19.3! You know my color. My notable occurrences include California, South Dakota and Alaska, USA; Russia, South Africa, Canada, India and Western Australia. You know what it feels like to hold me. I invite you to transfer that surety of recognition to the holding of other minerals.

Elemental Earth Grid:
California, USA: I emphasize pure optimism!
South Dakota, USA: I emphasize the treasure of the heart.
Alaska, USA: I emphasize power.
Russia: I emphasize ever traveling towards beauty.
South Africa: I emphasize knowing your own preciousness.
Canada: I emphasize the true richness of life.
India: I emphasize the striving toward perfection.
Western Australia: I emphasize sharing the joys of life with good, true friends.

Physical, Emotional, Mental Integration: Come by my fire and warm your soul. You have fire in you as well. If we join our flames, we will see the path ahead of us and it will *shine*......

Electrical Body Alignment: I will assist you in remembering and acting upon the fires of your chakras.

Affirmation of Support: *"I am an endless flame of life!"*

Dreamtime Doorway: The fire of spirit always extends itself to you, human-with-spirit.

Stone Story:

I wait in the cool earth

absorbing her fires,

stretching my flames

forging my body

solidifying my creatorheart.

I am here.

I love to be with you.

I love to feel what you are feeling

to know the spark of human.

It glistens upon the earth~its own special jewel.

I will frame your jewel

and we will worship the sun

the seasons

the flash of the ages,

all beauty

all wonder.

Wherever I am, joy leads.

Summary: Gold energizes us with warmth, happiness and creativity.

Goshenite

I am Be3Al2Si6O18, a variety of Beryl. I am the colorless variety with a hardness of 7.5 to 8 and a specific gravity of 2.36 to 2.91. I am used as a gemstone and a source of Beryllium. I am found in most all Beryl locations including Africa, Sri Lanka, USA, India, Burma, Korea, USSR, Columbia and Australia.

Elemental Earth Grid:
Africa: I emphasize purity and re-invigoration.
Sri Lanka: I emphasize the beauty of the land.
USA: I emphasize gentleness in strength.
India: I emphasize daily reverence.
Burma: I emphasize timelessness.
Korea: I emphasize beauty.
USSR: I emphasize the ideal.
Columbia: I emphasize bounty.
Australia: I emphasize brilliance.

Physical, Emotional, Mental Integration: Whatever happens I am here with and for you. I outlast all your illusions and resistances and just keep displaying your constant ideal. My light is not here to show you its sparkles, it is here to show you your way.

Electrical Body Alignment: I unite us with our chosen ideal.

Affirmation of Support: *"I am what I choose to be!"*

Dreamtime Doorway: When I sigh it is not because I wish for something else, it is because I admire what is.

Stone Story:

Ahhhhhhh, let us breathe together.

Not often do words find me.

They slip away in the light of my ways.

All before me is wonder.

All within is the same, just more.

The beauty of life inspires me to act upon the truth of who I am.

If you walk with me,

you will explore the passion of responsibility.

If you talk with me

I will sigh.

Summary: Goshenite simply and continually models its own perfection.

Green Kyanite

Yes, yes, it's true. In "Stones Alive!" we listened to Kyanite, already. And yes, those words do express the heart of Kyanite, including green Kyanite. Still, when it forms in green, instead of its usual blue......something different happens...... and its story offers us something just a little different than before.........something that exactly helps us in what we are doing and being today, right now. That is the heart of synchronicity—
the language of magic— that happens all across the earth every moment.........

I am Al2 SiO5, Aluminum Silicate, green in this case. I am a polymorph of Andalusite and Sillimanite. My hardness is 4.5 when parallel to my axis and 6.5 when perpendicular. My specific gravity is 3.58. I can be found in Brazil, USA, USSR and Africa. When you hold me, look to the realization of movement towards the heart.

Elemental Earth Grid:
Brazil: I emphasize the excitement of discovery.
USA: I emphasize the natural joy of open minds and hearts.
USSR: I emphasize whatever I am led to emphasize.
Africa: I emphasize innermost loves.

Physical, Emotional, Mental Integration: I am soft and I am strong. I am a mixture of so many things, and that is what I recognize and honor in you. I will hold all the unusual parts of you in so much admiration that you will look upon yourself anew, thinking, *'I really AM amazing!'*

Electrical Body Alignment: I align us with the most unusual parts of life.

Affirmation of Support: *"I am a rare treasure upon the earth."*

Dreamtime Doorway: I follow you to whatever doorway delights you................

Stone Story:

This is a glorious moment.

Life flows through us so delicately

***and** so powerfully*

that our hearts open to each other

as if we lived in a garden of trust.

Spirit joins so well in us

that we join with each other

even though

we look so different,

even though our languages

sound so different.

We embrace that!

We celebrate our differences so lovingly

that life itself smiles and surprises us,

"Here. Here is where you are the same—the heart."

That is the seed of every miracle ever born or imagined—

the utter uniqueness of life living in the same, perfect oneness.

Summary: Green Kyanite rejoices in our differences!

Hawkseye Velvet Tourmaline

I am an unusual Tourmaline found specifically in Arizona. I am black but also transparent and translucent in some respects. This is because I am composed of many, many parallel-aligned tubes that allow light to reflect and refract around them. This is somewhat like the condition that exists in star effects in other stones. Each of my crystals is a hollow tube. How does this happen? How is this possible? As yet a mystery. Enjoy.

Elemental Earth Grid:
Arizona, USA: I emphasize shapeshifting and time travel.

Physical, Emotional, Mental Integration: You are miraculous. I am miraculous. There is nothing about that that I will deny, so I invite you, RIGHT NOW, to join me in living **miraculously.** *How would you change your life if you knew every moment that you are an undeniable, unlimited miracle?*

Electrical Body Alignment: I link you to the union of body and spirit and miracles.

Affirmation of Support: *"I am a miracle!"*

Dreamtime Doorway: The doorway to the unknown lies within all of us. All we need to do is to look freshly upon our usual times and spaces and find the mystery that always lives alongside habit.

Stone Story:

I know who we are.

The source of the Hawkseye Tourmaline was revealed to me in a most unusual fashion. While exploring a remote mountain range in central Arizona, I spent some time in a very unique canyon. During the course of this geologic field excursion, I had spent time studying the geology from the edge of the mesa tops with the aid of binoculars in order to note the details of the geology in the canyons and valleys before mapping the area in detail on foot. I did not have aerial photos, so a semi-aerial view was helpful to note features which should have be checked more carefully later. This pre-mapping gives me a rough sketch of the larger scale geologic features and familiarizes me with the area prior to walking out the detailed geology.

This region is about 5000 feet in elevation, in the pinyon and juniper biotic zone, above the cactus filled upper Sonoran desert and below the cool Ponderosa pine forest. The area is alive with wildlife and a fairly thick growth of vegetation; rain-

(con't on next page)

Whether you understand it or not

I act upon this.

My world contains only wonder

and the impossibilities that linear reality can only hope for.....

I hope for nothing.

There is no need.

Everything that I require to create the most spectacular unimaginability

lives and breathes

in me

right now

just as I am

just as I am always.

I ask you now with full awareness and unerring clarity:

Will you join the world of miracles?

Summary: Hawkseye Velvet Tourmaline co-creates magic in our everyday world and beyond.............

Heliodor

I am Be3 Al2 Si6 O18, the yellow variety of Beryl. My hardness is 7.5 to 8 and my specific gravity is 2.36 to 2.91. I do not include specimens that are golden colored as they are simply called Golden Beryl. I can be found in Madagascar, Brazil, the USA, the Middle East and the USSR.

fall is sometimes plentiful and the temperature is mild.

The fall air was crisp and the pinyon trees had a good crop of pine nuts which were being enjoyed by most of the animals in the area. The trees which were laden with the most cones had a golden appearance due to the clusters of cones in the tops of the trees. I would tap the cones with a stick to release the pine nuts and avoid getting my hand covered with pitch. Fresh pine nuts are an excellent treat which I have enjoyed since childhood.

One morning I found an excellent vantage point to view a good portion of the canyon I was about to explore. While glassing the area with binoculars I noticed a group of four adult ravens flocking from pinyon to pinyon tree feasting on the pine nuts in the tops of the most heavily laden trees.

These large, intelligent, midnight black birds are known to have very special qualities and are revered by Native Americans. The low angle of the early morning fall sun would reflect off the shiny black feathers in silvery flashes as the ravens harvested the nuts and flew from tree to tree.

(con't on next page)

Elemental Earth Grid:
Madagascar: I emphasize living authentically.
Brazil: I emphasize the power of choice.
USA: I emphasize the unlimitedness of freedom.
Middle East: I emphasize the abundance of spirit.
USSR: I emphasize every smile.

Physical, Emotional, Mental Integration: I gently pulsate in all parts of you. If there is anything there that needs renewal, I shine upon it. Lifeforce loves you. I remind you of what you already know.

Electrical Body Alignment: I connect you with eternity.

Affirmation of Support: *"I feel the glow of spirit within me."*

Dreamtime Doorway: Ahhh! There are openings to love and abundance everywhere, because love and abundance is everywhere!

Stone Story:

Spirit remembers you

every moment

every way.

It is your path to forget this

for a blink.

It makes you no less exquisite

no less divine.

How do you know this?

Because spirit remembers you

and that memory is eternity.

Summary: Heliodor shines unconditional love upon us where we most need it.

The ravens were being very vocal and are known to scold other animals to drive them away from their territory and also to warn other ravens. To my surprise, I notice a large mature buck mule deer underneath the tree the ravens were feasting in. He was busily eating the pine nuts dislodged by the ravens which had fallen to the ground. The ravens would not feed on the nuts on the ground for fear of coyotes and other predators which are abundant in this area.

As the ravens flew from tree to tree, the deer followed for their free meal. As morning turned into afternoon, everyone got their fill of nuts. The buck ventured off to browse and nap while the ravens found a thermal to play in. A thermal is a warm column of rising air which allows birds to remain aloft without flapping their wings. I noticed this thermal was caused by the sun shining on a black outcrop of rocks comprising a small ridge on the south facing side of the canyon.

As I watched the pattern of the ravens and deer feed each day, I noticed the ravens spent a good part of the afternoon catching the thermal above the black out-

(con't on next page)

91

Hessonite Garnet on Smokey Quartz

I am Hessonite Garnet, a red-orange-brownish variety of Grossular and my hardness is 7 to 7.5 with a specific gravity of 3.59. (See "Stones Alive!" for information on Smokey Quartz.) Grossular is Ca3Al2(SiO4)3, Calcium Aluminum Silicate, and like the other Garnets forms cyrstals with 12 rhombic or 24 trapezoidal faces, or even in some combination thereof. As Hessonite Garnet I am one of the basic gems in Vedic Astrology. I can be found in Sri Lanka, Brazil and California as gem quality Hessonite (and have been called Cinnamon Stone), but here I particularly surfaced in China on Smokey Quartz. I invite you to feel your attraction to me as a marriage of multiple parts of yourself.

Elemental Earth Grid:
Sri Lanka: I emphasize incredible mystery.
Brazil: I emphasize following instincts.
California, USA: I emphasize the glory of exploring.
China: I emphasize letting go of pain to absorb more life.

Physical, Emotional, Mental Integration: We offer you perseverance when you have no energy. We offer courage when all you can see is fear. We offer you inspiration when all around and within you are dark. To accept our gifts, all you must do is go more deeply into all of life and death.

Electrical Body Alignment: I unite you with your own center of power.

Affirmation of Support: *"I remember my power no matter what."*

Dreamtime Doorway: I travel through and beyond the dark night of the soul.

Stone Story:

Sit down beside me.

The storm may go on a long time.

Let's watch from under these trees.

---

crop of rock. After a few days, my curiosity got the best of me and I was drawn over to explore the ravens hangout.

I was amazed to find a zone cut by black velvety tourmaline which contained a few veinlets of high quality hawkseye tourmaline. As I respectfully gathered these beautiful stones which shimmered in the sunlight, the ravens soared above me wondering what took me so long to come see what they were trying to reveal to me. I found several black shiny raven feathers among the hawkseye stones, both having a black color with a silvery sheen. I was grateful to be shown such an unique and special gem with such magical properties by the guardian ravens of the canyon.

~Robert P.

All life upon the earth holds death
and all death holds life.

It is only the illusion of separation
that allows you to believe
you can have one without everything else.
Your smiles birth from your tears.

Even when you feel calm
anger grows restless,
nearby.

We are, all of us,
every color
at once
right now.

When you feel, know, accept
the rainbow of life-death
intimately
profoundly
the storm will not shake your roots.

Summary: Hessinite Garnet on Smokey Quartz invites us to the source of strength.

Huebnerite

I am MnWO4, Manganese Tungstate. I am the Manganese rich member of the Wolframite group. I tend to be lighter in color and less dense than the other members of my group. My color is reddish brown and my hardness is 4 to 5.5 with a specific gravity of 7.2 to 7.6. I can be found in France, Germany, USSR, USA, China, Peru and Australia.

Elemental Earth Grid:
France: I emphasize will.
Germany: I emphasize certainty.
USSR: I emphasize practicality.
USA: I emphasize ruggedness.
China: I emphasize determination.
Peru: I emphasize connecting with divinity.
Australia: I emphasize the humor in the darkness.

Physical, Emotional, Mental Integration: Words are not my first language. I speak, now, simply, so that those of you, who have not met me, can meet me in your ease. Otherwise, I speak in acts and synchronicities that you create and that I support. I help you to connect your body to your soul ceaselessly. Now.

Electrical Body Alignment: I link you with the mystery of your own intent.

Affirmation of Support: *"I act upon my Spirit this and every moment."*

Dreamtime Doorway: You can find whatever you choose.

Stone Story:

> *I may seem too potent to some of you.*
>
> *Actually I am a being of the silence.*
>
> *I am soft yet unyielding.*
>
> *I travel gently so that I can see all possibilities.*
>
> *When I find what I choose to do and be*
>
> *I become it immediately.*

I merge with possibility until I am reality.

If you wish to speak with me

that is my language.

If you choose yourself fearlessly and fully

we will merge and we will create beyond ourselves.

If you do not know your own choices or potential

then I will point them out.

I will insist upon it.

I will discover your will.

And if that reflection is too powerful for you,

then it is your own life that is too much for you.

Summary: Huebnerite invites us to create our own lives.

Ivoryite

I am a natural substitute for Ivory that is suitable for carving and jewelry. I am a unique variety of an extremely fine grained mineral called Magnesite. I am a naturally occurring mineral and have not been altered by man. I have the creamy color, smooth texture and satiny luster of natural ivory. I occur in tabular beds approximately one inch thick, in pieces weighing 1/2 pound up to 5 pounds. My hardness is 5 to 5 and 1/2. I am composed of Magnesium, Calcium, Silica and Oxygen. I was deposited in an ancient highly saline sea similiar to the Red Sea in the Middle East. This type of ancient sea bed is called a sabka and allows the precipitation of the mineral Magnesite along with subsequent heat and pressure. I am found in Arizona.

Elemental Earth Grid:
Arizona, USA: I emphasize smiles.

Physical, Emotional, Mental Integration: Welcome. Where Ivory is delicate, I am strong. I remind you of its gentle art painted upon the earthscape so that you can pause your separation, your fear, your competition, just to be love.

Electrical Body Alignment: I show you the core of admiration.

Affirmation of Support: *"I adore every wonder of the earth."*

Dreamtime Doorway: The universe awaits you. It is ever open.

Stone Story:

> *For you who have known*
>
> *a breath of innocent love*

that took you over,

you know me.

I live awe, admiration and respect.

I invite you to take every complete breath of love

and carry them with you as the tools they are.

Let them build your house

and your communities.

Let them shape your laws

and write your plays.

They will help you in every question and decision ever known.

They are your true foundation of life upon the earth.

Use your tools.

Hone them with trust each day.

Share them immediately.

When they become your first thought and aid in any challenge,

your body will live countlessly young and vital.

Your breath will free itself from the top of your chest

 melting through blockages.

You will know what it is to be a human of awe.

Summary: Ivoryite helps us to release our unnecessary attachment to ego and to free ourselves continually.

During a particularly challenging time in my life (my father and my best friend both terminally ill) my niece Amy decided to get me something to cheer me up. She went to a metaphysical store because she knew that this is where she would find the perfect gift. She was in there for over an hour because she couldn't decide. There were so many beautiful pieces of jewelry but this one plain-looking ring kept "talking" to her. When she gave me the gift I felt honored when she told me the story of how she spent so much time and the process that she went through choosing the ring. It wasn't until I held the Lepidolite ring in my hand that I understood how perfect it really was. I immediately felt a sense of calm, my heart chakra softened and expanded and I felt a sense of hope. Another gift of this story was to see the look on Amy's face when I told her that she had listened to intuition to get me the perfect gift. This opened up a whole new realm for her.

A continuing story......

(con't on next page)

Lepidolite

I am $KLi_2Al(Al, Si)_3O_{10}(F, OH)_2$, Potassium Lithium Aluminum Silicate Hydroxide Fluoride, of the Mica group. I am an ore of Lithium and have a hardness of 2.5 and a specific gravity of 2.8. My usual color is varying shades of purple to pink. I can sometimes vary into white, gray or yellow. I am most notably in Brazil, Russia, Africa and California, USA. When you hold (or even gaze) at me, you may feel a sense of calm, patience, a possible interruption of your ongoing thinking process.

Elemental Earth Grid:
Brazil: I emphasize softness, the treasured feminine in all.
Russia: I emphasize reverence.
Africa: I emphasize the natural order of things.
California, USA: I emphasize tranquility after the storm.

Physical, Emotional, Mental Integration: I am beautiful, just like you. I know this; I remember this each moment. When you look upon me, I will affirm the beauty that is us: *Your body will remember and act upon this. Your mind will remember and speak of this. Your heart will remember because it never forgets; it will lead all of you into more…*

Electrical Body Alignment: I remind you to live in, and with, what is truly important.

Affirmation of Support: *"I forgive all."*

Dreamtime Doorway: In your most treasured moments, you will find the love to be more.

Stone Story:

I so love to have visitors. Are you surprised? I enjoy your company and you honor me by listening to the words that I offer.

Just like you, I am formed of unconditional love. We walk different roads in that and we still begin and end in the same place. Every step is perfect and belongs to life, itself.

I feel you stretching across my words, trying to understand. It is of no matter whether you understand or not. Today is a breath, a single moment, and an endless opportunity to grow more love upon the garden of the earth. If you accept that (understanding or no), you plant sweetlove on your journey. It is that simple. Everything is simple— ask your heart.

If you accept the gifts and the opportunities of love, then you will ever know what is important—

in each moment,

in each thought,

in each act,

in each feeling.

Then you will willingly, happily surrender everything else because it does not serve love, it does not grow more love: *Of what use would it be to life?*

Surrender everything and you will be left with love, because you are love.

Forgive everything else simply because you can.

Forgive and feel your heart stretch past these words, across the whole of the earth

in an enormous embrace.

You are more love.

That is the beauty that is life.

Summary: Lepidolite reminds us of love and forgiveness and all that truly matters.

When I decided to explore how certain rocks or crystals might help balance my daughter who has a mental illness, I contacted a woman who I buy stones from and told her of my situation. She recommended Lepidolite! My daughter now wears the Lepidolite ring of mine and I bought her a wand to hold in times of extreme stress. This stone is truly one of my favorites. I'm grateful for all the balance it has brought to my life and that of my family.

~Claudia A.

Personal Story

I absolutely love Lepidolite. It feels like unconditional forgiveness to me.

One day I was working at our room at the Tucson Gem Show. A lot of great people came by, until a guy we'll call, Bill, visited us. Nothing could make him happy. Everything he saw in the room was either too expensive, or not the right quality. I did everything I could to please him. And then I tried even more, until I felt like I had overdone it. Then I didn't mind that he wasn't happy— after all, I couldn't really please him anyway— but I didn't like the feeling in me that was trying too hard. I was expending way too much energy out of some old "people-pleasing" issue that I didn't want to be part of anymore.

Tohmas came to the room at the end of the day so that we could go home. I felt a little unhappy. As we were driving back, he handed me a bag, "It's a present for you." I opened it up, quietly. I unwrapped a good-sized Lepidolite, in the shape of **tree.** *It was me! I felt all that forgiveness flood over me and nothing else mattered. Everything was fine in my world.*

~Marilyn T.

Personal Story

Just thought I'd give you an update on your Lithium product. Our healer, Kathy, is using the Life Enhancer headband on her father who has Alzheimer's and is having positive results as he can now put words together.

I've watched him over the last couple of weeks where he had difficulty in folding her business cards in half the right way and can now package her products correctly.

Kathy says that she can see that the Lithium is healing the plaque in the brain caused by Alzheimer's.

~Janyce M.

Lithium Clay

I am Calcium Lithium Carbonate, hand-harvested, in the Southwest, USA, and I contain some of the highest Lithium content known. I am a Calcium structure where Lithium has replaced the Calcium. My crystals are more blocky and sharper than Calcite crystals, and I am a yellow to yellowish-brown to white color. In clay form, I am predominantly white.

Elemental Earth Grid:
Southwest, USA: I emphasize connecting to the earth.

Physical, Emotional, Mental Integration: I am here. I love when you use me; it gives me more life! Whatever you need, ask for it. I know how to fill in the space that wants something.......

Electrical Body Alignment: I unite you with your efficiently-running body!

Affirmation of Support: *"I give and receive whatever is needed."*

Dreamtime Doorway: This is your home. When you allow yourself to be full and welcome in your body, you will enter into the fullness and the welcome of the earth.

Stone Story:

I am harvested from the Earth Mother.

My heart never strays from there.

She pours out such sweet, unconditional love.

It stretches through the roots and stars of me and so far beyond I cannot see it all.......

I absorb it thoroughly, richly.

Being blanketed in her soft care, I offer the same to you,

for I know how and when and where she loves you as well.

I pass onto you her far-reaching support with all the joy that has shaped me.

I pass on her support through my body, through my being.

It awaits you.

Whatever you need to grow strong and stronger in this kind garden,

it awaits you.

Summary: Lithium Clay roots us into the unconditional support of the earth.

Lithium Crystals

I am Calcium Lithium Carbonate, hand-harvested, in the Southwest, USA, and I contain some of the highest Lithium content known. I am a Calcium structure where Lithium has replaced the Calcium. My crystals are more blocky and sharper than Calcite crystals, and I am a yellow to yellowish-brown to white color.

Elemental Earth Grid:
Southwest, USA: I emphasize whatever you need.

Physical, Emotional, Mental Integration: I support all of your biological processes according to what you need. Emotionally, I offer stimulation or calm— whatever promotes balance in this moment. I encourage you to feel and to use the healing qualities within you in every now.

Electrical Body Alignment: I link us to incredible gratitude for all.

Affirmation of Support: *"I am all that I need to be whole, right now!"*

Dreamtime Doorway: Everything that you are brings you what you need.

Stone Story:

I revel in beauty

which is every wave of life and feeling, joined.

It sweeps me away

in passions of delight.

Soaring through the currents of life

I twist and twirl

offering my geometries of love,

welcoming to my dance

all lovers who long for more…

We meet now

to exchange wonder.

There is nothing that we cannot caress with

our own special love.

Summary: Lithium Crystals easily show us how beautifully and naturally stones support us.

Personal Story

Tohmas had just come home from buying a lot of stones and he had done a particularly magnificent job. He gave me the largest rutilated quartz I had ever seen, and then I helped unpack an enormous, 100 lb + Amethyst Mountain, with completely intact, milky white Calcite crystals!!! Everywhere I looked there were new treasures.

Then he handed me a small, lavender-colored Lithium crystal. There were more stones to see, but I couldn't move. I literally couldn't move because something was going on with my body. My left forearm straightened out and coolness filled it. It wasn't uncomfortable, but it was very distinct. The chill moved up to my upper arm. I could feel every muscle and vein in it very clearly. Simultaneously the rest of my body wasn't cool; in fact every other part of me was warming up and tingling. It felt great.

I went back to work and my left arm felt strange but strong. I could wield it more consciously than usual. The feeling lasted for at least an hour. To this day, I don't know exactly why this happened, but I do know that Lithium will add heat or coolness to a chemical equation, according to what needs to be catalyzed. So I just trust that the Lithium Crystal added the cool to my arm and the heat to the rest of my body, to balance me just as I needed.

~Marilyn T.

Personal Story

"I purchased a Lithium on Chalcedony stone from AhhhMuse that can best be described as a "hand comforter." It fits perfectly in the palm of my hand and, thus, seems to radiate its effects much better than if I just placed it on my body. The first thing that struck me about the stone was the density of Lithium Crystals covering the Chalcedony. As I held it the first time, I was taken by the "need" to slow down. To me, the Lithium almost demanded it!

This wonderful stone has come in handy when I'm wound up at night and can't sleep due to the "busy brain" complex. I place the stone in my left hand (receiving energy) and allow its vibratory pattern to direct the soothing effect in my body. I encourage anyone who has trouble sleeping and/or needs a stone that allows them to slow down their harried life to locate a Lithium on Chalcedony stone and try it for themselves.

~Laurel D.

Magnetite

I am Fe3O4, Iron Oxide and am a natural magnet and a member of the Spinel group. My color is usually iron black with a metallic luster and my hardness is 5.5 to 6.5 with a specific gravity of 5.1. My crystals are typically octahedral, occasionally twinning and psuedomorphic. I can be found in South Africa, Russia, the USA and Argentina. When you look to connect with me, be aware of my grounded magnetism as well as my ability to psuedomorph.

Elemental Earth Grid:
South Africa: I emphasize contentment.
Russia: I emphasize here and now.
USA: I emphasize respecting the inherent beauty of all.
Argentina: I emphasize freedom in all choices.

Physical, Emotional, Mental Integration: With me, you root your soul into your body, fully, instantly. Then your senses awaken; they become messengers of this world and of everything else. Calm eases your metabolism and clears your breath. You are home.

Electrical Body Alignment: I link you to the spontaneous awe of being with and upon the earth now.

Affirmation of Support: *"I love living upon the earth."*

Dreamtime Doorway: I look for the old bitterness. It wants to be found. It wants to be found so that it can change now to the gratitude it has secretly ever been.

Stone Story:

Every body is a piece of the earth. When you accept that so utterly that you rejoice in the sheer wonder of it, then you are a peace of the earth.

Though some will see earthliving as full of limits, you will fly. You will soar while being ever more profoundly rooted in you and into the earth.

Being present with yourself and with the earth, who has given all of herself, strengthens you. It does not fill you with struggle, it overflows you with the sharpness to see the earth as she is: bounteous, loving, and spirit-with-a-form. Knowing the earth shows you how to know you: bounteous, loving and spirit-with-a-form.

Be with yourself. Be with yourself upon the earth. Separation slips away and limits are no more.

Summary: Magnetite brings us to the core of ourselves and the earth.

Mangano Calcite

I am (Ca,Mn)CO 3, a Manganese rich form of Calcite. I am a particularly beautiful pink variety from Peru.

Elemental Earth Grid:
Peru: I emphasize the healing in beauty and delight.

Physical, Emotional, Mental Integration: Peace.

When you come to me, I hold your hand. I hold your heart. Whatever struggles in you, I breathe with it. I sigh out loud, and I join with your struggle until nothing needs to feel that difficult ever again.

Electrical Body Alignment: I unite you with clear, nurturing breaths.

Affirmation of Support: *"I am full of forever calm."*

Dreamtime Doorway: You can travel anywhere on a sigh..........

(con't on next page)

105

Stone Story:

When you know love,
nothing worries you.

When you know peace,
you need nothing else.

When you first know yourself,
you discover fears, hurts
on the surface of pain
ever ready to give you an excuse for staying
struggle's captive.

As you go deeper into
yourself
it is impossible not to finally discover
Peace.

That is the core of life.
That is the core of you.

You can accept that or not
as you choose.

If you dare to accept that
miracle

and tell us about how she had gotten her Mangano Calcite yesterday when she was very sick. Deb went right to bed and rubbed the stone all over her belly. Within an hour, she wasn't sick at all.   And the next day she woke up feeling better than ever!

~Marilyn T.

what fear would dare

to control your destiny?

Summary: Mangano Calcite travels with us to the core of our nurturing.

Meteorite

82% of all Meteorite falls are Chondrites which are small bits of formerly melted minerals that have come together with other minerals to form a solid. In my form as Chondrites I am believed to be among the oldest rocks in the solar system. Most of my composition as Chondrite can be Iron, Enstatite, Sulfides, Plagioclase, Pyroxine and occasionally, Olivine. 7.8 % of Meteorite falls are Stony Meteorites (called Achondrites) and some believe these originate from the Moon or Mars. Howardites, Eucrites, and Diogenites are called HED meteorites and are said to originate on the asteroid Vesta. Chassignites, Shergottites, and Nakhlites are called SNC meteorites and are are said to originate on Mars. There are also many and varied mysteries that are associated with me (we have one variety that no matter how small it is broken up, when put under the microscope it is virtually made up of spheres and pyraminds and joinings of them) and I continue to display unknowns.

Elemental Earth Grid:
I emphasize the possibilities!

Physical, Emotional, Mental Integration: Where would you like to go? I will show you new worlds. With me, you can see the earth as a star and your body as a light upon it. Together we will find the ways to care for your gorgeous light.

Electrical Body Alignment: I show you how to root into the earth and the stars.

Affirmation of Support: *"I am a light upon the earth."*

Dreamtime Doorway: To travel with the stars, you must give up what you know in favor of what you will learn.......

Stone Story:

To travel here

sets me ablaze!

Within that fire,

life shows me its passion spiraling onto itself.

The pure preciousness of it

lights and lightens my eyes.

I must care for life

of every kind, way and possibility.

I am a gardener of the universe.

Summary: Meteorite gives us the chance to see and know ourselves freely.

Mookaite

I am Windalia Radiolarite, a fossiliferous sedimentary rock from Australia. I get my name from where I am primarily found, Mooka Creek in Western Australia. I can wear golds, reds, pinks, purples and burgundies and I can take on a high polish/glow. My sillification can form Opalite, Chert and Chalcedony. If you look into me microscopically, you will find that I am mostly composed of tiny remains of Radiolaria — an unusual skeletal structure of silica. When you hold me or gaze upon me, you may feel the strong Dreamtime connection with other worlds, while still being grounded in your body comfortably.

Elemental Earth Grid:
Australia: I emphasize all the worlds.

Physical, Emotional, Mental Integration: I remind us of our complete presence in the world and in every dimension, simultaneously. I share that caring for the physical body cares for the soul. That guides you towards hope and actions that inspire you even when you believe nothing can do that.

Electrical Body Alignment: I link us with every form of life that honors us.

Affirmation of Support: *"Everything reflects to me the wonder of the universe and of my wonderful, perfect place within it.*

Dreamtime Doorway: I will guide you wherever you wish to go. It is my honor. Just ask.

Stone Story:

I know you.

It pleasures me to watch you walk this beautiful star.

With every step

you sing a song

full of all the stars

that travel the world.

Deep in your heart

you breathe and smile

all the other songs~

of other worlds, yes,

and of this one

where you grant yourself

the form of your love.

Wonder!

With each step,

you bring other stars to this earthstar

to drink in the glory of

Grass

Trees

Children

The Moon dancing in your belly

Colors

Rain

Crystal Mountains

Unexpected courage

Oceans

Irises

Apples

Gold

Hugs

and all the endless forms

that you encounter love in here—upon this star--

within your body.

Through you the universe

caresses and listens to each of these

treasures.

Your courage to dance your life here

brings heart and love

to worlds that you pretend that you cannot see

so that you can focus on this one

~this sweet one now~

For that gift,

I offer love and

admiration untold—

until you caress and listen to me now.

Love.

Summary: Mookaite shares how to be multidimensional citizens of the earth.

Morganite

I am Be3 Al2 Si6 O18, the pink variety of Beryl. My hardness is 7.5 to 8 and my specific gravity is 2.36 to 2.91. I am named after J.P. Morgan and my color is the result of trace amounts of Manganese. I can be found in Brazil, Madagascar and the USA. When you hold me look to see what is in your heart.

Elemental Earth Grid:
Brazil: I emphasize glistening.
Madagascar: I emphasize fulfilling wishes.
USA: I emphasize unlimited bounty.

Physical, Emotional, Mental Integration: The ease is in your heart. It is not in others. It is not in the ways that you dream of secretly. It awaits you in your heart.

Electrical Body Alignment: I reunite us with the simplicity of love.

Affirmation of Support: *"I enjoy the gifts of love."*

Dreamtime Doorway: I am not always easy, but I am here. You do not need to TRY too hard to work with me.

Stone Story:

When you hold your friend's hand

worlds disappear.

You just know its warmth

and you want to hold it next to you forever.

The kindness of friends

the loveliness of nature

they touch

just as surely as a friend's hand.

They touch your heart

unveiling its vast arrays of treasures

sometimes unknown but ever ready.

Touching your own heart

is the forever

you dream of now.

Summary: Morganite quietly reflects the beauty of our hearts.

Mother Earth Spheres

I am exquisitely re-constituted Quartz with Cinnabar. (I may contain other "impurities" such as Barite or organic matter.) I hail from China with such profound life force that I am called, "Mother Earth Spheres." I know it is unusual to find such a creation as me here, in a space devoted to natural minerals, but I invite you to look beyond preconception and feel the strength and beauty of my lifeforce and my invitation to you to join me in deep, co-creative relationship with Quartz, Cinnabar, the Earth Mother and Humans. When you hold me or gaze upon me, you may realize some or more of the organizational properties that are inherent in the vibration of the Earth Mother as a constantly changing, respectful Being.

Elemental Earth Grid:
China: I emphasize the new ways mingling with the old for transformation.

Physical, Emotional, Mental Integration: I richly regenerate every part of your being, just as you choose. This catalyzes your dreams and any resistances to them. I align your thinking with efficiency, rather than just logic, alone. I help to organize communication between systems.

Electrical Body Alignment: I can align with the profundity of life.

Affirmation of Support: "Today I know who I am and that is enough. I am enough."

Dreamtime Doorway: An opening in the universe calls out to you. Will you answer it even though it looks and sounds like no other.......

Stone Story:

> *I sound across the ages.*
>
> *I speak of infinity*
>
> *as I am infinity.*

I speak with you

as you are infinity.

We come together

and even forever grows.

Touch me

to awaken the sleepiness in you

that forgets to remember.

We belong with forever

until we give away our power.

Summary: Mother Earth Spheres remind us to look at life with love, letting go of judgment.

Personal Story

When a friend of ours asked us if we were interested in these beautiful red spheres, we would have normally just said no. We had previously not been very attracted to any stone or combination that had been treated, altered, reconstituted, etc.

For some reason, now, these red spheres were different(They are reconstituted Quartz with the addition of Cinnibar.). We said, "Yes!" It just connected and made "sense." The minute the very large sphere came into our space, it took over and organized everything in a core vibrational way. Ok.

We have learned so much from our willingness to embrace these beings as "unaltered" manifestations of who they really are. The allowableness that it took for us to invite these "unnatural" forms into our lives has opened the doorway for many more forms of the mineral kingdom to come and play with us, as we choose to expand on our open-heartedness and appreciation of their forms respectfully. I feel this is the greatest gift we have received from the

Personal Story

In 2003 we were introduced to a new find (for us), the Mother Earth Spheres. When Lee was seeking information from the Sphere, she heard that this stone will go to those who need it and that the people that obtain it will know what it is for and what to do with it. Generally, the minerals that we sell come with a description of the mineral and the metaphysical properties that they contain. In this instance, the Mother Earth Sphere was telling us that those who need it and know what to do with it will find it and work with it.

Dave is a Reiki Master Teacher and has been blessed with the gift of working with Indigo, ADD/ADHD and special needs children. Early this year, Andrew, a marvelous 7 year old boy came to visit Dave. Dave did not have a regimen for Andrew to follow, but instead let Andrew take the lead. Pretty soon Andrew discovered our huge 83 pound Mother Earth Sphere. He placed it in the center of our healing room and then began placing other minerals in a circle around the Sphere. At

(con't on next page)

Mother Earth Spheres, beyond their organizational offerings. They have helped to teach us to honor the human part of co-creation in new ways based on the initial choice of the elements involved. They still organize the space, but "organize" now has the ever present potential to be defined in every new and expanded ways. Thank you.

~Tohmas T.

least 8 rows of different minerals were arranged around the circumference of the Mother Earth Sphere. Each mineral was selected and strategically placed by Andrew. The process took about 2 hours and when he was finished, he asked Dave to listen. Andrew tapped the Sphere with the zipper of his sweatshirt. He said, "Did you hear that?" Dave was a bit surprised that Andrew tapped the Sphere and wasn't prepared to hear anything. He told Andrew, "No, I'm sorry, I didn't hear anything." So Andrew tapped the huge Sphere again. This time Dave heard the din of the Sphere when it was tapped. "Ah, yes," Dave replied, "I did hear it!" and to this Andrew stated, "Good. This is for the healing of all mankind."

How blessed we were to be in the presence of this old soul, a 7 year old named Andrew. With this affirmation, we are believers that this mineral will fall into the hands of those that will know how to use it. And, we are firm believers that it is imperative to "Listen to Children."

~Dave and Lee H.

Nepalese Quartz Crystal

I am a variety of Quartz, SiO2, Silicon Dioxide, found in the Himalayan Mountains of Nepal. When you hold me you can feel the clean, clear coolness of the high Himalayas.

Elemental Earth Grid:
Nepal: I emphasize your highest potential.

Physical, Emotional, Mental Integration: I tone the sinuses and warm the heart. I open up possibilities until you expect miracles. Together, we promote life-long calm.

Electrical Body Alignment: I gently remind us that we all are masters.

Affirmation of Support: *"I love because I can."*

Dreamtime Doorway: The answer to anything is to perform every act fully, utterly, lovingly.

Stone Story:

Listen.

All things place themselves in the path of perfection.

Everything sings their single note of life force

walking in the world.

The music lands upon my soul

and grows it next to the roots of banyon-wonders

while also lifting me to the rings of Saturn.

All this I know and more

because I am a child of the earth

and I love this home,

which is all of us.

Summary: These Nepalese Crystals speak to our spirits.

Neptunite

I am $KNa_2Li(Fe, Mn)_2Ti_2Si_8O_{24}$, Potassium Sodium Lithium Iron Manganese Titanium Silicate, and am named after the Roman God, Neptune. My hardness is 5.5 and my specific gravity is 3.23. My color is black, to brown with a reddish heart. I can have well formed crystals that will flash my red heart. I can be found in Ireland, the USSR, Greenland, Canada and the USA. When you hold me the first thing you may feel is all things balancing all other things.

Elemental Earth Grid:
Ireland: I emphasize ever deepening feelings.
USSR: I emphasize belief.
Greenland: I emphasize the constancy of the heart.
Canada: I emphasize instantaneous feelings.
USA: I emphasize bonding.

Physical, Emotional, Mental Integration: When you hold me, you remember the wonder of water and the natural, unassuming flow of all life. My gift to you is to help you clear your emotions (and there are so many that you store needlessly) so that you can treasure the ones that truly belong to your heart.

Electrical Body Alignment: As you wish, I link you with the natural ebb and flow of emotions and their innate wisdom.

Affirmation of Support: *"I listen to my heart and act upon its dreams!"*

Dreamtime Doorway: Look into every form of water. That is you. You are mostly liquid and emotions.

Stone Story:

Today

we revel in the essence of each other.

How is this possible?

Not all of us have met.

Not all of us know each others' names.

Yet we are joined

for the sea of feelings flows around us

and within us

with constancy that imagination has not yet dared.

We are born of emotions

and we live in them

though our ways of expressing them

infinitely

unique.

If we listen to the waves

of feelings,

we will know each other

even when we do not understand the languages.

We will simply know each other.

Summary: Neptunite reminds us of the omnipresence of emotions within us all.

Orpiment

I am As2S3, Arsenic Sulfide, and am orange-yellow to yellow. I am very sensitive to light and will break down to a powder after continued exposure. My hardness is only 1.2 to 2 and my specific gravity is 3.5. My name derives from the Latin, *auripigmentum*, which means golden pigment. I have traditionally been used as a dye or pigment. I tend to form with my friend, Realgar, and can also have a distinctive odor due to my Arsenic content. I can be found in Eastern Europe, Western Europe, the USSR, the USA, Japan, Peru and Australia. When you hold me you can feel the pulse of ...

Elemental Earth Grid:
Eastern Europe: I emphasize delight in the little things!
Western Europe: I emphasize the magic of color.
USSR: I emphasize the healing in any experience.
USA: I emphasize child-likeness.
Japan: I emphasize energy.
Peru: I emphasize quality.
Australia: Yes!

Physical, Emotional, Mental Integration: We stand for all the wisdom that has been gathered through the ages and we absorb and proffer it in this time, this moment. Wisdom is eternal, like grace and truth. We support your timeless values and when you receive that your body unclenches and relaxes into timelessness as well.

Electrical Body Alignment: I point out to you that eternity is all around (and listening) and within you.

Affirmation of Support: *"I respect the ways of wisdom."*

Dreamtime Doorway: Some things you will enjoy; some things you will dislike. Either one is your trusted, sacred teacher.

Stone Story:

You measure life

in time

in the space

that you carefully allot it.

If I measured life

(and I do not)

it would be in

graciousness

love

and a smile that would stretch across forever.

Eternity ever reminds us

that love

is us

is forever

is the life

that never leaves us, even when we leave it.

Summary: Orpiment loves us to act upon timeless, unconditional ways.

Papagoite

I am $CaCuAlSi_2O_6(OH)_3$; Calcium Copper Aluminum Silicate Hydroxide. I am a rare copper mineral found in Arizona and the Messina location in South Africa. I am named for the Papago Indian tribe of Arizona. I am a rare four-membered silicate with four tetrahedrons linked into a ring as structure. My color is dark sky blue in crystals and I become paler in veins and inclusions. I tend to be associated with my friend, Ajoite. When you hold me or gaze upon me, feel my love freely.

Elemental Earth Grid:
Arizona, USA: I emphasize truth.
South Africa: I emphasize acceptance.

Physical, Emotional, Mental Integration: I am freedom. Welcome me and you will release the pent-up frustration and pain that longs to be gone. Welcome me and you will restore your own energy and will put your heart in charge of your life.

Electrical Body Alignment: I link your heart with truth right now.

Affirmation of Support: *"I am free!"*

Dreamtime Doorway: Deep inside of everything, past the denials and the politeness awaits the truth, clear, perfect, whole. Always reach for this. Always aim for this and you will find yourself.

Stone Story:

Yes, I am an ancient traveler. I know this Earthstar. I have praised it from far and near.

It gloriously allows so many beings opportunities to grow— and that always means more freedom.

Whenever you grow, it means that you are growing more freedom.

It means that you awash in life. It absorbs, caresses and then clears every part of you.

When you are more (when you grow), you expand and expand into life so far,

so far beyond yourself,

that you cannot go back

anymore.

You can only go forward.

You can only go to the home that you don't remember yet it worships every particle of you.

When you keep moving forward, you will no longer allow fear to shape your body

and crush your destiny.

You will never be satisfied with half a soul again.

You will stretch into space and you will know this Earthstar from roots to stars.

You will stretch into the vastness of you.

It is the journey of eternity.

Summary: Papagoite holds an ever growing vision.

Pectolite

I am $NaCa_2Si_3O_8(OH)$, Sodium Calcium Silicate Hydroxide. In my blue form I can be called Larimar although there is some confusion around all of this and doubt among some mineralogists because of other mineral influences. Larimar people also claim that Larimar is only found in the Bahamas. You get to decide. My hardness is 4.5 to 5 and my specific gravity is 2.7 to 2.9. I am white, grey, green, yellow, colorless and pale to sky blue. I can be found in the USA, the Bahamas, Canada, Scotland, England and Peru. I am likely to form with Zeolites and I do not necessarily bend and am brittle. Feel that brittleness when you hold me and see where it takes you.

Elemental Earth Grid:
USA: I emphasize all your traits.
Bahamas: I emphasize fire and water.
Canada: I emphasize capability.
Scotland: I emphasize connecting with others.
England: I emphasize efficiency.
Peru: I emphasize visions.

Physical, Emotional, Mental Integration: Remember when you were very small and you decided things about life because you were happy or hurt? I remember them with you. I celebrate your endless love and I nurture your wounds. But now that you know this, it is time: It is time for you to carry your love, fearlessly, out into the world and to let your pain slip away like the illusion it has always been.

Electrical Body Alignment: I unite you with the underlying strength at your core and at the core of all possibilities.

Affirmation of Support: *"I can take care of myself in anything."*

Dreamtime Doorway: Memory is a miracle. Do not let your mind take it over and smother its service. Memory teaches you who you are when you fearlessly align it with truth. Yes.

Stone Story:

So many Stonebeings visit you here. They celebrate you and the divinity that breathes in you and forms the body that you wear. My celebration of you is a gift. Let me set it beside you and whenever you wish to open it, it will spring to life— your life.

I will not say that you will always enjoy my gift.

I will say that it is shaped from the heart.

I will say that it is the witnessing of my soul and I gift it to you freely, always freely.

How many times will you find such a gift?

Here it is.

It lies next to us, unopened, yet ever open.

It awaits your touch, your free consent.

It will wait past forever and it will wait beyond patience into ever-new love.

It is free.

This gift is free.

It knows you. It remembers you. It sees you.

It is simply your gift.

Summary: Pectolite clearly sees all that we are.

Petalite

I am Li[AlSi4O10], a reddish aggregate found in South Africa, Canada, USA, Sweden, Brazil, Afghanistan and Western Australia. I can also be colorless, to white, gray and even greenish. My hardness is 6 to 6.5 and my specific gravity is 2.4. I am rich in Lithium and have been cut as gemstones in my colorless state. When you hold me the first thing you may feel is how everything really wants to be if it were not held back by separation.

Elemental Earth Grid:
South Africa: I emphasize gifts.
Canada: I emphasize being carefree.
USA: I emphasize embracing.

(con't on next page)

Sweden: I emphasize satisfaction.
Brazil: I emphasize optimism.
Afghanistan: I emphasize trust.
Western Australia: I emphasize laughter.

Physical, Emotional, Mental Integration: I tingle your body. I show you the smile in you that is ever ready to be shown and to be USED! Wherever you are too stiff, I ease that part into sweet grace.

Electrical Body Alignment: I join you with delight.

Affirmation of Support: *"I bring love to every moment."*

Dreamtime Doorway: I lift myself up to my most beautiful, perfect state!

Stone Story:

> *Walking through life*
>
> *you look so serious.*
>
>
> *Take my hand.*
>
> *Ease is around every corner*
>
> *you just have to breathe a little more*
>
> *to find it, to wear it.*
>
>
> *You sharpen your senses*
>
> *with fear*
>
> *when you can expand them*
>
> *with joy.*
>
>
> *Remember*
>
> *you do not have to earn divinity.*
>
> *it goes wherever you go.*

Summary: Petalite turns our hearts and our eyes ever upward.

Pipestone

I am Catlinite, a reddish brown metamorphic claystone argillite. I am a mineral made up of Diaspore, Pyrophyllite, Muscovite and Hematite, along with traces of Anatase and Chlorite. I am named after George Catlin, the American artist who, in 1836, recorded the Sioux legend of Pipestone: *"At an ancient time the Great Spirit, in the form of a large bird, stood upon the wall of rock and called all the tribes around him. Taking out a piece of the red stone, he formed it into a pipe and smoked it, the smoke rolling over the whole multitude. He then told his red children that this red stone was their flesh, that they were made from it, that they must all smoke to him through it, that they must use it for nothing but pipes: and as it belonged alike to all the tribes, the ground was sacred, and no weapons must be used or brought upon it."* (Excerpted from "Life and Adventures of Frank Grouard" by Joe DeBarthe.) My most famous home is Pipestone, Minnesota although I can be found in other places including Arizona. My softness of 2.5 on the Moh's scale (about the same as the human fingernail) allows me to be easily shaped. When you touch me, look for the sacred within.

Elemental Earth Grid:
Minnesota, USA: I emphasize living in your center.
Arizona, USA: I emphasize the power of being.

Physical, Emotional, Mental Integration: If you can feel me, listen to me; you will also hear the deepest parts of your body. All children of the Earth Mother have bodies that hold the sacredness of being alive, of giving their spirits through their bones and their hearts. When you hold me, your heartbeat will smile. It will breathe more fully and you will be able to not only hear its rhythm, you will know its song, and you will dance it throughout your life.

Electrical Body Alignment: I can link to the most ancient wisdom.

Affirmation of Support: *"I am truly alive and divine in this body."*

Dreamtime Doorway: Smoke yourself. You take time to know the distractions. But will the distractions carry you into infinity? Smoke yourself.

Stone Story:

Please.

Listen to my voice.

It does not belong to me.

It unfolds from the spirit that moves in all things.

This sweet voice that can reach anything

across time, space and even fear,

echoes the love of all spirits.

It only knows kindness.

Whatever I say will gift you whatever your soul needs

and whatever the deepest part of your heart craves.

Listen.

My voice harmonizes with the voice

in the pit of your belly

in the beat of your heart

in the spreading of your bones

and the full flowing of your blood.

We are the ancient ones.

We are the wisdom that has planted itself in the Earth Mother

and yet has the freedom to move, to grow!

Let your footsteps ring with this truth.

I will meet you there with one voice

and many bodies.

Summary: Pipestone ever appreciates sacredness.

Prehnite

I am $Ca_2 Al_2 Si_3 O_{10}(OH)_2$, Calcium Aluminum Silicate Hydroxide. I have been named after my "discoverer," Colonel Hendrik von Prehn. I am usually a pale green or yellowish-green although I can also be found as grey, white, red or colorless. My hardness is 6 to 6.5 and my specific gravity is 2.9. I can be found in the USA, South Africa, Namibia, China, Canada and Australia. When you hold me you may feel my watery-ness.

Elemental Earth Grid:
USA: I emphasize music.
South Africa: I emphasize dance.
China: I emphasize union with all things.
Canada: I emphasize allowability.
Australia: I emphasize the journey.

Physical, Emotional, Mental Integration: One of the ways to open up the gifts of my heart is to play music for me. I am here to breathe with your heart, to ever remind you that life flows through you ever more abundantly, as you keep opening your heart. When we walk together, we will feel all emotions. It is a challenging, precious journey that can stretch your heart into forever.

Electrical Body Alignment: I help your heart to speak the language of spirit to all parts of your being.

Affirmation of Support: *"All my actions show my heart to me and the world."*

Dreamtime Doorway: Just feel. Dedicate yourself to that.

Stone Story:

Please. Come sit with me. Hold me close. Let's just watch the sun ride across the sky and how all of life dances with it in its own perfect way......no words between us until we have witnessed and absorbed this parade of life.

Welcome! We know our hearts and now we are home together. Just to walk this earth in this powerfully quickening moment demands such courage that your heart steps to the forefront of all that you do. To truly live upon the earth now you must open your heart. To thrive you must keep opening your heart over and over and over. Absorb this. My words come with love and logic cannot explain it. If you cannot feel this yet, then come back again, over and over again.

I am here.

I await your open heart and we will name the mysteries with smiles.

Summary: Prehnite urges us to keep opening our hearts.

Psilomelane

I am Ba(Mn+2)(Mn+4)8O16(OH)4, Barium Manganese Oxide Hydroxide. I am a Barium bearing Manganese specimen, made up mostly of the mineral Romanechite. I am black, to brownish gray with a hardness of 5 to 6 and a specific gravity of 4.4 to 4.7. I can sometimes appear banded with alternating layers of grey Pyrolusite. I can be found in Western Europe, the USSR, the USA and India. When you hold me you may well get a sense of time, or some version thereof.

Elemental Earth Grid:
Western Europe: I emphasize quiet presence.
USSR: I emphasize nothing and everything.
USA: I emphasize being in the body.
India: I emphasize facing everything.

Physical, Emotional, Mental Integration: I know you from the depths of your being. I am calm with your struggle. I am present with your denial. I am love when you are afraid.

Electrical Body Alignment: Together we join with the Center Stillness.

Affirmation of Support: *"I am whole."*

Dreamtime Doorway: The treasure lies within.

Stone Story:

The peace of the world

does not touch you.

I wear it

we are one.

You long for the relaxation

that comes with a still, observing heart.

Yet

you are here living with separation.

If it was possible for you to be one with anything

that may be it.

When you yearn for forever calm

know that you all must do

is to choose to join

everything.

Summary: Psilomelane shows us the core of stillness and acceptance.

Quetzalcoatlite

I am $Zn_8Cu_4(TeO_3)_3(OH)_{18}$, Zinc Copper Tellurite Hydroxide, a rare, bright blue mineral named after the Aztec god, Quetzalcoatl. I am a minor ore of Tellurium and I come from the Moctezuma area of Sonora, Mexico. My hardness is 3 and my specific gravity is 6.1, very heavy for a translucent mineral. In addition to my Mexico location, one specimen has also been found in Tombstone, Arizona.

Elemental Earth Grid:
Sonora, Mexico: I emphasize patience.
Arizona, USA: I emphasize brilliance.

Physical, Emotional, Mental Integration: When you hold me, you know reality. You *feel* me in your toes and your bones. This immediacy invites all parts of your being (particularly your mind) to accept what is and to respond with your biggest, brightest dreams.

Electrical Body Alignment: I link you with your own co-creatorship.

Affirmation of Support: "*I respond to everything with joy, trust and creativity.*"

Dreamtime Doorway: You will forget divinity. You will sleep through wonder. You will do all of these things and much more.....and whatever you keep doing is your continual, free choice.

Stone Story:

Here I am.

I am a being of the ages..........like you. We have known each others' ways and tests. I do not expect you to remember because you want to do so much first.

I am patient.

I am timeless.......... I am. I am here. Whatever my choices I accept my beingness. I just accept.

You will know so many things because you have the gift of awareness, the spark of ever mutating consciousness: A wonder to behold, a challenge and a privilege to live.

Will you nurture your experiences with awareness?

It awaits your intent.

The awareness is timeless infinity.

Whenever you wish to claim it, to use it,

to shape it with your uniqueness

it is here and now.

Summary: Quetzalcoatlite shares with us the honor of responsibility.

Personal Story

Rainbow Boji®

When I met Joe he gifted me two Boji® stones about the size of a small ball (just a little smaller then a golf ball), they were partners of course, male and female. I kept them at work and used them in my treatments with other stones for some time. One day I was going through my purse to find some other stones I carry in a small pouch, when inside this pouch was a very small (size of a marble) Boji® stone. I thought how sweet of my husband to gift me this little fella in my purse. When I got home I said, "thank you" and held out my baby Boji® stone. He then explained that he was not the one who gifted me this new being, he assured me it was not him. I then spent many days asking everyone I knew, clients included; "did you place this little Boji® stone in my purse?" No one ever claimed to have placed him there and in time I realized he was, just was to be, in my life. The years passed and I spent many days holding onto this little soul and touching the magic of life we encounter each day. He was such a reminder to me that

I am Boji®. I am here in this world by design and I bring to you an energy that is unique and intentional. I am a concretion stone, a combination of Palladium and Pyrite. While most minerals combine the masculine and feminine aspects into a single stone, I evolve into separate gender manifestations, as well as in androgynous forms. My usual appearance (as Boji®) is dark, mostly black to brown and I come as spheroids, either in female, as mostly smooth, flat, flying-saucer-shaped, or as male, in bumpy, geometric platelet protrusions from a smooth substrate. As Rainbow Boji®, I am very different in my coloration, appearing much like Rainbow Hematite showing off many, many colors. My colors can predominate singly or can be a true rainbow mulitude. I also occur frequently as a single Boji®, unpaired, androgynous.

Elemental Earth Grid:
Kansas, USA: I emphasize efficient communication.

Physical, Emotional, Mental Integration: It is simple. I help you to see what makes you truly glitter, shine and glow! Some things inspire you because you have learned it so. Yet further within you are more inspirations
that just like you and you, them. Together we find them and the real you of your dreams.

Electrical Body Alignment: I link you to the core of all communications.

Affirmation of Support: *"I am truly alive!"*

Dreamtime Doorway: Insist upon being you. I do.

(con't on next page)

134

Stone Story:

I help you to balance yourself. This we do, together, first. Then you are able to really hear me and to touch the love in my every word. I come to you to show you utter health expanded outward and inward into true vitality.

True vitality knows you and fuels you when you drop all the ways that you have taken on just to survive. Each of you carries them. You compromise infinitesimal pieces of your soul so that you can keep your body intact. Yet this is not necessary. Do you hear me: it is not necessary to give away your soul to keep your body! In fact it is impossible.

When you do not completely honor the full power and uniqueness of your being and body, both, you welcome in death where only life used to be. A piece at a time, you invite more and more death until your body is a stranger to you and the only thing that is left to you is to die as easily as you can.

Ask for more life. Respect your soul utterly. It will always lead you to the unique bliss that you are created for and are. Its light will show you the delights of life even when fear haunts you and makes death seem inevitable. It is not. You are.

Summary: Rainbow Boji® sparkle with endless inspiration!

Personal Story

I have changed my life a lot since I have met Boji®. I think without Boji® we wouldn't start our business. Taka was very much into minerals but I was not. I feel like Boji®. And Rainbow Boji® remind me that I was with minerals before.

For me, before I met Rainbow Boji®, I was a very blinded, boxed in, in Japanese society. I feel like Boji® opened me up and the Rainbow Boji® opened me up more to the minerals Spirits and to people. With Boji® I can be very good antenna. I always have Rainbow Boji® with me and sometimes I wear as a necklace and I feel like I am getting the message. And also my body gets stronger senses. In Tokyo, I am very much around people and so many minds and so many negative vibration, so to me Boji® protect me from these vibrations in Tokyo. It is very important for me to have Boji® in Tokyo. A lot of people in Japan are starting to make Boji® bracelets and necklaces to wear.

miracles do happen and that we just need to acknowledge them and sit with them in real time. The story continued for me until just last month. I was lecturing at DIHA (The Desert Institute of the Healing Arts) in Tucson, Arizona. I always take stone gifts for the students and facilitator of the group when doing lectures or teaching. Well, it happened this day that there was one extra person in the group then I had expected, so I took out of my purse my little pouch of stones and laid them on the table for David to choose one. He asked me about each stone and how they came to me; I explained my time with these stones and opened my heart for him to take the one he was drawn to. David chose the little Boji® stone. In the past this might have been hard on me to release him to a new home; but my soul was excited to know that David would embrace this little being with love and anticipation of finding this Boji® stone a mate.

~Mary N.

Also, from my customer, I have heard many farmers like Boji® very much. Like organic farmers. They have never known about minerals and live in old area of rural Japan but sometimes they must come to Tokyo and then they need to wear Boji® to deal with the city.

I also have a how to say Boji® flashback: It's like when I was at the pyramid harvesting (at the mountain where Boji® are found). After hunting Boji®. I go back home and before sleep I see the pyramid mountain and the Boji® . I see like movie. It still happens after sometimes now as flashback - like printed on my brain. I am just very much connected to Boji® energy. I feel Boji® more and more and so can say that am always with Rainbow Boji® and connected to source. Especially when we are driving car. I see scenery and then suddenly I see the pyramid mountain, it is always coming to me. After I know about Boji® energy, I feel like it release my fear to be here (in body as human) as human.

~Moto S.

Personal Story

In the summer of 2003, I joined my sister of the heart, Karen (and our friends Moto and Taka) on a visit to Boji® land. I was so excited as it had been quite a few years since I had been there. I was also concerned over my ability to keep up on the hike. The past 2 years had been very challenging as my walking had been extremely painful. A doctor had told me I had bone spurs in both of my feet.

The night before we were to hunt the Boji®, I had a dream. In the dream I was walking along and on the ground glistening in the sun appeared a Rainbow Boji® shaped just like a foot. I picked it up, sat down, and took turns placing it on the bottom of both my feet.

When I awoke the next morning, my thoughts were filled with a knowing that my feet had been healed. I shared my dream with my friends as we proceeded to pack our food and water for the long journey ahead of us. The day was a scorcher at 100 degrees, with little to no shade for us. We took a muddy bath in a small lake before we set out on foot to hunt the vibrant Boji®.

Perhaps an hour had passed as we walked on the dusty dirt and I had found a few small brown Boji® here and there. Then, from the corner of my eye I saw a gray lump of dirt that I knew I had to check out. It was stuck to the ground

---

Personal Story

Boji® are incredible. To me, no other stone relates more or better to human bodies. It balances us quickly and easily. Even people who say they don't "feel" stones, they feel Boji®.

I knew the regular Boji® long before I had even seen a Rainbow Boji® (Comparatively speaking they are rarer.) I saw them at our booth at the Tucson Gem Show. I listened to them without thinking about it. When people came into our room and were interested in the Boji®, I had them hold two regular Boji®, one in each hand. It balanced them nicely. Then I took a Rainbow Boji® in my hand and it asked me to run it over the person's body, without actually touching them (which I did after I had asked the person's permission, of course.). As I did it, the Rainbow Boji® would always pause my hand over a particular part of the body. Then it would tell me why that part of the body needed work, and I passed that onto the person. Often times, the Rainbow Boji® would pick out old misalignments, like someone

(con't on next page)

136

like glue so I decided to plant myself next to it. My friends turned around to look at what I had found. Karen said, "Could be a clam shell. It's probably not a Rainbow." We took turns for a while gently picking the dirt away from around it until it was free. A big lump of dirt with bumps – Boji® bumps! Hmmm.

It sure was heavy and big and grey. If I was going to keep up, it was time to pack it and go. My companions were already out of sight! Soon I was feeling kind of funny. I needed shade and water for awhile, so I found a clump of rock and decided to take a break.

My friends left me there for quite awhile. After some time I had chipped away for what seemed like hours, carefully removing the dusty dirt. For the next 10 days we soaked and scrubbed and continued to free this grey Boji®. Sparkles began to appear: gold, blue, green. This labor of love had revealed a Rainbow Boji® shaped just like my foot! I placed the Boji® on the bottoms of my feet just like in my dream and to this day I have been able to walk pain free!

~Shakti

Personal Story

The Boji® and the Rainbow Boji® have been great stone friends in my life and they certainly have attracted amazing people and stories to me. For instance, one time we were doing a show and this fellow came up to our booth and stood there a long time, holding a Rainbow Boji® to his forehead, silently. Now we had never met this man before and we weren't quite sure what he was doing.

After quite a while, he told us, "These stones are very special. They come from a 'ring' where they are in contact with lots of celestial beings." Kip went onto describe the land where we gather the Rainbows accurately. Then he told me that if we wanted to get in contact with those celestial beings, we needed to put the Rainbows in a circle, around the pyramid where I meditated.

Now he really got my attention, cause I certainly had never told this guy that I meditated under a pyramid, on my deck (with my dog, who loved it!). So the very next time that I could, I put a large ring of Rainbow Boji® all around my pyramid. As I put the very last one into place, I could feel it. It was absolutely incredible. It was so potent that my dog growled and wouldn't go near the pyramid for the first and only time ever.

~Karen G.

being "pigeon–toed" and how that original imbalance was also negatively impacting other parts of the body. Sometimes the stone would speak of old injuries and how they had never healed fully. So far, everybody who has experienced this recognized what was said and appreciated the information.

~Marilyn T.

Rhodozite

I am (K,Cs)Be4Al4(B, Be)12O28, Potassium Cesium Beryllium Aluminum Borate. I am a pale yellow, to grey, white or colorless. I can be found in Madagascar and in the Ural Mountains of Russia. My hardness is 8 and my specific gravity is 3.3 to 3.4. I am a small little ten-sided stone that can be quite intense. When you hold me, look to your own feelings and respond-ability.

Elemental Earth Grid:
Madagascar: I emphasize support.
USSR: I emphasize constancy.

Physical, Emotional, Mental Integration: I translate, bridge, and empower. Look for me when you seek true balance in any area.

Electrical Body Alignment: I link with the universe.

Affirmation of Support: "I am harmony."

Dreamtime Doorway: I am here. I am a part and a partner in this journey.

Stone Story:

Let me be where the need asks for me.

When you do not understand something,

call me.

I will speak the word that you do not know of

that will join you with clarity.

When you fear something,

call me.

I will show you the path where courage and fear

travel together

each accepting the other.

When you need to integrate something,

call me.

I will point out your heart

where only union exists.

I offer the direction

you must travel it.

Summary: Rhodozite bridges us to where we are going next.

Roselite

I am Ca2(Co, Mg)(AsO4)2 - 2H2O, Hydrated Calcium Cobalt Magnesium Arsenate, a pink to rose-red to dark-red mineral. My name comes from an 18th century mineralogist, Gustav Rose. I have a hardness of 3.5 and a specific gravity of 3.5 to 3.7. My color comes mainly from Cobalt, much like my friend, Erythrite.

Elemental Earth Grid:
Morocco: I emphasize glorious imagination.

Physical, Emotional, Mental Integration: Yes. I ease, soften and sttrreetchhh your breathing. I sharpen your senses to match your ever-growing consciousness and I firm up your body, your focus and your intent, simultaneously.

Electrical Body Alignment: I link you with refreshing energy.

Affirmation of Support: *"I am love, beauty and perfection."*

Dreamtime Doorway: This is it. This is the initiation. It is all an initiation and you are everything you need.

Stone Story:

Many stones help you to change

beyond yourself.

I come to you

because you already live as

ever increasing perfection—

I support that and record that

in the timeless stonelibraries of wisdom.

In every way

in every moment,

my heart accepts you utterly.

As you feel this

you blossom like an eternal rose.

*You **know** your perfection*

and you grow more.

Summary: Roselite recognizes the divine perfection in our humanness.

Rutile

I am TiO2, Titanium Oxide, with a hardness of 6 to 6.5 and a specific gravity of 4.2 to 4.3. I am very metallic-like and can be red, brownish-red, yellow and iron-colored to black. I am found in Europe, Africa, the USSR, the USA, Brazil and Chile. When you hold me or gaze upon me, be aware of the electrical alignment of whatever is present for you, now.

Elemental Earth Grid:
Europe: I emphasize fun with work!
Africa: I emphasize vitality.
USSR: I emphasize stamina.
USA: I emphasize constant momentum.
Brazil: I emphasize a much needed boost.
Chile: I emphasize wildness.

Physical, Emotional, Mental Integration: I know the pulse of your electricity, the flow of your blood. If you ask, I will clarify them, tone them, and fill them with passion. You have a body so that you can unfold its wonders and dance with them in every act.

Electrical Body Alignment: I join you with the lifeforce vibrating in you.

Affirmation of Support: *"I act with LIFE!"*

Dreamtime Doorway: Though we may not know it, we always have friends that will support us. They will come just at the moment that we want to give up and they will remind us that energy is endless.

Stone Story:

All beings carry a story.

Within them and all around them soars energy

to carry that story to all corners and circles of the world.

When you fill yourself with the passion of a fulfilled heart

you fill that energy with the same.

When you fill yourself with fear and doubt,

you paralyze that energy—

your story is hushed.

Even when you don't feel *like it,*

Feed your being the finest hope and faith.

Then the story of your life will fly to all others

graciously allowing the story of life, itself

to be told to you,

to be gifted to your brave heart

and then the most incredible dreams will land upon you

to be created with ever growing joy.

Summary: Rutile moves us to positive, conscious action.

Sahara Sand

I don't have a chemical composition to present to you here. And even if I did, it would probably vary widely depending on the exact location where you gathered me and which camel peed on me. I simply have a strong personality and in the form that lives here with Twintreess, I am a reddish-golden color and you can feel my heat and my earthiness regardless of your seeming location or temperature. I invite you to bury yourself in me.

Elemental Earth Grid:

Africa: I emphasize electricity.

Physical, Emotional, Mental Integration: My fineness will sift through your blockages, reminding you to breathe.....to know you have choice......to release fear, as you wish. I will help you to clear yourself though your defenses pretend to have forgotten how.

Electrical Body Alignment: I join you with electricity!

Affirmation of Support: *"I am free and clear!"*

Dreamtime Doorway: Within the earth awaits whatever we need. If you need to be refreshed, a river appears. If you need to clear your deepest confusion, a vast desert offers itself to you. It filters your uncertainty until you know that you know.

Stone Story:

I am the fire in the sand. I hold the pure heat and the intense light of the sun in infinitesimal particles. Between them life breathes exquisiteness! Hold me and you hold the space for more passion than you have dared to imagine.

143

The passion comes to every being who lets go of the war-within.

The passion comes to every being who lets go of fear-as-a-god.

The passion comes to every being who lets go of separation-before-life.

The passion breathes within all of us.

It will flame you when you move your stubbornness from its path.

Let pride fuel the fire and you will be un-owned by petty need or desire.

Bury yourself in the deep sand and you will stop holding anything

that is holding you back from life!

Summary: Sahara Sand introduces us to the fullness of life this moment.

Personal Story

Talking Sand.

When I first arrived in the Sahara desert 33 years ago on the pink sand dunes of Mazuga in Morocco I got lost in the beauty of the sand. Instead of just having a pile of sand by my door, I decided to find a nice door with a nice house behind it near the dunes. Sitting and letting the sand run between my fingers from one hand to the other I enjoyed the slight prickling and the wonderful designs. I found a message: Wisdom. But I did not know what to do with it. This time (in my life) I was still after adventure.

So many years had gone by; I had moved to the north to grow up my children. We always had a pile of sand next to the door. When I returned to the Mazuga sand dunes again, I got lost again, again; this time in a sand storm. The dunes have one body about 10 miles long. The local people, the nomads, know exactly where the head is and the feet. I got lost around the belly and tried my best to reach the highest dune. The storm cleared up and I had a breathtaking look to Algeria. I turned around and oriented to some faraway light which must have been a little town. When the sand talked, the wind was his tongue.

When extraordinary things happen to us, we try to find an explanation. The sand said, "Move." I said, "What? You? Sand?" I asked in disbelief. I am always ready for new games and adventures. Between all these serious people on

massage or loving touch or anything else could access— only the creeping cold, death-cold could. I was beginning to come to a state of separate reality. Of course I was in no mortal danger, but it felt so. To be blocked, frozen to such a degree that these areas could not be felt came to me as a blazing truth, I had agreed to that. Until that moment I had no idea about it. The sand supported me, kept me safe. To be buried in sand, this cold sand must have been a blessing compared to the feelings trapped there in my body, that of betrayal, that of worthlessness and being un-loved. After that it occurred to me that I have a fire in my belly and all I had to do was to turn it up— that was the second-to-last night there. I thought it would have been possible to be cold anywhere now and I would be able to handle it.

All through this time since— now 10 months— my shoulders are continuing to unfold. It is a very reassuring sensation to know that I have uncovered the ancient "cold."

Thank you Sahara.

~Margherita V.

the planet there are not so many which are ready to play, even the children. So here's the game: I started the sand wiggle, which is a dance to shake the sand out of your pants…because the sand asked me to move. So I shook the sand out of my pants and out of my flute and played a sandy blues: chanting, singing, dancing in the dunes; making designs and standing on my head. It didn't move him at all. I got the message again: Move me, <u>ME</u>! I asked the sand, "How? In my pocket, in kilograms, in tracks, in containers?" The sand replied, "As much as possible to America." Then I exclaimed, "America!" and fell back on my back laughing and dancing with the sunshine on my feet because they were up in the air. I then asked, "Where in America?"

"Everywhere. And first Arizona."

I told him, "This is ridiculous. You are flying tons worth, day and night, summer and winter, in higher atmospheres over the Atlantic. You come down in the South American rain forest and are found melting the American glaciers. And sometimes you are on top of our cars."

For awhile I talked about everything I knew about sand. I even wrapped under his nose the story about how my third son almost died in a sand storm going to fill a bottle of sandstorm from the highest dune. Eventually I run out of facts and stories and look around. Sand is everywhere from beige yellow, to orange, to peach pink , to purplish-red, to dark red, to purple, calm and beautiful, not a single sound, nothing.

Part II: I filled up my pockets, empty water bottles and everything which held sand and left heavy. My next visit at sunrise, I went up to the highest dune filling up two sacks, as much as a camel could carry. So I somehow managed to ship this to America to distribute there. I invented the Sahara Sand laptop which is fossilized agate or marble with a small rim to hold half a kilo of sand where I then place some Moroccan stones, some crystals, and some little sandstones. During the Tucson Gem Show in February, I walked around with small bags of sand to give to nice people with a friendly smile (like you!).

In spring I visited the Sahara Sand again. He is also a great healer. I told him he had to pay his ticket for his transportation (for distribution). For an answer, I watched a small dust devil just around me. The inspiration he gave me is that I discovered lots of playful sandy things. For example, I throw it up in the air and see what designs he makes. I put him next to doorways. I put him in soles in shoes. And of course, I put him in the laptops. It is all there, just know how you see it and use it. I also had the feeling that the sand knew a lot more about me than I knew about him. My great love for sand made me move my ass and open up new worlds to explore and many games to play without rules. So this is not my only great love. When I look at it this way how any sand fits on the face of the planet, he or she always invites us gently to lay down and relax. Also, in the concrete age, sand holds together our houses; sand in movement in higher atmosphere I see as a part of Mother Earth's astral body. There are particles you can see like floating veils.

In the beginning of October, I went to the desert again in good company of two friends, Sahara lovers like me. We drove out to the dunes on a nice clear afternoon and stopped two miles before on a new place which is built on a small hill which is the only one all around. I sat and watched the changing colors of the dunes in the afternoon light. The whole dunes' body stretched out long, enormous, 10 kilometers. A mist came up from the Algerian border mixed with the setting sun creating layers of veils – purple, pink and turquoise, moving, moving with the sun's rays and in long shadows. So I glimpsed the beauty and the wholeness and all I could do was breath, that's it. That's all there is at the beginning and at the end, finally, breath.

When we headed back, our usual Inn had a big sand dune right in front of the entrance. I could not see anything else, except for a brand new, gleaming, aluminum chair on top of it. Fantastic! We were the only guests (in room number 5). A sand storm came up. The days were still burning hot. So I just drank my water and read my books for 3 days. Some men walked in the distance, digging a well in the dunes. I walked out there and looked. There was sweet, light Mazuga water there– the best drinking water in my life. I talked to the well diggers for a while and watched the water make designs with the sand like lava. I filled my bottle and went as high as I could to the top to hear the sand talk. He said to me, "You did not come for sand this time. You came for water." I drank as much as I could and I filled up with as much water as possible and I felt good – so well. Nothing hurt anymore. This is one of the most beautiful journeys I have ever had with many miracles on top and below.

~Rashida A.

Samarium

I am the Element Samarium. My symbol is Sm and my Atomic Number is 62. As a member of the Lanthanoids group, I do not occur naturally in mineral form. I am most often found in Xenotime, Monazite, and Bastnaesite and Samarskite. I am named after the mineral, *Samar-*

skite, which was named for Vasili Yefrafovich von Samarski-Bykhovets (1803-1870), Chief of Staff of the Russian Corps of Mining Engineers. My current technological uses are: carbon-arc lighting for the motion picture industry; a permanent magnet material with one of the highest resistances to demagnetization known; optical lasers, alloys, headphones, and as an absorber in nuclear reactors.

Physical, Emotional, Mental Integration: Look for me in your own hands. When you understand what genius you hold there, then hold me, too. I will recognize all your true capabilities, and because I recognize them, I will urge your body to ground them in your entire being and to root them into the earth for full support and manifestation.

Electrical Body Alignment: Together we will find the unusual creativity that you need to keep evolving.

Affirmation of Support: *"I am a human miracle!"*

Dreamtime Doorway: The chances to change dramatically may not seem to come along often but what does it matter if you are ready when they come.......

Stone Story:

Don't think about me.

I'm not here for you just to hear my story.

If you truly want to know me,

*then know **you.***

You must unfold the fullness of you.

Yes, I know that you do not understand that:

How can you find what you don't know exists?

That is the question for this age.

To insist upon its answer is to lead yourself

into the massive evolution that is your destiny.

Yet no one can truly tell you what that is

for evolution is not something you can project,

it is a gigantic leap into life

into the abyss.

In mid-air, you will find

your evolution

and it will find you.

Summary: Samarium catalyzes our unknown genius.

Scheelite

I am CaWO4, Calcium Tungstate, an ore of Tungsten (which means "heavy stone"). I am appropriately named after Karl Wilhelm Scheele, the "discoverer" of Tungsten. My hardness is 4.5 to 5 and my specific gravity is 5.9 to 6.1. I can be grey to white, yellow to brown, orange-ish, and sometimes colorless. Some of my notable occurrences are in the USA, Brazil, China, Tasmania, and Australia. I form in pseudo-octahedral crystals that are tetragonal and dipyramidal. In a green variety known as Cupro-Scheelite part of my calcium is replaced by copper, hence the color change. Large crystals of Scheelite have been found in Japan completely altered to Wolframite and are called, Reinite.

Elemental Earth Grid:
USA: I emphasize intent.
Brazil: I emphasize bounty.
China: I emphasize no judgment.
Tasmania: I emphasize independence.
Australia: I emphasize possibilities.

Physical, Emotional, Mental Integration: I offer myself to you. Because I listen to your body profoundly, I know how to speak to you in the ways that will most comfort and bolster you when you feel utterly depleted. I can re-fill you. I can soothe you. I can help you, as much as you allow it. My gifts will inspire you to extend perfect trust.

Electrical Body Alignment: I join you with the workings of your body and the intent of your spirit, simultaneously.

Affirmation of Support: *"I am perfectly aligned."*

Dreamtime Doorway: This is your path. Walk it with awareness.

Stone Story:

> *I wear many forms. My Spirit speaks to you from this golden Stonebeing because that is what your heart welcomes now. But if you need something different to inspire you to your true greatness, I will offer that as well. Sometimes I walk as a healer or I flow as a quiet river. Other times I fly overhead, and you will recognize me if your need is sharp.*
>
> *My spirit travels among many forms. You do not need to understand this. What you need to touch is that I am here. I come as the friend that can truly help you. However you need to see me is how I will appear. I accept you completely, absolutely. Perhaps I even know you better than you know yourself and there is nothing within you that cannot feel my compassion and my peace.*
>
> *To evolve as you are already doing, you must have strong support— support that will rise when you fall and smile when you cry. That is me. Those are the faces that I give to you. Look for me when you do not know how to carry on. Expect me.*
>
> *I come to hold you so that you can hold unconditional love in all of your body and spirit together once again.*

Summary: Scheelite unconditionally bonds with us and supports us.

Silver

I am Ag, the Element, Silver. Native Silver is somewhat rare so most Silver used today is extracted from other silver-bearing minerals. One of the current high demands for Silver is in the photographic industry thanks to my special abilities to respond to light. My hardness is low at 2.5 to 3, but my specific gravity is very high at 9.6 to 12. As a native element, I can be found in Europe, Norway, Canada, the USA, Mexico, Bolivia/Peru/Chile, the USSR and Australia. Also, as a native element, I tend to be found in a wire or hook shape.

Elemental Earth Grid:
Europe: I emphasize embracing the earth.
Norway: I emphasize what is not understood by the mind.
Canada: I emphasize boundaries.
USA: I emphasize mothering.
Mexico: I emphasize reflection.
Bolivia: I emphasize union.
Peru: I emphasize hidden desires.
Chile: I emphasize solitude.
USSR: I emphasize relations.
Australia: I emphasize traveling.

Physical, Emotional, Mental Integration: When you were growing inside of your mother, you were absorbing the world through water and feelings…patiently taking in its ways before you were strong enough to leave the womb.

I am that same patience, that same receptivity and gently I will draw it out from you so that you can birth yourself new each night, and dawn with each day.

Electrical Body Alignment: We align with the moon.

Affirmation of Support: "Peace."

Dreamtime Doorway: I slip into you, as you allow and we ride our dreams into forever.

Stone Story:

> *Melt*
>
> *into the rivers*
>
> *inside*
>
> *the earth*

Soften

your reason

Smooth

your pain

Allow the tides and the ripples

to wash your disbelief

and carry the weight of you

into a realm

where bodies and spirits

are respected as

One.

Summary: Silver encourages us to grow our nurturing and to find family wherever our heart belongs.

Sphalerite

I am (Zn, Fe)S, Zinc Iron Sulfide, an ore of zinc. My hardness is 3.5 to 4 and my specific gravity is 3.9 to 4.2. I can be yellow, brown to black, reddish and green and less commonly white to colorless. I am named after a Greek word meaning, *treacherous rock*, because of the difficulty in correctly identifying me. I am special in that I have six directions of cleavage and that I can twin in unusual ways. I can be found in the USA, Morocco, Spain, England, Peru, Eastern Europe and the USSR. When you hold me you may have to look and feel deeper, past the initial charge you feel, to find my true connection.

Elemental Earth Grid:
USA: I emphasize empowerment.
Morocco: I emphasize responsibility.
Spain: I emphasize strength.
England: I emphasize justice.
Peru: I emphasize caring for the body as a vessel of spirit.
USSR: I emphasize potential.

Physical, Emotional, Mental Integration: Hold me. I am **power** in your hand. Do you choose to know life and love? Hold me and offer me your truth. I will offer you mine and it will warm even the stiffest, coldest part of your being and it will stretch your mind to almost unbelievable possibilities that would like to travel with you now, heart-to-heart.

Electrical Body Alignment: I link you to the knowingness that life and power fills all of us, as much as we believe and allow.

Affirmation of Support: *"I live with and act upon power."*

Dreamtime Doorway: We all live this earthwalk together. Let us choose to be present with each other and then hold hands and hearts.

Stone Story:

Yes.

I am honored to meet you.

I am honor.

Let us not hide from our power and wonder.
The truth tells us relentlessly
* we shine as infinitesimal lights in a star-filled firmament—*
each one perfectly glowing,
each one powerfully, gloriously making up the earth
and the heaven.

What are you doing with your power?

How do you honor it?

This is the only moment

that power and love know

and live in.

Summary: Sphalerite claims its power right now.

Sphene

I am Calcium Titano-Silicate, CaTiSiO5. My crystals are generally thin and wedge-shaped, resulting in my name which is derived from a Greek word meaning, *"wedge."* I am also called, *"titanite."* My colors can be yellow, green, brown, red or black. My hardness is 5 to 6 and my specific gravity is 3.3 to 3.6. Twinning is common for me, especially when I am found in Pakistan. I am also found in Italy, Russia, the USA, Mexico and Brazil.

Elemental Earth Grid:
Pakistan: I emphasize miracles as a way of life.
Italy: I emphasize risking everything for your dreams.
Russia: I emphasize unexpected creativity.
USA: I emphasize new inspiration.
Mexico: I emphasize celebration.
Brazil: I emphasize what is precious.

Physical, Emotional, Mental Integration: Yes! I sparkle upon every incredible inspiration you have ever had. When you really stretch your purest dreams into reality, I grin, and that grin lights up all your chakras and every meridian in your body so that you can attract whatever you truly wish!

Electrical Body Alignment: I link you to the twinkle in your eye........

Affirmation of Support: *"I can do anything!"*

Dreamtime Doorway: Look amongst every wish and impossible dream, there you will find the footprints of your spirit looking for you.

Stone Story:

When spirit made the world

there were all manners of beings.

They were strong or quiet

or impossible.

They all had a place

that served them

and delighted the heart of life.

My place?

My place is to stand high and low

and glow upon it all

and give sparks

to those who honor

the heart of life

no matter how

impossible.

Summary: It demands that we dream BIG!

Spinel

I am MgAl2O4, Magnesium Aluminum Oxide, with a hardness of 8 and a specific gravity of 3.6. I can be found in Germany, Sweden, Italy, the USSR, Sri Lanka, Thailand, Burma, the USA, Brazil, Australia, Pakistan and Afghanistan. I am typically pinkish-red and historically have been sometimes confused with Ruby. I am famous for my twinning capacities and my red color comes from the element Chromium. I can also be yellow to brown, blue to violet, and when black am called Pleonaste or Ceylonite.

Elemental Earth Grid:
Germany: I emphasize connecting with spirit.
Sweden: I emphasize attainment.
Italy: I emphasize wish fulfillment.
Sri Lanka: I emphasize perfection.
Thailand: I emphasize patience.
Burma: I emphasize perseverance.
USA: I emphasize youth.
Brazil: I emphasize triumph.
Australia: I emphasize following one's heart.
Pakistan: I emphasize presence.
Afghanistan: I emphasize all possibilities.

Physical, Emotional, Mental Integration: We come to you only to enliven you. If you focus only on fear, then all you will know of us is the offering of more energy to do with as you please. Yet, if you choose to open yourself to MORE, then we shall unfold our treasures before you. We will tell you of immortality. We will show you how to strengthen your chakras and to grow them deeply into the earth. Whatever you uniquely need to come to life with power and MORE, we will present it to you. Now.

Electrical Body Alignment: We link you with your kundalini.

Affirmation of Support: *"I am full and overflowing with Life."*

Dreamtime Doorway: I deepen with every experience.

Stone Story:

> *Some beings come to you*
>
> *to help you,*
>
> *to support you.*

I come to you acknowledging

your ceaseless perfection.

I insist upon it.

If you wish to know more of it,

listen:

See as I see.

Accept everything

and everything will bring you unheralded gifts

miracles

that only lay down before the endlessly willing.

I know that you are immortal.

Eternity lays in wait all around you.

It breathes profoundly, perfectly, in your smallest action.

Will you deny this?

Will you accept eternity?

Summary: Spinel points out the eternity all around us and within us.

Stillbite

I am a mineral of the Zeolite group, Hydrated Calcium Aluminum Silicate, $CaA12(SiOi)6+6H20$. My name comes from a Greek word meaning, *"to shine."* I can be abundant in the volcanic rocks of Iceland and Nova Scotia appearing white; I can occur salmon-pink with green Apophyllite in India. I can also be found on the west coast of the USA. My hardness is 3.5 to 4 and my specific gravity is 2.1 to 2.2. My structure has a unique Zeolite ability to allow large ions and molecules to reside and actually move around inside of me. I have places and ways where these large ions and molecules and water can travel in and out, therefore allowing me to act as somewhat of a chemical strainer or purifier.

Elemental Earth Grid:
Iceland: I emphasize purity.
Nova Scotia: I emphasize acceptance.
India: I emphasize stillness.
USA: I emphasize co-operation.

Physical, Emotional, Mental Integration: Softness am I. Do you think that is weak? Absorb my gifts; know what it means to consciously, clearly choose to yield to love. That is the basis of every strength. I breathe this into your organs, your eyes, your dreams, and the relentless pains.

Electrical Body Alignment: I link you with your perfect place in life.

Affirmation of Support: *"I am in harmony with all."*

Dreamtime Doorway: All emotions are allowed.

Stone Story:

> *Yes.*
>
> *I ever say yes*
>
> *for every question that comes to me*
>
> *comes from Life!*
>
> *Life comes disguised as sweet despair or quiet bliss.*
>
> *I know they are all the same.*
>
> *The pain and the ecstasy spiral together*
>
> *with the same spirit*
>
> *with the same grace*

and sometimes, different faces.

What could I refuse?

I say yes to all.

I say yes to you before you have asked the questions

that permeate your days and invade your night.

Ask.

Yes.

Summary: Stillbite models perfect service.

Sulphur

I am S, the Element Sulfur. I am very soft with a hardness of 2 and a specific gravity of 2 to 2.1. I have an unmistakable yellow color and an odd reputation because of my odor. The odor occurs when I mix with water and a gas is formed. When dry, I do not emit this strong odor. I can be found in Michigan/USA, Poland, Chile, Mexico, Indonesia, and the USSR/Middle Asia.

Elemental Earth Grid:
Michigan, USA: I emphasize uniqueness.
Poland: I emphasize senses.
Chile: I emphasize new possibilities.
Mexico: I emphasize omnipresence.
Indonesia: I emphasize self reliance.
USSR: I emphasize progression.

Physical, Emotional, Mental Integration: I align with your solar plexus. When you hold me, pause. Wait. Breathe. Ask yourself freely, letting go of all expectation and judgment, *"How does this stone connect with me?"* Then you will find the integration that awaits us together.

Personal Story

I came out of a dream one morning seeing myself using my little Sulphur crystal on my hands; I was drawing the meridians down each finger with it. It felt quite wondrous and as I woke up, I wondered what I would use this for. It seemed very purposeful.

Later on that morning, I found myself getting unreasonably irritated by some stuff that was going on. I was becoming pretty angry, and trying to back off from it so that I could figure out where it was coming from. I asked for some help with this, and suddenly saw myself using the Sulphur again.

I went and got it and started drawing it along the meridians in my arms and my hands — drawing it towards my fingertips the way I saw it in my dream. It was very soothing. I felt the Sulphur moving through me and consuming the fire of the anger in its own fire.

Then the Sulphur talked to me about boundaries and about caring for myself. I placed it on my solar plexus and felt myself gently warming up. All the little

(con't on next page)

Electrical Body Alignment: I support you linking your heart and your power as if you have never known them as separate.

Affirmation of Support: *"I breathe powerfully in all moments and all events."*

Dreamtime Doorway: Whether you believe it or not, your power is the doorway and it may be the doorway to anything. When you change your thinking to accept this, you are your power.

Stone Story:

Welcome.

For you to hear my heartwords now

it is the season of your growing power.

I come simply

to witness that you are changing, growing

and stretching into the power that has

always

been yours —

that always has been you.

If you find yourself fading from my words,

stop now.

Breathe.

Feel the wholeness of you—

embrace it with every single part of your being

as if it were a precious, perfect child.

You have felt afraid of your power,

knots of tension and irritation relaxed and I settled and was able to breathe deeply. I saw the difference between having a boundary that I constantly guard and fend others off from, and having a place that is so solidly and comfortably me, that there is no question of defending it. It is just the place that is me and that is all there is to it. What a different perspective! I am very thankful to Sulphur for this gift and blessing.

~Maggi P.

your wholeness

yet that is only a habit of other times already gone and still unneeded.

Let your fears fly to the winds!

Watch them go freely, knowing

you are watching your freedom growing as well.....

Breathe as deeply as life.

Breathe more.

You and your power are one.

How do you walk the world now?

Summary: Sulphur shows us the ways of power.

Terbium

I am the Element, Terbium. My Atomic Number is 65 and my symbol is Tb. As a member of the Lanthanoids group, I do not occur naturally in mineral form. I am most often found in Cerite, Gadolinite and Monazite. My Element itself was isolated only recently even though I was discovered in 1843 by Gustav Mosander in Sweden as an impurity in Yttrium Oxide. I am named after the town he lived in, Ytterby. In current technology, I am used in lasers, alloys, solid state devices and as a stabilizer in some fuels.

Physical, Emotional, Mental Integration: Some of you pretends that you are not spirit. I show these parts to you, for they so want to be rewritten. They ask for their freedom, for all of you! And with it, they will align your balance so that you can travel all worlds.

Electrical Body Alignment: I unite you with strength that you never knew was/is you.

Affirmation of Support: *"I can do anything!"*

Dreamtime Doorway: When challenges stretch you, see what comes to the surface. That is your answer.

Stone Story:

Every being lands upon the earth

clear and glimmering with purity.

This innocence never leaves.

It simply hides in you when you believe the world is not safe.

Bit by bit the buried innocence builds up

until it demands to be in the world.

It wants all of you to see with unreasonable awe.

It wants you to explode

with unplanned miracles and gleeful dreams.

Your innocence knows all of these things

even though you have not let it stand in your world.

Its strength is the strength that you have hoped across ages

to know

to be.

Summary: Terbium lets us find the core of our unexpected gifts.

Thulium

I am the Element, Thulium. My Atomic Number is 69 and my symbol is Tm. As a member of the Lanthanoids group, I do not occur naturally in mineral form. I am most often found in Monazite. I am the least abundant of the earth elements, and am about as rare as Silver, Gold, or Cadmium. I am named after *"Thule,"* an ancient name for Scandinavia. In current technology, I am used in alloys, x-ray equipment and microwaves.

Physical, Emotional, Mental Integration: Let's go! We're on adventure for sure. You'll see the impossible and hear the unimaginable. You shake your head at me: You're THINKING. Let it go! Join your mind with your heart and your spirit until they live seamlessly.

Electrical Body Alignment: I unite you with Life as the adventure.

Affirmation of Support: *"I am an intrepid explorer!"*

Dreamtime Doorway: During the peak of doing something fully, find me.

Stone Story:

> *Let's not sit in this book*
>
> *too long.*

> *Come all the way OUT*
>
> *into the world.*
>
> *Feast your imagination.*

> *Come all the way IN*
>
> *into you.*
>
> *Flame your inspiration.*

> *I will not be your guide*
>
> *I will travel with you*
>
> *to touch what has never been before.*

Summary: Thulium shows us how to live life, instead of calculate its path in our minds.

Vanadinite

I am Pb5(VO4)3Cl, Lead Chlorovanadate, a yellow, brown, orange-ish, but mostly red mineral coming mostly from Morocco. I am also found in Austria, Yugoslavia, the USSR, the USA, Argentina, South Africa and was first discovered in Mexico. My hardness is 3 and my specific gravity is 6.5 to 7.1. A variety of Vanadinite containing much arsenic is called Endlichite.

Elemental Earth Grid:
Morocco: I emphasize passion.
Austria: I emphasize appreciation.
Yugoslavia: I emphasize the foundation of things.
USSR: I emphasize geometries.
USA: I emphasize vitality.
Argentina: I emphasize creativity.
South Africa: I emphasize life.
Mexico: I emphasize support.

Physical, Emotional, Mental Integration: Around me, your breath and blood surge together, uniting your intent with the fullness of being and creativity. I insist that you build your dreams and watch them grow into a garden that feeds your body and soul forever.

Electrical Body Alignment: I link you to empowered creativity.

Affirmation of Support: *"I create whatever I truly wish."*

Dreamtime Doorway: Deep within your belly, every instinct leads you home.

Stone Story:

> *I am beautiful to you.*
>
> *I am beauty*
>
> *because nothing in me is unaligned.*
>
> *All of my being answers*
>
> *to the same, unwavering delight.*
>
> *If I have thoughts*
>
> *they are my feelings.*
>
> *If I have feelings*
>
> *they are my spirit.*
>
> *I know I am spirit*
>
> *and that creates everything I am.*

Summary: Vanadinite shows us how to build beauty and art.

Wolframite

I am (Fe, Mn)WO4, Iron Manganese Tungstate. I am Huebnerite and Ferberite. When I am Huebnerite, I am Manganese rich. When I am Ferberite, I am Iron rich. Generally speaking, I am called Wolframite unless either my Manganese or Iron reaches 80% or beyond, then I am referred to as either Huebnerite or Ferberite. My color as Wolframite is dark brown to black, very metallic, and my hardness is 5 to 5.5 and my specific gravity is 7.1 to 7.8. I can be found in the USA, China, Australia, Burma, Canada, Russia, Korea, England and Bolivia.

Elemental Earth Grid:
USA: I emphasize certainty.
China: I emphasize being guided.
Australia: I emphasize being able to do anything.
Burma: I emphasize power.
Canada: I emphasize service.
Russia: I emphasize determination.
Korea: I emphasize leadership.
England: I emphasize commitment.
Bolivia: I emphasize unlimitedness.

Physical, Emotional, Mental Integration: I catalyze the change visible only in our most powerful dreams. I root you and care for all parts of your being during tremendous transformation. Together we clarify your purpose, action and presence. Ho!

Electrical Body Alignment: I link your breath and body with your beautiful potential.

Affirmation of Support: *"I am that I am and the universe encourages me thoroughly."*

Dreamtime Doorway: I absorb the energy of all possibilities and I respond.

Stone Story:

Come to my sweetness.

Look around.....

We rest in high mountain meadows

among wild-run flowers.

Or if you prefer~

we bury our toes and roots in sand

by a sun-splashed ocean.

Whatever you need of the earth and its finery,

I help you to attract it.

Listen, my friend,

you come here to shape miracles

and mold unimaginable destinies—

Don't you suppose that you are meant to have

all that you need to create this soulbeauty

here and now?

Here and now

the bounty of the earth awaits you.

Sketch the dream and it will paint in the colors.

Add the passion

and I will travel thoroughly blessed

with you.

Personal Story

I want to tell you about the saga of my Wolframite. When I received it, I felt that if I so much as handled it for a while, I might have to confront some STUFF I didn't want to let go of. This stone has stayed on my patio since I got it. When my son came for a visit one and a half weeks ago, he immediately hung on to the Wolframite and took it to bed with him. He didn't let it out of his sight all the time he was here. He is at a real crossroads in his life and I think that the Wolframite crystallized in his mind what he should be doing, at least in the short term.

The Wolframite is still on the patio.

I will let you know when I am ready to do some work with the physical stone. When I worked with the Stonessence of Wolframite in January and February, my whole world was turning upside down. I think I am a bit afraid of what I might unearth about myself this time around.

~Starr H.

I come to help the magical co-creators.

If you know who you are

then I am with you

here and now

Summary: Wolframite invites us to join our power, our purpose, and our passion.

Personal Story

It was the end of June that I first met Marilyn and Tohmas in Denver. I already had a couple of precious stones from them but in Denver I met Wolframite and Yttrium Fluorite. I bought two pieces of each.

It is now the end of September and I feel as though in the intervening time I have been catapulted along my path.

In this moment, as I write, I am sitting beside a beautiful waterfall, one Wolframite in my left hand, the other in my right hip pocket.

Just before Wolframite came into my life I had the inspiration to create a crystal grid around my painting table and myself when I channeled my Healing Paintings.

The crystals I bought were to be mailed, so I had to wait.

On their arrival I was very excited. The first night I concentrated on the Yttrium with Fluorite, the second night I added the Wolframite. All night as I slept I was aware of very powerful energy movements taking place in and around my physical body.

The stones are so powerful!

I awoke to realize that they are to play an important role in my crystal grid——they have been a part of the grid almost constantly since that day.

During this period I have channeled eight new paintings, powerful crystal energies are held within them. Then last week I traveled to England with my new artwork and seven of my most important working crystals. One Wolframite came amongst the seven, the other remained within the grid to form

---

Personal Story

I had the opportunity to first meet this incredible stone at the Tucson Gem & Mineral Show in the Twintreess room. I was feeling "spaced out" after spending so much time with the crystals and minerals. When I picked up the Wolframite there was a warm, powerful energy that went through the central core of my being continuing down to the center of the earth, taking with it the interference I had picked up during the day. My thinking was much clearer and I was grounded.

I use this particular stone on a regular basis during meditation. It enables me to go to the central core of my being while remaining grounded. It's truly one of my favorite stones!

~Joyce M.

an energy connection back to the grid. We visited The Chalice Well, at Glastonbury, a sacred ancient healing spring, where I performed a ceremony with my art and the crystals. Then to Avebury where again the Wolframite took an active part. Finally Stonehenge was visited, where the crystals were walked around the perimeter of the stone circle before being placed quietly on the ground.

My Wolframite now carries the energy of these ancient and sacred places, and has left it's blessing with them. I also know that as long as the Wolframite remains connected to the crystal grid, the crystal grid will be connected to the energy of those sacred places.

I had always thought the piece carried an image, but had never found it. Two days after Stonehenge, as I shared my story with a friend, we both clearly saw a polar bear in the white quartz. Today the polar bear is difficult to see, it has transformed into a unicorn.

I have returned to the US with increased clarity, encouragement and awareness of my path of service.

I thank Wolframite for coming into my life and aiding me on my journey.

~Barbara E.

Xenotine

I am YPO4, Yttrium Phosphate. I am one of the few Yttrium containing minerals and I also can sometimes be slightly radioactive. I have a hardness of 4 to 5 and a specific gravity of 4.4 to 5.1. I can occasionally be confused with the mineral Zircon. I am usually brownish, but can be grey, green, yellow or reddish. I can be found in Madagascar, Brazil and the USA. When you hold me, feel the penetrating power of Yttrium.

Elemental Earth Grid:
Madagascar: I emphasize healing.
Brazil: I emphasize directness.
USA: I emphasize feeling safe.

Physical, Emotional, Mental Integration: I offer my love quietly. Whatever you truly need, I offer you that. As you change, I change my gifts to you.

Electrical Body Alignment: I link you with hope.

Affirmation of Support: *"Whatever I need comes to me."*

Dreamtime Doorway: If you want the help of your guardians, ask.

Stone Story:

The world hovers over you.

You feel tiny.

Size, strength, money

all the things that you felt

would keep you safe

are simply the learnings of an eternal soul.

Every moment

spirit fills you.

It renews you endlessly.

Angels and guides surround you.

Whatever you need is here.

It is now.

Summary: Xenotine helps us with whatever we need.

YAG
(Yttrium Aluminum Garnet)

I am Y3Al5O12, Yttrium Aluminum Garnet. I am a man-made crystal and am currently used widely in laser technologies. As a gem, I am also valuable as I am easily cut and can resemble a diamond. I am typically rich in Rare Earth Elements and can be grown in as little as 4 - 8 weeks. I was initially grown in the late 1950's but didn't achieve much popularity until decades later. I have a hardness of 8.5 and a specific gravity of 4.55. I am available in many colors and I cut and polish much like garnet.

Physical, Emotional, Mental Integration: I find your strengths and I unify them for you, until they become a point of focus, health and balance. I show you how to use your strengths to form the life of your choosing.

Electrical Body Alignment: I link you with all your abilities.

Affirmation of Support: *"I do whatever needs to be done."*

Dreamtime Doorway: From the unknown something comes to meet you. You are conditioned to fear, but are you also free to find the miraculous?

Stone Story:

> *I am born of earth and I am born of humans.*

> *I join all the worlds with my being. Because of this I own strengths that were unknown before this moment. They aim me towards what needs to be done and everything I do swims into the river of life, peacefully.*

There is no need for understanding in this. I allow. I accept. All that I am changes with all that is. My strengths do not lock me into one place where change would crush me.

Instead they move me like an eagle on the wind.

Powerfully.

Gracefully.

The flow of evolution lives in me. I share it with all. If you accept life and the circle of constant change then my strengths will merge with yours. All of your gifts will rise to your fingertips, poised to be used with one word.

Yes.

Summary: YAG supports us in this amazing evolution.

Yttrium

I am the Element, Yttrium. My Atomic Number is 39 and my symbol is Y. As a member of the Lanthanoids group, I do not occur naturally in mineral form. I am in most all Rare Earth Element minerals and have even been isolated in Moon rocks. My name derives from the town of Ytterby in Sweden. In current technology, I am used in microwaves, television tubes, lasers, to increase the strength of alloys, and as a gemstone in the form of Yttrium Aluminum Garnet, a simulated Diamond.

Physical, Emotional, Mental Integration: I embrace you. You think you are imperfect. I show you the wonder of you and every change that is possible. I enter them into your breath and with them you can transform your core.

Electrical Body Alignment: I link you to prana and to all peace.

Affirmation of Support: *"I am ever perfect."*

Dreamtime Doorway: All healing belongs to ourselves.

Stone Story:

> *Welcome.*
>
> *So many thoughts and wonders*
>
> *fly through you*
>
> *at our meeting.*
>
> *Incredible.*
>
>
> *I require*
>
> *no expectations.*
>
> *Just meet me.*
>
> *Just reach across yourself and smile.*
>
> *I have nothing to offer you*
>
> *except the peace of your destiny*
>
> *where you have already*
>
> *arrived.*

Summary: Yttrium presents us with the core of our own healing.

Yttrium Fluorite

I am purple Fluorite with a strong addition of the Rare Earth Element, Yttrium. I can be found in Nevada and in Mexico. I have strong Fluorite properties (see the Fluorite section under "Families") with the added enhancements of Yttrium. (See "Yttrium" in this section.) In Nevada, I am found in a rare botryoidal form in the zone of a giant volcanic caldera. My crystals grow from the center out, much like a cone. When you hold me, feel my energy under "tension" that wants to come out.

Personal Story

Found myself attracted to a pendant about two years ago and I didn't know why. It wasn't fancy or showy, it was a simple piece of Fluorite with Yttrium in gold wire wrap. On the days that I wore my new pendant I discovered that there were portions of my day that were very peaceful and loving. I'd try to figure out what was happening, and would come to realize that what I was experiencing in my body was the wonderful influence and experience of Yttrium with Fluorite.

~Joyce M.

Elemental Earth Grid:
Nevada, USA: I emphasize relaxation.
Mexico: I emphasize balance.

Physical, Emotional, Mental Integration: I recharge, lighten and in-spire lifeforce flow. I support the evolution of the new DNA. I help you to integrate belief and overall health spontaneously. I amplify auras gently embrace full emotional body transformation.

Electrical Body Alignment: I align our energy libraries.

Affirmation of Support: *"I reach down to my core to manifest the love I AM."*

Dreamtime Doorway: I come quietly. There is no fanfare, that way we can talk beyond the surface and go right to the deepest part of your pain.

Stone Story:

> *I do not often speak words, so I thank you for this sweet opportunity to know you and for you to know me just a little bit better.*
> *Ever better actually.*
>
> *Life brings me to your heart and mind's door.*
>
> *It is the season for those who can reach across time and space easily to stretch into each other's realities and meet.*
> *Hello~*
>
> *Even in this simple introduction, I extend my heart out to your heart, though you may think that you only are reading words. Hmmm. When I offer my heart all my energy pours out into the possibilities and we cannot help but know each other. If you believe nothing is happening, I understand. Your body will store our meeting for when your energy stretches past time and space and in that flash, you actually will hear my voice return with these words. You actually will see my face (such as it is). Your heart will shake next to mine and together we will remember just exactly what you need to grow at the speed of light. So be it.*
>
> *If you already hear, see and touch me, truly I am honored. Our books of life read each other and exchange the wisdom of the age as it has always been done and yet, now it is with the newness of this conscious-ness. There I ever will meet us. See you again and again.*

Summary: Yttrium Fluorite teaches us the meaning of integration qui-etly and gently.

Zircon

I am ZrSiO4, Zirconium Silicate with a hardness of 7.5 and a specific gravity of 3.9 to 4.8. I can be most any color: brown, yellow, red, green, blue and also colorless. In my blue form I am called Starlite. I am NOT Cubic Zirconia, although I have been used to simulate Diamonds in many ways. I can be found in the USA, Canada, the USSR, Norway, Brazil and Pakistan.

Elemental Earth Grid:
USA: I emphasize freedom of choice.
Canada: I emphasize dedication.
USSR: I emphasize recognizing your values.
Norway: I emphasize well-earned rewards.
Brazil: I emphasize rhythm.
Pakistan: I emphasize connecting with the earth and beyond, simultaneously.

Physical, Emotional, Mental Integration: When you hold me, I show you all possibilities from all moments. Some of these potentials you do not want to meet, but when you do, you can change your destiny. I show you the energy of immediate, profound transformation......if you choose.

Electrical Body Alignment: I link you with life and death, at once.

Affirmation of Support: *"I live life utterly, always."*

Dreamtime Doorway: Walk with, and like, your sacred witness.

Stone Story:

All through the ages, beings have evolved. Your stories do not record this completely. Sometimes the changes have been so profound that some life forms left the earth instantaneously.

Humans have evolved even more than they can remember. After all, you cannot see how dramatically you are transforming when you are in the middle of it— you're just too busy doing it!! When you have flown further down your path and landed upon the mountain's top, you will finally be able to look back and smile, and whisper, "What a journey! What a journey I have been and what a journey I will be!!"

Until you sit triumphantly on that mountaintop, listen to me. Hold my heart next to yours. It, too, will whisper to you. It will tell you of every sweet glory that you are wearing, whether you recognize it or not. It will sing your epic adventure, even before you know it yourself. And this will carry you to the next mountain and the next and the next.

Summary: Zircon recognizes our evolution, as it is occurring.

Personal Story

About a Personal Stone.

In 2004, I gladly accepted an invitation to the "Freedom Intent" workshop. I stated my intent, packed some clothes along with "my" stone and ventured to the Wilderness Lodge with a bunch of strangers to face my selves.

Now, "my" stone had been a very sacred part of me for a couple of years prior to the "Freedom Intent." (It is still a very sacred part of me.) I was at the Fairburn Agate beds looking for agates. The 360 degree view around me was hills upon hills of stones. I dug around hoping to find an agate when I came upon the most peculiar looking rock. It was just lying right out in the open for me to find. It was round with a flat face that had an imprint on it that looked like an eye. It stuck out, so I just shoved it in my pocket. I really had no idea, at that moment, how significant this little guy would become in my life. I just thought it looked cool.

In a later evaluation of the rock I became baffled. It was imprinted so perfectly – like it could have been carved. On the side it had an imprint of an arrow or tree.

It looked different to every person I brought it to. Some said for sure it was carved while others were convinced it was carved only by Mother Nature. At any rate it was my #1! I imagined many scenarios with this little stone and all of them led to me finding "my" stone. Ahhh, I love my stone!

So back to the Freedom Intent. I have always had severe cramping during my moontime and was asking Twintrees about it. I learned that when I am not occupying my body there is a parallel that surely will. For many years I have offered her, freely, as much of my lifeforce as she wants. Specifically I feel her in my abdomen and reproductive organs. She feels aggressive, assertive, and sexually charged. It feels as though she uses these feelings to get what she wants. She is very present in my intimate relationships.

Going through this process (of writing this experience down) has not been easy. I chose to forget a lot of information about her and me. I refused to believe that my precious stone was linked to my parallel (though somewhere deep inside of me it felt like it). Looking at those parts of myself have not been on my priority list— that is, until now: How would I have a relationship (with myself or anyone else) based on freedom if I let my autopilot-parallel run the show? Especially using tactics that compromise my spirit.

So, after stopping the story and starting again, my truth is that stones are recordkeepers. They hold information that change lives— like "my" precious helped change mine. My truth is that the stone I found that day in those hills found me! We came together to bring a piece of myself home to be loved. We co-created an opportunity for me to see where I give my lifeforce away. I had been just as attached to my parallel as I had been to my beloved stone. So when the earth asked for it back, I was less than eager.

When I was in the hot springs (at the workshop), one day, looking at my stone, I knew our time was up. It was undeniable yet so much of me wanted to put it where I could find it again. Before I knew it my attention was drawn elsewhere and my stone was gone. It was ready to leave and it did. I looked all around the pool but it was nowhere to be found. It shapeshifted right out of my hands.

I used to take 6-8 Ibuprofens a day during my moon. Since I chose to be responsible for my own lifeforce energy I have not taken anything anymore. I rarely get any cramps now; I feel healthy, strong and responsible.

Thank you precious stone!

~Charity B.

Welcome to the Second Half of the Journey

This book offers itself to you as a thrilling adventure in listening. When you read here, you can actually *absorb* the glorious, vibrational gifts of the stones, by truly listening with your heart to their own words. The more you listen, the more you connect with the stones, yourself— in the absolutely unique ways that fulfill you and incredibly expand all your possibilities. That way, even when you're not actually "reading" this book, you will still keep listening to the Stonebeings: Their words and vibrations will grow inside you (as you wish) and you will **watch** the incredible evidence of their gifts in your reality. Listen to your whole being and you will find the magic of the stones, and the earth, in you, nurturing you, expanding your most amazing creativity.

The second half of this book builds upon the first and consciously furthers your opportunities to expand your learning and growing with the stones. First of all, Hawkseye Velvet Tourmaline moves beyond its introduction of itself (in the A-Z section), with new words that spontaneously land in the middle of other texts, to surprise you, to catalyze you, and to magically spur you on to new listening. There is no way to truly explain that. It simply is. Drink in their messages, knowing that they come directly to <u>you</u>, and that they can spark your journey with all other stones immediately, profoundly. Watching for their wisdom is like watching for a miracle: *It will come in a blink, be inexplicable, and what it will give you may speak to you forever*.

Then we move from stones, A-Z, to stones in combinations and "families" of stones ("The Families" Section and the "Stone Combination" Section). When stones join with stones, their intents and energies multiply profoundly, exponentially, and alchemically. That means that their support of you also expands exponentially, along with your ability to listen.

Pause here.
Breathe fully.
Appreciate the deepening of this glorious miracle.
Feast upon it all.

Totem Stories from Hawkseye Velvet Tourmaline

You honor me joining me here.

Your listening has brought you (and me!)

to this world that I sculpt

the one that I bring with me

on this bold adventure

that I AM.

This black that I wear hungrily absorbs all colors

all possibilities....

It is my shaman's cloak.

I am a shadowy nebula

in a firmament exploding with silvers, azures, scarlets—.

faces that tell the wonder of growing,

living,

dying

and endlessly living

as stars.

In my darkness,

I highlight everything else

so that I can seed myself in anonymity

and then grow into worlds upon worlds.

My palette lies patiently empty so that I can paint

any wish upon myself.

When I grow

I grow dreams.

Stone Families

Listening to the Families of Stones

When we speak of families of stones, we mean one particular type of stone as it is found in one particular part of the world, like Bolivian Amethyst. It is similar to Amethyst found anywhere else; yet, its geographical placement also gives it unique characteristics. Therefore listening to a stones' geographical placement (its "family") helps you to explore stones from yet another view.

First of all you can listen to one entire family of stone, like Bolivian Amethyst, and feel the inherent, spontaneous relationship between all Amethysts from that country. When that pulsates within you, not only will you know those stones more intimately, you will also know that part of the earth and perhaps even the other plants, animals and stones that live there. You can directly experience the union of all life on the earth that, unlike humans, does not experience "separation," through mind processes that focus on the individual above all else. Then you can create this harmony in your own life, as you choose…even if you don't quite understand it…even if you don't know exactly how to do it…even if you are afraid of it. Listening to stones in this exponential way immediately invites you to *feel* as connected to all life, as you truly are. When you learn that, what wisdom could evade you?

Another way to listen to stone families is to explore the differences between them, like Bolivian Amethyst versus Brazilian Amethyst. Each stone family specifically relates to the part of the earth that births it. Bolivian Amethyst and its gifts automatically form according to the conditions of the land around it. That way it can best serve the needs of all the beings that also live in the same area, under the same conditions. For example, this is why herbalists prefer to work with local herbs: they inherently possess the healing qualities for the diseases most prevalent in those areas. Listen to the uniqueness of the stone families. If you let them, they will show you how all life upon the earth shapes itself to harmonize with the land from which it comes. Learn how that serves that place and simultaneously serves the whole of life upon the earth.

When you read the "Families" Section, you will find the following categories to help you absorb their wisdom:

Physical Description: As in the stones in the A-Z section, this is where you find the common physical and geological traits of all stones of that type.

Elemental Dance: This will tell you what the stones in that geographical area have in common with each other. We call it "Elemental Dance" because the elements of life (fire, earth, air, water, ethers/spirit) make up every form of life, and upon any particular part of the earth, the elements will dance uniquely there. They will balance everything in their own special way and this imprints the stones and gives their stone family its common traits.

Tools for Listening: After you have listened to the basic qualities of the stone families, go further: Here you will find tasks to actually incorporate the energies of stone families in your life. You will integrate the energies as you listen to them.

Each of these categories comes to you as a tool in your stone listening, like spelling and sounding out of words once helped you to learn to read. Fully absorb and appreciate each of these tools, each time you encounter them. Don't allow your mind to get "used to them" or you'll miss their energetic gifts. They will focus and fine-tune your listening and develop it as an ever-growing practice in your life.

Here are other, overall tasks (or Tools for Listening) with which to explore stone families:

- Begin with "Stones Alive!" (the initial book) and read about the individual stones featured in the "Families" section here.

- Absorb those energies. Flow with them. Find the connection that they have for you.

- Ask the stones to show you how those energies fit into your life. Listen.

- Make a list of all the stones and the stone families in this section—do not read anything else. Then, by yourself, listen to each stone family and find the qualities that they each have. For instance, write down the qualities of Bolivian Amethyst and when you're ready, note the special energies of Brazilian Amethyst, and so on…

- Read the "Families" section. Explore all the similarities and the differences between the stone families. Give yourself the fullest view of these stones and what energies make them up.

- With the notes from your stone family listenings, explore your completely personal connection to them. With that relationship, deepen your conversation with all of life.

Amethyst

Africa

"When you touch me, you find joyous upliftment and the awakening of all possibilities."

I am the purple variety of Quartz, SiO2, Silicon Dioxide. As Quartz, I am the most common mineral on the Earth Mother and am found most everywhere. I can be the most varied also when it comes to form and color. My hardness is 6.5 to 7 and my specific gravity is 2.57 to 2.64. For our purposes here below I am specifically speaking as Amethyst from Africa.

Elemental Dance: All Amethyst bridges us with spirit, with magic, and with unimaginability. The fire and air elementals in it link immediately and profoundly with the ethers. When you hold Amethyst, feel this for yourself, for how you feel it will show you how you join with your spirit with your uniqueness.

I, African Amethyst, joyfully focus on linking you and all your experiences with spirit. The etheric elemental in me lives and grows very actively. It catalyzes you as continually as you will allow, urging you to see the sacred....see the sacred.....see the sacred......and then all you see is sacred.

I am a profound part of the incredible evolution that you are dancing in now.

With all my essence, I realize that your re-birth feels devastating.

So I will not offer you pity to weigh you down on your adventure.
Instead I urge you to receive my compassion.
My compassion is a thousand stories, unfolded, and in each one you
are the hero — you are growing courage.
Every hardship fills you to the brim with Herculean strength (It takes
that much just to be a human now.), and then you
overflow
overflow
overflow
until you are the evolution and it is everything of wonder that you
didn't remember how to ask for until
courage showed you the way.

Tools for Listening:
In each life, spirit beckons to you.
It comes in so many countless forms, each moment.
Most often it lands upon your consciousness like a question:
Who am I? What am I supposed to do with my life?

Now the opening exists.
If you're listening to these questions, then they will show you how to
listen to/for the answers.
They will show you tools to help you find/be the answers.
Like now.
Like this moment, while you're reading this.
Recognize the feeling of this opening, of this possibility. FEEL what
your own listening feels like
so that you can return to it, like a good home, over and over again.
In the silence of listening, there is a void.
In nature, a void doesn't stay one for long; it attracts something else
to fill it.
You fill it. Fill the void with everything that supports you.
Fill your life with every inspiration you can imagine and allow.
Fill your walls with quotes that awe you. Cover your shelves with
books that remind you of miracles!
Yet don't crowd the void **just to fill it.** Only put there what you truly
love — what speaks to you of the delight of being alive!
Then listen to all your tools and all your support.
Listen and absorb every one and the respect that you listen with will
build your life.

Bolivia

"When you touch me, you find joyous upliftment and the awakening of all possibilities."

I am the purple variety of Quartz, SiO2, Silicon Dioxide. As Quartz, I am the most common mineral on the Earth Mother and am found most everywhere. I can be the most varied also when it comes to form and color. My hardness is 6.5 to 7 and my specific gravity is 2.57 to 2.64. For our purposes here below I am specifically speaking as Amethyst from Bolivia.

Elemental Dance: I know you, for I ever stay close to my center stillness. By living there, everything comes to me. Kindness always visits me and awareness cannot stay away. And if you are tuned into spirit, even your presence comes to me. Nothing of love will stay away, for I focus on the stillness to ever give love a good home with me.

Tools for Listening:
Be close to the stillness.
Sit in the silence.

Once you are there, you will hear everything, and suddenly you will realize something: Some of what you hear is noise!
You can hear noise, **but you do not have to listen to it.**
The beauty of living in the stillness is that it offers you clarity.
If you accept the clarity, you always find **choice.**
You have choice about what you listen to in each moment.
You have choice about where you place your focus and whether or not you will keep placing your focus there.
You have choice about where you will travel and who you will be on the journey.
Your focus will attract what will visit you along the way.

Be close to the stillness and find your choice. Listen to it.

Brazil

"When you touch me, you find joyous upliftment and the awakening of all possibilities."

I am the purple variety of Quartz, SiO2, Silicon Dioxide. As Quartz, I am the most common mineral on the Earth Mother and am found most everywhere. I can be the most varied also when it comes to form and color. My hardness is 6.5 to 7 and my specific gravity is 2.57 to 2.64. For our purposes here below I am specifically speaking as Amethyst from Brazil.

Elemental Dance: I link my fire with the fire of the Earth Mother so that it will give you grounding and a tender love of your body that you hoped a devoted partner would give you. Around me, your senses will root more deeply and more deeply until you soar! Every caress, every aroma, every sound, every sight, all food and drink, are here to remind you....to remind you to remind you...to remind you....to remind you.

To remind you of what?
Everything is here to remind you of the divine
and your senses are the gateways to discoveries.
Listen to them as you would a sage and you will learn your spirit-answers.

Tools for Listening:
Pick one sight, or sound, or smell, or taste or touch.
Make it a simple one.
Maybe even make it a very common one.
Once a day visit a very specific manifestation of that sense.
Let's say that you picked looking at a tree.
Daily, look at that tree.
Keep looking at it for a pre-determined time, at least.
Relax.
Some days it will be easy. Some days it will be hard. The complexity of it will be determined by the amount and the stubbornness of your

defenses.

As you do this task, your defenses will rise to the surface, for they will try to stop you from being simple (Being simple means that there is nothing between you and life, but love.).

That's when JUST seeing the tree means that your senses are the gateways to spirit.

The longer you just see what is with you this moment, the less you will need judgments. They will slip away like an old coat, once comfortable, but definitely out-grown now. You may feel cold without it at first, but life **will show you new, even better ways to keep warm,** always.

Keep looking at the tree until you find the whole world there.

Mexico

"When you touch me, you find joyous upliftment and the awakening of all possibilities."

I am the purple variety of Quartz, SiO2, Silicon Dioxide. As Quartz, I am the most common mineral on the Earth Mother and am found most everywhere. I can be the most varied also when it comes to form and color. My hardness is 6.5 to 7 and my specific gravity is 2.57 to 2.64. For our purposes here below I am specifically speaking as Amethyst from Mexico.

Elemental Dance: I listen to the earth. Then I will know exactly how to combine (and to keep combining) with her to make more crystalline beauty. In this part of the Earth Mother, so much lush loveliness thrives and grows and grows. Stones, plants and animals richly abound here. Witness and enjoy.

Tools for Listening:
Spend a day truly noting every lovely thing that you see.
When you see it, stop.
Breathe.
Breathe with the flower

from roots to stem
to petal
and then from petal
to stem to roots
and then together, caress the earth with your breaths.
Do this until life force tingles you,
till you know you are alive
and that each thing that you see greets you with equal life and verve.

At the end of the day
in the silence of your own space
re-see every lovely thing that stopped you.
Stop.
Breathe with each one.
Breathe with each color.
Breathe each shape.
Absorb it all until breath connects you all.
You are interwoven inhales and exhales and you can never be fully
separate again.

When you feel challenged, visit these lovely beings.
Breathe with them.
Ask them for their gifts. Listen.
Offer your gratitude.

Nevada, USA

*"When you touch me, you find joyous upliftment and the awakening of
all possibilities."*

I am the purple variety of Quartz, SiO_2, Silicon Dioxide. As Quartz,
I am the most common mineral on the Earth Mother and am found
most everywhere. I can be the most varied also when it comes to
form and color. My hardness is 6.5 to 7 and my specific gravity is
2.57 to 2.64. For our purposes here below I am specifically speaking
as Amethyst from Nevada.

Elemental Dance: Come to me here where the water lies far, far beneath the surface and the fire lives everywhere else. If you are like me, you accept the fire as plentiful fuel. With it, we will shape sculptures from life. We will paint every thought of awe upon the earthcanvas until we are creators divine.

Tools for Listening:

Everything you do is the act of an artist.
Can you believe that?
If not, just pretend it is so.
Look at everything as if you were Matisse.
Listen to everything as if you were Mozart.

Now what do you notice? See? Imagine?
Focus.
Focus upon the highest artform you can attain.
Be it.
Write your life as if you were Shakespeare.

New Mexico, USA

"When you touch me, you find joyous upliftment and the awakening of all possibilities."

I am the purple variety of Quartz, SiO_2, Silicon Dioxide. As Quartz, I am the most common mineral on the Earth Mother and am found most everywhere. I can be the most varied also when it comes to form and color. My hardness is 6.5 to 7 and my specific gravity is 2.57 to 2.64. For our purposes here below I am specifically speaking as Amethyst from Mule Creek, New Mexico, USA. I have formed (very unusually for quartz) in an old volcanic caldera and have grown in many different ways: seed crystals, scepters and side-growth scepters, "twins," and enhydros. We all appear to have grown as individuals. There are no real quartz veins here, no apparent clustering or quartz base with crystals growing up out of it (although there is Calcite present in places to hold some of us together), so all my crystals seem to be trying to double terminate.

Elemental Dance: If you knew what I know, perhaps you would speak less. Maybe you would naturally listen because there is so much to listen to and it just keeps growing. The Earth Mother holds an infinite space for every miracle. Whatever can be imagined is utterly supported and loved.

I am loved beyond reason and I am just one glint of that love.

Tools for Listening:
Know that you are honored.
Inhale that into every bone, muscle and hair.
Feel the honoring crystallize you
into your perfect body
and feel that perfection stretching into.....infinity.........

Now.
What will you do with the lifeforce that you call your own?

When you drink in the pure respect of the Earth Mother and of life, you find that no lifeforce is just your own.
It mingles and breathes with all other life.
In some way of its own it shares itself with you and with others, all at once.
As you enter it ever more deeply, you enter the union of all as well.

In your own story, you are the writer,
the scenery,
the reader, the actor,
the book holding it — and then, all of it, and none of it.

Russia

"When you touch me, you find joyous upliftment and the awakening of all possibilities."

I am the purple variety of Quartz, SiO2, Silicon Dioxide. As Quartz, I am the most common mineral on the Earth Mother and am found most everywhere. I can be the most varied also when it comes to form and color. My hardness is 6.5 to 7 and my specific gravity is 2.57 to 2.64. For our purposes here below I am specifically speaking as Amethyst from Russia.

Elemental Dance: Deep within the Earth Mother I am, deeper than the roots of mountains. I grow away from the air so that you will see what it is to be free from endless thought. My instincts keep me growing strong and sharp; I do not need any logic or judgments to shape me. Instead I will grow into what is needed and if you are listening to me now, you feel that. You feel how to breathe without measurement or calculation.

Tools for Listening:
Make today a Listening day.
Go everywhere you wish and focus on listening to whatever comes before you asking for your attention.
Bring no tools to record any of this.
Make no plans.
Just let listening guide your steps and choose the times
that you sit,
or look,
or eat.

Be free.
Just let your listening shape you.
Let it tell you who you are and in what respectful ways you will act:
When you become something that you are not usually,
just accept it.
Accept it completely.
Watch it.
Learn from it.
Absorb the grace in everything —
no need to think it through, no need to schedule your feelings or friends.
It is easier for miracles to surprise you when you don't have to control the possibility of them first.

Thunder Bay, Ontario, Canada

"When you touch me, you find joyous upliftment and the awakening of all possibilities."

I am the purple variety of Quartz, SiO2, Silicon Dioxide. As Quartz, I am the most common mineral on the Earth Mother and am found most everywhere. I can be the most varied also when it comes to form and color. My hardness is 6.5 to 7 and my specific gravity is 2.57 to 2.64. For our purposes here below I am specifically speaking as Amethyst from Thunder Bay, Ontario, Canada.

Elemental Dance: I focus upon the Etheric Elementals that shape my existence. As I choose that, allow that, and then enhance it, bliss fills my being. I exalt in the endless worlds before me. As I travel them, I find they reflect the endless worlds within me. Me! They live in me.

The bliss of me goes soft. It stretches out to every tip of me and I am peaceful contentment — no need to go, no need at all. I am all that I could have wanted.

Tools for Listening:
Get a tape recorder, a small one that you can take everywhere for a week.
As it occurs to you, record every single thing in your life that goes well — is a wonder to behold.
No need to limit, to logic, to shape your recording
in any particular way.
Let the sound of its inspiration lead you onward and onward.
If you repeat some of the topics, no worries: they want to keep coming to you! Hooray!

See how the witnessing of wonder shapes your life.
It grows in awe and delight.
Let it.
You can choose it

and as you choose your contentment, the wonder never stops growing.

Uruguay

"When you touch me, you find joyous upliftment and the awakening of all possibilities."

I am the purple variety of Quartz, SiO2, Silicon Dioxide. As Quartz, I am the most common mineral on the Earth Mother and am found most everywhere. I can be the most varied also when it comes to form and color. My hardness is 6.5 to 7 and my specific gravity is 2.57 to 2.64. For our purposes here below I am specifically speaking as Amethyst from Uruguay.

Elemental Dance: I am tucked away from people because I find it so easy to grow shiny and strong by myself. There is nothing in me that needs validation to prove my points, to prove my facets, to prove my clusters. Right now, I listen to me as the focus of life and then all is here with me, as well.

Tools for Listening:
Your life belongs to you.
Though you share it with others in many, many ways, the fullness of it rests with you.
It always has and it always will.
That is what responsibility means; it is your ability to respond to being your own life.

Accept this.
Accept this utterly.
Remind yourself of this at the dawn and at the sunset of each day.
Remind yourself with the full power of responsibility and unlimited lifeforce.

Now what will you do?

Try this: Schedule a time every week that is solely for you. No exceptions. It is a date that you keep with and for yourself. Honor it. If it must change its time and space for something else, then re-schedule it with complete respect.

Fill your time for/with you with whatever you choose.
Perhaps it will be a time to swim in the things that you truly adore that others don't,
or things that you don't want to do with others.
Luxuriate in it all.
Enjoy the completeness, the wholeness of you.

Calcite

China

"I grow with myself, I grow with others. I grow to Celebrate Life that forever grows."

I am CaCO3, Calcium Carbonate, one of the most common minerals on the Earth Mother, making up approximately 4% of her crust by weight. My name comes from the Greek word, *"chalix,"* their word for lime. My hardness isn't very much at 3 and my specific gravity is 2.6 to 2.8. Calcite is abundant, widely distributed and varied in its forms. For my purposes below I am speaking to you specifically as Calcite from China.

Elemental Dance:
Come to me. I so love meeting you.
Come very close.
It will take all of us,
together,
to reflect the light
of life.

Tools for Listening:
Be a child.
Just see everything as a moment to play, to laugh, to cry, to sleep,
as that moment wishes.
Yes.

Now share that.
Share that with whomever comes to you with that moment.

Tell them your stories while you walk and hold hands.
Trade lunches.
Share your favorite toys.
Together write your intermingled stories of each other
and color them.

Just find everything of this journey that you can share
and do it.

India

"I grow with myself, I grow with others. I grow to Celebrate Life that forever grows."

I am CaCO3, Calcium Carbonate, one of the most common minerals on the Earth Mother, making up approximately 4% of her crust by weight. My name comes from the Greek word, *"chalix,"* their word for lime. My hardness isn't very much at 3 and my specific gravity is 2.6 to 2.8. Calcite is abundant, widely distributed and varied in its forms. For my purposes below I am speaking to you specifically as Calcite from India.

Elemental Dance: Yes, I am so soft. My softness lets
every ray of light come through me and dance.
The colors twirl and
suddenly I am shaped of rainbows and spectacular dreams.

Tools for Listening:
When you listen to someone, just go soft all over.

It means that you have to decide, up front, that you could like them. It means that your body will sigh and relax all over. You will sit contentedly and listen contentedly.
It means that you can't talk until there's a space for it that asks for it, that really wants it.

It means that you don't even need to talk.
It means if there is something said that you don't like, it'll just go by without harming you.
It means that you don't have judgments to make you hard.

Madagascar

"I grow with myself, I grow with others. I grow to Celebrate Life that forever grows."

I am CaCO3, Calcium Carbonate, one of the most common minerals on the Earth Mother, making up approximately 4% of her crust by weight. My name comes from the Greek word, *"chalix,"* their word for lime. My hardness isn't very much at 3 and my specific gravity is 2.6 to 2.8. Calcite is abundant, widely distributed and varied in its forms. For my purposes below I am speaking to you specifically as Calcite from Madagascar.

Elemental Dance: Come look, come look!
Colors are exploding all around me!
Inside of me rainbows shake and pulsate.
If you watch them and hold them,
they shoot outside of me and land on whatever is accepting.........

Tools for Listening:
Today you have just been appointed the "Sacred Support for Miracles."
The title is official (appropriate costume is optional but encouraged.).

Your job is to do the "Oooh's" and "Ahhhh's" for every miracle that happens next to you.
For instance, a new baby is born, offer the appropriate awe.
If somebody next to you wins $2 in the lottery, celebrate.

You get the idea.
When you get the hang of it, you will be like a Madagascar Calcite,

recording and reveling in miracles.
Take your practice and your enjoyment of supporting miracles and use those memories
to connect with the heart of that stone.
Compare notes.

Mexico

"I grow with myself, I grow with others. I grow to Celebrate Life that forever grows."

I am CaCO3, Calcium Carbonate, one of the most common minerals on the Earth Mother, making up approximately 4% of her crust by weight. My name comes from the Greek word, *"chalix,"* their word for lime. My hardness isn't very much at 3 and my specific gravity is 2.6 to 2.8. Calcite is abundant, widely distributed and varied in its forms. For my purposes below I am speaking to you specifically as Calcite from Mexico.

Elemental Dance:
Hooray!
I can be any color my imagination picks.
I can be anything.
Even though I will reflect every one else's hues (happily),
I will still revel in the color that is
me.

Tools for Listening:
Look in the mirror.

Keep looking in the mirror.

You will find parts of you that you like and parts that you don't.

Keep looking.

Listen to your dislikes and your likes. Let them tell you their stories. Be glad for them (after all they are a part of you.).
When you have absorbed them all, decide for yourself: Do they matter? In other words, do they make up the form/matter of me?

Now that you have listened, gladly, to everything that you can see and can't see about you,
relax.

Smile.

Can you offer every single part of you appreciation?

Keep looking in the mirror as you choose and as you decide.
How do you look with your choices?

USA

"I grow with myself, I grow with others. I grow to Celebrate Life that forever grows."

I am CaCO3, Calcium Carbonate, one of the most common minerals on the Earth Mother, making up approximately 4% of her crust by weight. My name comes from the Greek word, *"chalix,"* their word for lime. My hardness isn't very much at 3 and my specific gravity is 2.6 to 2.8. Calcite is abundant, widely distributed and varied in its forms. For my purposes below I am speaking to you specifically as Calcite from the USA.

Elemental Dance:
I am soft,
yet I am sharp.
I am common
yet I am unique.
I am clear,
yet I am colorful.

I am so like you, I am nothing and I am everything.

Tools for Listening:
How would you like to listen?
If you keep looking for new ways (for listening always needs to keep being new), you will still pick them from your habits, your likes — in other words, from what you know.
How can you pick fresh ways to listen?

Get some Calcite from the USA.
Keep one and give one to someone else who will do this task with you.
Each of you will write a list of every way that you can think of to listen respectfully.
While you're writing, keep the calcite close by to align you, both, in clarity and purpose.

Exchange lists.
Thank each other and your Calcite friends.

USSR

"I grow with myself, I grow with others. I grow to Celebrate Life that forever grows."

I am CaCO3, Calcium Carbonate, one of the most common minerals on the Earth Mother, making up approximately 4% of her crust by weight. My name comes from the Greek word, *"chalix,"* their word for lime. My hardness isn't very much at 3 and my specific gravity is 2.6 to 2.8. Calcite is abundant, widely distributed and varied in its forms. For my purposes below I am speaking to you specifically as Calcite from USSR.

Elemental Dance:
I spring from the earth who knows us completely, utterly.
There I have seen your secrets that have left all memory,
yet
I store them.
I record everything about you
and when you listen to me
now
I set them free.
I place my timeless witnessings of you into the sun of this day
and let them shimmer with new freedom.

Tools for Listening:
Listen to yourself.

Nothing may be more profound than that.

When you quietly, freely listen to yourself, you will discover what you
repeat endlessly
and what you don't say.
You will hear your volume,
your tone
and your inflection,
and you will explore what they mean.

Listen to yourself.

Then you will know you
and what you bring to your listening of everything else.

luorite

Argentina

"This is my time to be on the planet. I say, 'Awaken and remember, our struggle can be released.' "

I am CaF2, Calcium Fluoride, a mineral of many, many colors. My hardness is 4 and my specific gravity is 3.1 to 3.2. I exhibit perfect cleavage in four directions. I was originally called, *"fluorospar,"* by miners, Flour Spar and Ore Bloom, and received my name because of my common use as flux in processing. Actually my name comes from the Latin word, *fluere,* "to flux." I am speaking to you below specifically as Fluorite from Argentina.

Elemental Dance:
Life is delicious!
No matter how many ways we ingest the glory of it,
the feast is endless.
Life is gorgeous!
No matter how many vistas we point out,
the earth grows more mountains,
more flowers,
more springs
to decorate herself with.
Life is love. No matter how many friends we share it with,
it expands into
infinity, forever.

Tools for Listening:
In your listening, you will learn many things.
You will thrill to some; you will cringe at others.

If you choose to deepen your listening, and therefore your learning,

deliberately
continually
freely
delight in it all.
Choose.
Enjoy how much you don't like some of what you have learned!
Enjoy how well you listen.
Enjoy that you have found time to listen.
Spread enjoyment to every part of your listening — leave no part
unembraced.

Your joy always brings more joy and expands its source: listening.

Brazil

*"This is my time to be on the planet. I say, 'Awaken and remember, our
struggle can be released.' "*

I am CaF2, Calcium Fluoride, a mineral of many, many colors. My
hardness is 4 and my specific gravity is 3.1 to 3.2. I exhibit perfect
cleavage in four directions. I was orginally called, *"fluorospar,"* by
miners, Flour Spar and Ore Bloom, and received my name because of
my common use as flux in processing. Actually my name comes from
the Latin word, *fluere,* "to flux." I am speaking to you below specifically as Fluorite from Brazil.

Elemental Dance:
If you come to me with need
I will care for it.
If you come to me with dreams
I will shield them from distractions.
Whatever aid you wish
I offer it
before you can ask.

Tools for Listening:
However you are listening is your choice.

Respect it.
Expose it to no attention, approval, focus or words,
unless they encourage it,
nurture it,
allow it the freedom
to stretch itself
and flourish as it will.

China

"This is my time to be on the planet. I say, 'Awaken and remember, our struggle can be released.' "

I am CaF2, Calcium Fluoride, a mineral of many, many colors. My hardness is 4 and my specific gravity is 3.1 to 3.2. I exhibit perfect cleavage in four directions. I was orginally called, *"fluorospar,"* by miners, Flour Spar and Ore Bloom, and received my name because of my common use as flux in processing. Actually my name comes from the Latin word, *fluere,* "to flux." I am speaking to you below specifically as Fluorite from China.

Elemental Dance:
Whether they realize it or not,
everyone has someone to look out for them.
For you,
I am one of those beings.
Here,
take my love,
I give it freely
so that it will soften your unnecessary cares.

Tools for Listening:
When you listen to stones,
ask them for their help.
Ask them to help you
to be freer

to be clearer
to be more loving.

Then listen.

How does it feel?

When you learn and memorize knowledge intellectually,
your way to prove your learning
is by repeating the knowledge, later, exactly as it was given to you.

When you listen from the stones and learn as you wish,
the wisdom enters your heart. It spreads out into your life
and is shared with all other willing hearts.
If you need to prove your wisdom,
it will come in your ability to share it later
in your own new and unique way.

England

"This is my time to be on the planet. I say, 'Awaken and remember, our struggle can be released.' "

I am CaF_2, Calcium Fluoride, a mineral of many, many colors. My hardness is 4 and my specific gravity is 3.1 to 3.2. I exhibit perfect cleavage in four directions. I was orginally called, *"fluorospar,"* by miners, Flour Spar and Ore Bloom, and received my name because of my common use as flux in processing. Actually my name comes from the Latin word, *fluere*, "to flux."   I am speaking to you below specifically as Fluorite from England.

Elemental Dance:
I feel the emotions of all others
yet I stand firm in free detachment.
My clarity is the gift with which I honor spirit
and the aid I offer to all in need.

Tools for Listening:
Listening is received most clearly
in a calm peace.

Choose to listen
when your heart beats easily
and your breath draws deeply and effortlessly.

Then you will receive most clearly
the grounded wisdom of the stones.

Morocco

"This is my time to be on the planet. I say, 'Awaken and remember, our struggle can be released.' "

I am CaF2, Calcium Fluoride, a mineral of many, many colors. My hardness is 4 and my specific gravity is 3.1 to 3.2. I exhibit perfect cleavage in four directions. I was orginally called, *"fluorspar,"* by miners, Flour Spar and Ore Bloom, and received my name because of my common use as flux in processing. Actually my name comes from the Latin word, *fluere,* "to flux." I am speaking to you below specifically as Fluorite from Morocco.

Elemental Dance:
I join with other minerals
to extend our beauty
our strength
our wonders.

When you hold me, you hold the exponentiality of the ages

rising in this single moment
of love.

Tools for Listening:
Do you know others who truly wish to listen to stones?

Then join hearts and intents.
Listen with the union of your combined wisdom
and willingness.

Listening and learning together
grows more life.

USA

"This is my time to be on the planet. I say, 'Awaken and remember, our struggle can be released.' "

I am CaF2, Calcium Fluoride, a mineral of many, many colors. My hardness is 4 and my specific gravity is 3.1 to 3.2. I exhibit perfect cleavage in four directions. I was orginally called, *"fluorospar,"* by miners, Flour Spar and Ore Bloom, and received my name because of my common use as flux in processing. Actually my name comes from the Latin word, *fluere,* "to flux." I am speaking to you below specifically as Fluorite from the USA.

Elemental Dance:
Surely you can find me most anywhere.
The Elementals make sure that I am common
for your need
for balance
and for continual learning
is great.

Tools for Listening:
When you listen to stones,
surround yourself with them.
They can help you to ground yourself
so that all of your efforts can be filled with ease.

As you listen with the stones,
feel the etheric roots they have
descending deep into the earth.
Through them,
know the earth's rich support and continual renewal.

The more familiar your body grows with the stones,
the more readily it will find a common language of respect.

USSR

"This is my time to be on the planet. I say, 'Awaken and remember, our struggle can be released.' "

I am CaF2, Calcium Fluoride, a mineral of many, many colors. My hardness is 4 and my specific gravity is 3.1 to 3.2. I exhibit perfect cleavage in four directions. I was orginally called, *"fluorospar,"* by miners, Flour Spar and Ore Bloom, and received my name because of my common use as flux in processing. Actually my name comes from the Latin word, *fluere,* "to flux." I am speaking to you below specifically as Fluorite from the USSR.

Elemental Dance:
Deep within the mother
I await.
I wait past times and cares.
I wait past limits and comforts.
None of this translates to me
for I am carved of a single intent.

I offer balance to all beings upon the Earth Mother
to create the equality of peace for all.
This will I record.
This I await.

Tools for Listening:
For ages upon ages,
Stonebeings have given sweet service to the earth and her beings.
One of their special gifts is to encourage acting upon respect.

Join them.
Join them in the gifts they provide.
When you meditate,
offer peace to every part of the earth
equally
unconditionally.

Listen through the support you offer
after you have offered peace.

henakite

Brazil

"No matter what you see, you are surrounded, gloriously, by infinite guides and angels."

I am Be2SiO4, Beryllium Silicate, with a hardness of 7.5 to 8 and a specific gravity of 2.96 to 3. I can be colorless/clear, yellowish, pinkish or brownish. I am a Beryllium mineral and my name comes from a Greek word meaning, *deceiver* — relating to how easy it is to confuse me with Quartz. For our purposes below, I am speaking to you as a native of Brazil.

Elemental Dance:
I insist.
I travel to the center of energy
as if distraction never existed.
I know what life tells me
and I do as it asks.

Tools for Listening:
Listening comes to us in countless, different ways.
Each of us hears what is offered to us with our uniqueness.

If you do not know how your listening lands yet,
just insist that it is coming to you regardless.
Know that the gifts of stones
are with you.

One day your insistence will lead you right to them.

Madagascar

*"No matter what you see, you are surrounded, gloriously, by infinite guides
and angels."*

I am Be2SiO4, Beryllium Silicate, with a hardness of 7.5 to 8 and a
specific gravity of 2.96 to 3. I can be colorless/clear, yellowish, pinkish or brownish. I am a Beryllium mineral and my name comes from
a Greek word meaning, *deceiver* - relating to how easy it is to confuse
me with Quartz. For our purposes below, I am speaking to you as a
native of Madagascar.

Elemental Dance:
Yes.
Oh yes.
Life on the earth glistens.
It shapes me absolutely
and my every twist and turn is
Wonder.

Tools for Listening:
Listening with stones is like life.
When you come to it empty,
it fills you.

This moment is the moment of listening.
You have arrived at it.
Let go of your expectations
and fill yourself with glorious expectancy.

Nambia, Africa

"No matter what you see, you are surrounded, gloriously, by infinite guides and angels."

I am Be_2SiO_4, Beryllium Silicate, with a hardness of 7.5 to 8 and a specific gravity of 2.96 to 3. I can be colorless/clear, yellowish, pinkish or brownish. I am a Beryllium mineral and my name comes from a Greek word meaning, *deceiver* - relating to how easy it is to confuse me with Quartz. For our purposes below, I am speaking to you as a native of Namibia.

Elemental Dance:
There is fresh evolution upon the Earth Mother.
Change breathes through us
like a wildfire.
This season shapes us
like lava from a volcano.

Tools for Listening:
You know yourself.
Yet do you know how much you are changing?
Right now?

Most of our transformations do not reach our understanding
until after we have breathed through them thoroughly
and worn them a while.
Remember this.

You are changing dramatically, more dramatically than anyone knows
how to tell you.
It is beyond the table of knowledge that already exists.
To find out how you are changing,
listen.

Listen to the changes, themselves.
Listen to stones, the eternal witnesses of change.

Russia

"No matter what you see, you are surrounded, gloriously, by infinite guides and angels."

I am Be2SiO4, Beryllium Silicate, with a hardness of 7.5 to 8 and a specific gravity of 2.96 to 3. I can be colorless/clear, yellowish, pinkish or brownish. I am a Beryllium mineral and my name comes from a Greek word meaning, *deceiver* - relating to how easy it is to confuse me with Quartz.   For our purposes below, I am speaking to you as a native of Russia.

Elemental Dance:
You find me now
because I have a gift.
The energy that I proffer
is of making the impossible
possible.

Tools for Listening:
Make a wish list
from your biggest vision possible.
Let each of the wishes
speak from your truth.

Put your list in a special place.
Place stones on top of it.

Listen as the stones and the wishes speak to you
about how to make them so.

USA

"No matter what you see, you are surrounded, gloriously, by infinite guides and angels."

I am Be2SiO4, Beryllium Silicate, with a hardness of 7.5 to 8 and a specific gravity of 2.96 to 3. I can be colorless/clear, yellowish, pink-ish or brownish. I am a Beryllium mineral and my name comes from a Greek word meaning, *deciever* – relating to how easy it is to confuse me with Quartz.   For our purposes below, I am speaking to you as a native of Colorado, USA.

Elemental Dance:
This is the moment.
Rise the newness within you.
Let it walk into the world
and point out the changes
that must be
that have not yet been imagined.

Tools for Listening:
Listening to stones is such a strange, new experience.
Yet you are doing it.
If you are making this possible for yourself.
What other unimaginables can you help to happen.
Live in readiness of miracles.

# Pyrite

Australia

"Squeeze my hand when you know what you want in life. Then open your hand and there it is."

I am FeS2, Iron Sulfide. My hardness is 6 to 6.5 and my specific gravity is 5 to 5.2. My color is brassy yellow to golden yellow and I am frequently tarnished. I am also known as "Fool's Gold" because of my color and feel. I come in many, many interesting shapes and sizes. I contain a high percentage of iron along with sulphur. For our purposes below I am speaking to you as a native of Australia.

Elemental Dance:
I am the foundation
for so many things.
Build upon me.
Build upon me
what you truly want
and live more life.

Tools for Listening:
Listening is a practice of life
like anything else that you choose to do.

If you want to receive the fullness of its gifts,
you must invest in it fully.
Give it a strong foundation in your life:
Give it a special time and space.
Enter it with a willing heart.
Use all the tools and resources available to help you.

If you nurture its foundation, you can build magic upon it.

Brazil

"Squeeze my hand when you know what you want in life. Then open your hand and there it is."

I am FeS2, Iron Sulfide. My hardness is 6 to 6.5 and my specific gravity is 5 to 5.2. My color is brassy yellow to golden yellow and I am frequently tarnished. I am also known as "Fool's Gold" because of my color and feel. I come in many, many interesting shapes and sizes. I contain a high percentage of iron along with sulphur. For our purposes below I am speaking to you as a native of Brazil.

Elemental Dance:
I give you beauty.
Light flashes around me in showers of glitters.
Each one is a star,
a perfection of life
to be enjoyed here
and now.

Tools for Listening:
You have all the wonder and all the resources
to do and be what you choose.

You may not know that all the time.
You may not realize it fully.

Listen.
The world will tell you of what you already have
if you give it your heart and your ear.

Greece

"Squeeze my hand when you know what you want in life. Then open your hand and there it is."

I am FeS2, Iron Sulfide. My hardness is 6 to 6.5 and my specific gravity is 5 to 5.2. My color is brassy yellow to golden yellow and I am frequently tarnished. I am also known as "Fool's Gold" because of my color and feel. I come in many, many interesting shapes and sizes. I contain a high percentage of iron along with sulphur. For our purposes below I am speaking to you as a native of Greece.

Elemental Dance:
Life is kindness.
No matter what you think
your heart will find constant signs
of its infinite beauty.

Tools for Listening:
When you get discouraged
and think you can't do something
listen.
Just sit and listen.
Life will show you its unwavering
support.
You just need to be still enough
to receive it.

Peru

"Squeeze my hand when you know what you want in life. Then open your hand and there it is."

I am FeS2, Iron Sulfide. My hardness is 6 to 6.5 and my specific gravity is 5 to 5.2. My color is brassy yellow to golden yellow and I am frequently tarnished. I am also known as "Fool's Gold" because of my color and feel. I come in many, many interesting shapes and sizes. I contain a high percentage of iron along with sulphur. For our purposes below I am speaking to you as a native of Peru.

Elemental Dance:
I come from a part of the Earth Mother
that honors geometries.

Listen to my shape
it is a river of life itself.

Tools for Listening:
So many ways to listen to stones............

One day focus on stones of a certain color.
Another day focus on stones of a certain shape.
Listen to each corner, crevasse and point.
Each one has a story,
each one a gift for those willing to receive it.

South Africa

"Squeeze my hand when you know what you want in life. Then open your hand and there it is."

I am FeS2, Iron Sulfide. My hardness is 6 to 6.5 and my specific gravity is 5 to 5.2. My color is brassy yellow to golden yellow and I am frequently tarnished. I am also known as "Fool's Gold" because of my color and feel. I come in many, many interesting shapes and sizes. I contain a high percentage of iron along with sulphur. For our purposes below I am speaking to you as a native of South Africa.

Elemental Dance:
Ah you see my shimmers........
remember they are there
even when the sun is visiting elsewhere.

Tools for Listening:
Whenever you are rewarded for all your fine efforts
and enduring practice,
remember them.

Remember the rewards.
Too often, we focus (even inadvertently)
on the challenges, or even on what challenges could yet come.
This is because we have built fortresses of defenses
that want to keep us from pain.
Yet to ever look for hurt is to find it.

Remember the rewards.
Remember the rewards at every step of the journey
and you'll find more.

Spain

"Squeeze my hand when you know what you want in life. Then open your hand and there it is."

I am FeS2, Iron Sulfide. My hardness is 6 to 6.5 and my specific gravity is 5 to 5.2. My color is brassy yellow to golden yellow and I am frequently tarnished. I am also known as "Fool's Gold" because of my color and feel. I come in many, many interesting shapes and sizes. I contain a high percentage of iron along with sulphur. For our purposes below I am speaking to you as a native of Spain.

Elemental Dance:
Yes I come to you.
The world is a treasure chest
and I am but
one
of the golds that awaits you.

Tools for Listening:
Whatever you can do to revel in the delicious bounty of the Earth Mother,
do it!

As you drink it all in

appreciate it even more

Your life is a bounty!

USA

"Squeeze my hand when you know what you want in life. Then open your hand and there it is."

I am FeS2, Iron Sulfide. My hardness is 6 to 6.5 and my specific gravity is 5 to 5.2. My color is brassy yellow to golden yellow and I am frequently tarnished. I am also known as "Fool's Gold" because of my color and feel. I come in many, many interesting shapes and sizes. I contain a high percentage of iron along with sulphur. For our purposes below I am speaking to you as a native of the USA.

Elemental Dance:
This is it.
This is the moment
created
to reap your harvest.
Whatever you have sown
it is flowering
and shares it bouquet with you
now.

Tools for Listening:
Are you listening?
Are you listening to the stones here in this bookmiracle?
Are you doing it?

Now.

When you wait for anything
you will wait for your rewards.

Listen now
and the worlds open to you
this moment.

USSR

"Squeeze my hand when you know what you want in life. Then open your hand and there it is."

I am FeS2, Iron Sulfide. My hardness is 6 to 6.5 and my specific gravity is 5 to 5.2. My color is brassy yellow to golden yellow and I am frequently tarnished. I am also known as "Fool's Gold" because of my color and feel. I come in many, many interesting shapes and sizes. I contain a high percentage of iron along with sulphur. For our purposes below I am speaking to you as a native of the USSR.

Elemental Dance:
You think so much, so constantly
you are not truly aware of your body
and all the wonders it is telling you about.
Enter your own body
its path ever meets spirit.

Tools for Listening:
Listen.
Now deepen your listening,
also focus on your body
the receptacle of your listening.

If you THINK about the listening,
you will project your own biases upon it.
If you simply wait for communication
to come to you,
you will feel it in your body.
You will receive it as it was offered.

uartz

Africa

"I expand energy!"

I am Quartz, SiO2 , Silicon Dioxide. As Quartz, I am the most common mineral on the Earth Mother and am found most everywhere. I can be the most varied also when it comes to form and color. My hardness is 6.5 to 7 and my specific gravity is 2.57 to 2.64. For our purposes here below I am specifically speaking as clear (or uncolored) Quartz from Africa.

Elemental Dance:
Shapes I have many for I serve many needs.
I hear every call for help
and I amplify them so beautifully they ring across the land
like a song,
"Know your freedom and you will answer your needs."

Tools for Listening:
As you learn your ways of listening
challenges will arise.
Sometimes you will think, *'If only such and such didn't happen, I could listen perfectly.'*

Every time you think this
you deny the gifts of courage and stamina.
Wherever you find challenge, you will also find unexpected
courage and stamina
also arising,
also teaching you.

If you listen to their gifts,

challenge eventually can do nothing but
focus even more resources and love
upon your intent.
Listen strongly and respectfully to any difficulties
and their gifts will connect you with all of life even more.

Argentina

"I expand energy!"

I am Quartz, SiO2 , Silicon Dioxide. As Quartz, I am the most common mineral on the Earth Mother and am found most everywhere. I can be the most varied also when it comes to form and color. My hardness is 6.5 to 7 and my specific gravity is 2.57 to 2.64. For our purposes here below I am specifically speaking as clear (or uncolored) Quartz from Argentina.

Elemental Dance:
Remember to play.
In all your work,
in all your focus
in all your being
play
so that the muses will find you
and sing their symphonies
through you in sweet joy.

Tools for Listening:
To listen to stones
you are learning so many rituals of respect:
Be still.
Be focused.
Be brave.
Be new.

Also remember this. All beings upon the earth hold a space for forever-joy.

They do this to keep their hearts open to the unexpected.
For humans this is most crucial.
The hope of joy allows fear to be one of their teachers,
instead of the only one.
In the most incredible moment
put play into your work.
Its joy will open your heart
and your striving will transform to ease.

Arkansas, USA

"I expand energy!"

I am Quartz, SiO2, Silicon Dioxide. As Quartz, I am the most common mineral on the Earth Mother and am found most everywhere. I can be the most varied also when it comes to form and color. My hardness is 6.5 to 7 and my specific gravity is 2.57 to 2.64. For our purposes here below I am specifically speaking as clear (or uncolored) Quartz from Arkansas.

Elemental Dance:
I am the voice of land upon land.
To you her ways seem slow,
steady
easy to ignore.

I shout her wisdom
through every part of her flesh
and it echoes in your bones
to hold your body strong!

Tools for Listening:
When you go out in nature
bring a piece of Arkansas quartz
with you.

Ask it to shout out to you

Personal Story

It was a few nights before our crystal digging honeymoon. I wished I had a Merkaba meditation to take along, one that would be sweet and simple enough to practice before falling asleep in a cold tent.

My wish was granted just a little later that night, when I held one of our clear, double-terminated quartz crystals to say hello. I said, "Hello." The crystal said, "Come on inside."

By doing so, I found myself standing in the center of the crystal, root and crown chakra aligned with its two terminations. After a strong pulling and tingling sensation over crown and root, I felt all chakras being aligned simultaneously and acting pretty much like a double helix, the crystal energy merged with mine in up and down spiraling motions.

Now the crystal told me to open the heart chakra wide and project love energy, to let this be the "horizontal connector." (God/Spirit does not live "above"; it is important to remember that our connection with

(con't on next page)

the gifts and the wisdom of the Earth Mother.

Then listen.
Let go of expectations.

Do this with sacredness and love
and the earth will answer you through stone.

Australia

"I expand energy!"

I am Quartz, SiO2, Silicon Dioxide. As Quartz, I am the most common mineral on the Earth Mother and am found most everywhere. I can be the most varied also when it comes to form and color. My hardness is 6.5 to 7 and my specific gravity is 2.57 to 2.64. For our purposes here below I am specifically speaking as clear (or uncolored) Quartz from Australia.

Elemental Dance:
I help you to bring to you
whatever you need.
Sometimes you know what it is
sometimes you don't.

Either way
the gift comes from respect –
how you receive it is

All That Is happens on the horizontal plane as much as on the vertical.)

We were completely merged now and through the radiating heart energy I felt fully connected and one with All That Is. This was not only a very blissful state, but also the ideal setting for doing my work.

To me, Quartz is not only a great teacher, but family.

Quartz taught me to stop asking what it could do for me, but to ask, "What can I do for you?"

Thank you.

~Dunyasha

the gift you give yourself.

Tools for Listening:
Carry an Australian quartz with you.
See what happens around you.

Listen to the events that offer themselves to you.
Listen through the language of circumstance
to see what life and spirit are offering to teach.

Brazil

"I expand energy!"

I am Quartz, SiO2, Silicon Dioxide. As Quartz, I am the most common mineral on the Earth Mother and am found most everywhere. I can be the most varied also when it comes to form and color. My hardness is 6.5 to 7 and my specific gravity is 2.57 to 2.64. For our purposes here below I am specifically speaking as clear (or uncolored) Quartz from Brazil.

Elemental Dance:
Listen to me as well as you can.
I hold the space for a continent.
I anchor its dreams
with a wild expansion
that marks all its stones, plants and animals.
They smile
with the fire
of the ancient ones.

Tools for Listening:
Hold quartz from various places on the earth.

Listen to each one carefully and timelessly.

What are the differences between them?

What qualities of that part of the earth can they show you now?

How can you use those gifts wherever you are?

Personal Story

I was teaching outside of New York City on my 41st birthday. On the last day of the course one of the students asked me if she could bring in her crystal so I could see it and tell her what it was. I said, "Sure, bring it in at lunch and at the end of the day we can take a look." In my mind I was thinking it would be like most crystals, small, maybe the size of my hand and of course I was curious to see what kind of being this was.

After lunch in the corner of the room I saw something covered with a towel that looked like a small trash can or something. I figured she brought her stone in a plastic box or something. The rest of the day went well and the students loved learning all about LaStone Therapy. A few of them were not so sure about all the spiritual aspects of this type of stone work so they elected not to stay for the closing ceremony at the end of the day.

I asked the students to clean up the room and would the student with the crystal be willing to place her in the middle of the room on the floor and then we'd all sit in a circle around the crystal. I put on a CD of "OM" and came to the circle to sit down.

Well you can imagine my surprise when I saw this being sitting in the middle of our circle; "A crystal she said she wanted me to see." I do not think to this day I have seen such a crystal of this size and clarity. She stood about two feet high with one perfect point; she was about 9 inches across, clear on top except for rainbows of color flickering within each of the lines that burst with life within her. As my eyes moved down her body I could see the rainbows beginning to darken as the crystal herself was changing color to various shades of brown and the bottom of this being was dark brown and yet you could see these rainbow colors within the density of the darkness.

I told the students I think it is a Smokey Quartz, but I was not fully sure for there were so many rainbows within this being. Then I asked the students to close their eyes and hold hands - left one up to

Father Sky, and right one down to Mother Earth. We began to chant with the "OM" that was continuously playing in the background. About 20 minutes went by and my back began to hurt (not surprising after four days of class). I did not want to break this trance we all seemed to be in. As always, spirit spoke to me: "Open your eyes and look". So I took a breath and did, still chanting "OM". As my eyes opened I saw the most amazing light show happening: the crystal was changing colors and expanding in size both above and below and in width, as if it was breathing with us.

I stopped chanting and just watched in amazement, for up to this moment in my life I would get flickers of color, images of beings in the room with me - not moments of being able to study what I was witnessing. Now before me was this crystal breathing with the rhythm of our chants. Again the voice said, "Open your eyes." As I heard this message I began to not only see this being breathing but I could see colors shifting with the expansion of the crystals breath. From the bottom of the crystal came the deep color of purple and as the breath expanded, the color traveled up the crystal and moved into the color blue. With this expansion came the color green to the tip of the crystal and as we all exhaled the colors faded and the cycle began again. Over and over again I watched this crystal breathe with us, from purple to blue to green and then back again; over and over, in what seemed like a life time.

Again the voice came and said, "Open your eyes." Now keep in mind my eyes have been open since the first message, but spirit wanted my eyes to see more. So I looked deeper into the crystal all the while it was breathing and expanding in size and the colors purple, blue, green where rising and falling with our breath. Now beyond the crystal I could see lines of liquid magenta leaving the crystal at every single angle that the crystal's body was made of. These liquid lines of magenta were moving from the crystal, through the bodies of the students, and reaching into the walls that surrounded us in this room. These magenta lines were straight off the crystal expanding the distance of the room. Between these straight lines were lightening strikes of color connecting the magenta lines with cobalt blue lightening that seemed to be moving in all directions.

By now my mind was in a whirl wind of color, breath, and amazement. I had never before had the opportunity to study the matrix of anything. Until this day I would get glimpses of a shadow or spirit near me, or colors coming and going to and from my client's bodies. Never before could I study them closely or even get a second glance at them, and yet here I sat for what seemed like a very long time and was actually studying this crystal's life, its colors, the expansion of breath swelling up within her core and the matrix as it traveled through our bodies and into the walls that protected us from the outside world. I took in a deep breath and listened as the students continued to "OM." My next thought was to give thanks, to let all the Gods and Goddess' know how grateful I was to have been able to witness such a phenomenon, to be a part of such a blessing - and this blessing was surely not for me alone. I spoke with Spirit and asked, "Do I dare speak, do I dare ask the students to open their eyes to this glorious moment, do I dare take the chance of this magnificent show stopping when I open my mouth to speak"?

With a deep breath I spoke out loud, "Take in a deep breath, keep holding hands and open your eyes slowly and look into the crystal." Slowly the students stopped the chanting of "OM" and opened their eyes. To my pleasure the light show I was watching did not stop; all that had been happening from this crystal continued to do so - the purple, blue, green expanding with the breath of the crystal; the magenta and cobalt blue matrix was still moving from the crystal through our bodies and into the wall.

I spoke again: "Does anyone see anything from this crystal?" One of the students said he could see it expanding like if it was breathing. None of the other students would say anything. I asked them if they wanted me to describe what I saw and they all said yes. So for the next several minutes I described in detail what was happening, and all along to my amazement, the crystal and I continued to be one in this experience.

I took another deep breath as I came to the end of my explanation, although I am sure I could have sat there for hours watching such a blessed event. Then, all of a sudden, the woman who brought the crystal put her right foot on the base of it and all stopped - even my own breath stopped. I was stunned and did not know for sure what to say. After a moment of silence I looked up at the clock and it was 5:57 pm, the exact moment of my birth 41 years ago. We had started our circle at 5:00pm and 57-minutes had passed and a life time for me. A journey with the world of crystals that I had not yet dreamed of, had just been gifted to me by the Universe and I will forever be grateful and humble to the whole experience of that night in New York and the gifts that came to be part of me.

~Mary N.

233

China

"I expand energy!"

I am Quartz, SiO2, Silicon Dioxide. As Quartz, I am the most common mineral on the Earth Mother and am found most everywhere. I can be the most varied also when it comes to form and color. My hardness is 6.5 to 7 and my specific gravity is 2.57 to 2.64. For our purposes here below I am specifically speaking as clear (or uncolored) Quartz from China.

Elemental Dance:
With my one song,
I bring together
lands and beings
of so many kinds.

With my one song,
to many beings
I present one language
of kindness.

Tools for Listening:
Listen to as many different kinds of beings as possible.
Speak simply.
Speak respect.

Then see the sameness they share.

Now carry some Chinese Quartz with you while you listen to so many different beings.

What more have you learned about differences and commonalities?

Madagascar

"I expand energy!"

I am Quartz, SiO2, Silicon Dioxide. As Quartz, I am the most common mineral on the Earth Mother and am found most everywhere. I can be the most varied also when it comes to form and color. My hardness is 6.5 to 7 and my specific gravity is 2.57 to 2.64. For our purposes here below I am specifically speaking as clear (or uncolored) Quartz from Madagascar.

Elemental Dance:
My sweet place lies in the Dreamtime.
This crystalline voice echoes across the ethers
and sounds upon the land
in the hearts of
shamans
dreamers
and adventurers.

Tools for Listening:
Go into the Dreamtime,
the place your spirit travels the worlds
while your body rests.

Before you lay yourself down to sleep
listen to the Madagascar Quartz.
Let its energy imprint you
just before your nightly travels.

WHAT HAPPENS TO YOUR DREAMS THEN?

Mexico

"I expand energy!"

I am Quartz, SiO2, Silicon Dioxide. As Quartz, I am the most common mineral on the Earth Mother and am found most everywhere. I can be the most varied also when it comes to form and color. My hardness is 6.5 to 7 and my specific gravity is 2.57 to 2.64. For our purposes here below I am specifically speaking as clear (or uncolored) Quartz from Mexico.

Elemental Dance:
With my presence,
constant change visits you
and stays with you.

The way of peace also comes
when you accept
the constant change
that is the footprint of life itself.

Tools for Listening:
Today you will be given millions of opportunities to change.
There are so many,
some of them you won't even notice consciously.
Others will face you straight-on and demand that you change.

Listen to the opportunities.
For one full day, listen to all of them that you can.
Find out what their gifts are.
Revel in them.
Even if you are afraid of them, revel in them.

Recognizing the opportunities to change means you are more alive.
Greet them that way.

Nepal

"I expand energy!"

I am Quartz, SiO2, Silicon Dioxide. As Quartz, I am the most common mineral on the Earth Mother and am found most everywhere. I can be the most varied also when it comes to form and color. My hardness is 6.5 to 7 and my specific gravity is 2.57 to 2.64. For our purposes here below I am specifically speaking as clear (or uncolored) Quartz from Nepal.

Elemental Dance:
From here, from some of the highest mountains on the Earth Mother,
I see life.
I see it with my heart.
So many manifestations of other hearts
some open,
some closed,
others still learning to open.

As I watch and keep opening my heart through everything
I smile
for I know that my willing heart will draw others to it.
Soon all I see is
a garden of hearts blossoming in the sunlight.

Tools for Listening:
Who do you admire?
Right now picture in your heart a being that you look up to truly.
Thank him/her for the glorious inspiration that he/she offers.

Now wear that inspiration.
Go out into the world and act as if you were that person, in the ways that utterly fuel your spirit.
Be those amazing qualities.
Keep being them.

Listen.
Then act upon your finest ideal.

Pakistan

"I expand energy!"

I am Quartz, SiO2, Silicon Dioxide. As Quartz, I am the most common mineral on the Earth Mother and am found most everywhere. I can be the most varied also when it comes to form and color. My hardness is 6.5 to 7 and my specific gravity is 2.57 to 2.64. For our purposes here below I am specifically speaking as clear (or uncolored) Quartz from Pakistan.

Elemental Dance:
Hold me.
Ever will I remind you to follow your spirit.
It travels with you even when you believe otherwise.
Spirit lives beyond beliefs and morality
and dances with you in your sweetdreams.

Tools for Listening:
When you meditate,
encircle yourself with quartz.

Listen to the gifts that they can offer you in that space.
When you meditate,
you enter a realm they live in
quiet, still and timeless.

When you become like a crystal in your meditation,
how will you grow and change?

Sri Lanka

"I expand energy!"

I am Quartz, SiO2, Silicon Dioxide. As Quartz, I am the most common mineral on the Earth Mother and am found most everywhere. I can be the most varied also when it comes to form and color. My hardness is 6.5 to 7 and my specific gravity is 2.57 to 2.64. For our purposes here below I am specifically speaking as clear (or uncolored) Quartz from Sri Lanka.

Elemental Dance: Can you feel it?
I capture the warmth of the sun
and hold its glow in my body.
When you touch me,
the flame engulfs you.
You remember life
until there's no need to remember anything else.

Tools for Listening:
Where do you listen the most easily?

Pick a gorgeous day to sit and simply listen (by the water, the mountains, the trees, whatever you wish).
Lay in the sun and let it melt your resistances effortlessly.
Breathe more deeply in the clean, invigorating air.

Be as a crystal
that absorbs all the gifts of nature
to form its body and being
and amplify those gifts to perfection
and listen.

Switzerland

"I expand energy!"

I am Quartz, SiO2, Silicon Dioxide. As Quartz, I am the most common mineral on the Earth Mother and am found most everywhere. I can be the most varied also when it comes to form and color. My hardness is 6.5 to 7 and my specific gravity is 2.57 to 2.64. For our purposes here below I am specifically speaking as clear (or uncolored) Quartz from Switzerland.

Elemental Dance:
Purity lives in the mountains yet.
I echo that untouched perfection.
If you cannot go to the mountain,
listen to me
and we will be there
hand in hand.

Tools for Listening:
Listening means to come to this moment with all that you are
in calm acceptance
ready to receive what life is offering.

When you cannot listen easily
it can be because there are parts of you that still live in old, unresolved hurts
and when you get quiet, all you really are hearing are their voices
whether you recognize them or not.

Before you come to the listening, relax.
Completely relax everything.
Listen to all the voices in you first.
Hear their stories and give them your acceptance.

Then all of you will come to this moment
and listen to everything else, as well.

USSR

"I expand energy!"

I am Quartz, SiO2, Silicon Dioxide. As Quartz, I am the most common mineral on the Earth Mother and am found most everywhere. I can be the most varied also when it comes to form and color. My hardness is 6.5 to 7 and my specific gravity is 2.57 to 2.64. For our purposes here below I am specifically speaking as clear (or uncolored) Quartz from the USSR.

Elemental Dance:
I am old old,
yet I am not a day long.
As I be the fullness,
I am not time,
I cannot be measured
and the finery that I know is all
now.

Tools for Listening:
True listening happens in a special space,
it does not need time, form, or expectations of any kind.
In fact, it frees us from them
and allows us to simply be.

When you listen to/with quartz
consciously set free the expectations of you,
and anything that defines you.

How will you listen if you can be anything at all?

Rose Quartz

Brazil

"Everywhere we are, we create beauty, grace and poetry."

I am the Rose variety of Quartz, SiO2 , Silicon Dioxide. I am a specific Rose Quartz native to Brazil. As Quartz, I am the most common mineral on the Earth Mother and am found most everywhere. I can be the most varied also when it comes to form and color. My hardness is 6.5 to 7 and my specific gravity is 2.57 to 2.64. For our purposes here below I am specifically speaking as Rose Quartz from Brazil.

Elemental Dance:
My heart stands strong.
Your defenses tell you that if you feel too much
you will be weak and vulnerable.
All of my feelings
bolster me
until I can bear anything.

Tools for Listening:
When you are most afraid
let your feelings talk to you.
Listen.

When fear seems strong
you think about so many options,
but what if your mind's thoughts are already based upon fear?

Maybe you're adding fear to fear
and there's nothing original or creative in that.

Feel.
Open your heart.
What else do you know besides fear?

India

"Everywhere we are, we create beauty, grace and poetry."

I am the Rose variety of Quartz, SiO2 , Silicon Dioxide. I am a specific Rose Quartz native to India. As Quartz, I am the most common mineral on the Earth Mother and am found most everywhere. I can be the most varied also when it comes to form and color. My hardness is 6.5 to 7 and my specific gravity is 2.57 to 2.64. For our purposes here below I am specifically speaking as Rose Quartz from India.

Elemental Dance:
Yes, yes, listen.
So much of the quartz of the world wears masculine energy.
I focus on the feminine.
To know me is to touch the divine mother
and linger in that gentle embrace.

Tools for Listening:
Wait for it.
Wait timelessly for the stories and the wisdom of the stones.
They will come to you.
They carry ancient earth records within them.

If you show your willingness
they will find you,
they will ever find you.
Show your willingness
with the timelessness of an open heart and a soft body.

Madagascar

"Everywhere we are, we create beauty, grace and poetry."

I am the Rose variety of Quartz, SiO_2 , Silicon Dioxide. I am a specific Rose Quartz native to Madagascar. As Quartz, I am the most common mineral on the Earth Mother and am found most everywhere. I can be the most varied also when it comes to form and color. My hardness is 6.5 to 7 and my specific gravity is 2.57 to 2.64. For our purposes here below I am specifically speaking as Rose Quartz from Madagascar.

Elemental Dance:
Life is an adventure with endless mountains.
First you are up then you are down.
No matter where you walk
if you see the flowers applauding your steps,
you sweeten the adventure
and expand your senses.

Tools for Listening:
Listen to beauty.
Many of us think that beauty visits our eyes alone
yet beauty is life joining our spirit.
When it enters our soul
it wafts out of our senses
enriching every part of our being.

Listen to beauty with your eyes closed.

South Dakota

"Everywhere we are, we create beauty, grace and poetry."

I am the Rose variety of Quartz, SiO2 , Silicon Dioxide. I am a specific Rose Quartz native to South Dakota, USA. As Quartz, I am the most common mineral on the Earth Mother and am found most everywhere. I can be the most varied also when it comes to form and color. My hardness is 6.5 to 7 and my specific gravity is 2.57 to 2.64. For our purposes here below I am specifically speaking as Rose Quartz from South Dakota.

Elemental Dance:
I am the bones of your elders.
Every hope that your grandparents
held for you
lies in my heart.

I am the bones of your elders.

Tools for Listening:
So many have gone before you.
Though their bodies have gone back to the earth
it is not too late to learn from their wisdom.

The stones are the voices of their stories.
They hold sacred their rituals
and their ways of honoring.

If we are to continue on this Earth Mother
we must join with her.
We must respect her spirit and her generosity, as our elders did.
Through listening to the stones
we can find that path.

 Selenite

Personal Story

One summer, during the Festival of the Little People celebration, Marilyn and Tohmas and the dogs and I brought hundreds of pounds of Selenite to bath with us in Lake Superior. I have lived on this lake for 12 years and still have never felt the water as warm as it was that day. It was like bath water. One by one, we unloaded those stones and lowered them into the lake. I don't know if it was the one that came to live with me or one of it's mates but I remember Tohmas lowering this particularly large piece into the water and watching it clear right before our eyes! It was as if Lake Superior transformed something in all of us, in me, that day as we looked on up to our knees in this amazingly warm water charged by Selenite beings all around us.

To this day, from that group, I have a companion Selenite that was unique in that it was sculpted by water after it came out of the Earth in a beautiful wave pattern, within and on its surface.

I remember when Marilyn called to tell me the Selenite was coming. (Often times over the

(con't on next page)

Australia

*"I am large in your eyes
and small in the wonders possible."*

I am Selenite from Australia. I am Gypsum, $CaSO_4-2(H_2O)$, Hydrated Calcium Sulfate, very soft with a hardness of 1.5 to 2 and a specific gravity of 2.3 to 2.4. My name, Selenite, is related to the moon and I form in massive ways related to saline water.

Elemental Dance: I emphasize independence in feelings.

Tools for Listening: When listening to anything

 you hear yourself as well as anything else.

Your feelings merge with everything else naturally.

Before you listen to stones, clear yourself.

Meditate.

Relax.

Let go of everything.

Then you are free to listen to what else presents itself to you.

Chile

"I am large in your eyes
and small in the wonders possible."

I am Selenite from Chile. I am Gypsum, $CaSO_4-2(H_2O)$, Hydrated Calcium Sulfate, very soft with a hardness of 1.5 to 2 and a specific gravity of 2.3 to 2.4. My name, Selenite, is related to the moon and I form in massive ways related to saline water.

Elemental Dance: I emphasize the need for solitary peace. For in solitude there is aloneness and in that calm you never grow lonely.

Tools for Listening: Go to your favorite quiet place.

Say nothing.

Say nothing for a pre-determined specific period of time.

Relax.

There is so much life to listen to and enjoy.

Breathe it all in and revel in the stories.

Madagascar

"I am large in your eyes
and small in the wonders possible."

I am Selenite from Madagascar. I am Gypsum, $CaSO_4-2(H_2O)$, Hydrated Calcium Sulfate, very soft with a hardness of 1.5 to 2 and a specific gravity of 2.3 to 2.4. My name, Selenite, is related to the moon and I form in massive ways related to saline water.

Elemental Dance: I emphasize the celebration of every feeling! As water shapes me, so emotions shape you. You think them a luxury

last many years, I would just feel the need to call Marilyn and Tohmas and invite new friends home: "M & T, I think there are some stone buddies there for me. Send them home to me!) The way Marilyn tells the story, she and Tohmas went to meet the Selenite for the first time and when they first saw my particular unique water-worn friend, Marilyn said, "Cool. You're going home with …" to which Tohmas replied, "its Cari's!"

I have heard that story a couple of different ways a couple of different times now, and what I feel every time I reflect on it and how I felt the first time, was a deep sense of honor to be selected by such an amazing being. The beauty of these beings, what they offer, and what they are, astounds me again and again.

~ Cari C.

247

for a quiet day, yet I tell you they form your reality the way bones hold your body.

Tools for Listening: Today is a full day of celebration of feelings. Note every emotion as you have it. Pause. Let it fill you. Then affirm, "Through my feelings, I find my Spirit." Every emotion has a story with which to teach you something new, something to be celebratred.

Mexico

*"I am large in your eyes
and small in the wonders possible."*

I am a specific Selenite from the Cave of the Giants in Chihuahua, Mexico. I am Gypsum, $CaSO_4 \cdot 2(H_2O)$, Hydrated Calcium Sulfate, very soft with a hardness of 1.5 to 2 and a specific gravity of 2.3 to 2.4. My name, Selenite, is related to the moon and I form in massive ways related to saline water.

Elemental Dance: I emphasize the glories of the Earth Mother. Through me, you feel her inner being. You know her heart. She lives as unconditional love; she gives us all so that we can have home and family as long as we are here.

Tools for Listening: Every moment the Earth gives to you so you can have life and beauty.

Today, find every way to give back to the Earth:

Recycle.

Use only non-toxic products.

Offer her thanks and rituals.

Treat her with respect.

On the next day, see how your actions affect your listening.

Morroco

> *"I am large in your eyes*
> *and small in the wonders possible."*

I am Selenite from Morocco. I am Gypsum, $CaSO_4 \cdot 2(H_2O)$, Hydrated Calcium Sulfate, very soft with a hardness of 1.5 to 2 and a specific gravity of 2.3 to 2.4. My name, Selenite, is related to the moon and I form in massive ways related to saline water.

Elemental Dance: I emphasize adventure! With all my heart I open. I open to wonder. I open to everything with the awe of love.

Tools for Listening: You are a being of wonder. Create for yourself a ritual to celebrate everything. When you have performed it, create another one, even more glorious.

USSR

> *"I am large in your eyes*
> *and small in the wonders possible."*

I am Selenite from the USSR. I am Gypsum, $CaSO_4 \cdot 2(H_2O)$, Hydrated Calcium Sulfate, very soft with a hardness of 1.5 to 2 and a specific gravity of 2.3 to 2.4. My name, Selenite, is related to the moon and I form in massive ways related to saline water.

Elemental Dance: I emphasize passion. Inside me, I know all for I feel all.

Tools for Listening: Create a storytelling circle.

Invite your friends.

Tell them that you will only exchange the stories that truly excite, the ones that feed your real magnificence.

Then tell your stories.

No one can talk during the stories.

After all the stories have been shared,

all share your wonder and awe.

Utah

> *"I am large in your eyes*
> *and small in the wonders possible."*

I am Selenite from Utah, USA. I am Gypsum, CaSO4-2(H2O), Hydrated Calcium Sulfate, very soft with a hardness of 1.5 to 2 and a specific gravity of 2.3 to 2.4. My name, Selenite, is related to the moon and I form in massive ways related to saline water.

Elemental Dance: I emphasize sureness of feelings. I know who I am.

Tools for Listening: Make a list of the basic beliefs

 that you know and trust.

These are the foundation of your life

and therefore of everything that you know and do.

As you listen to the stones,

find out if any of the beliefs change or grow.

Totem Stories from Hawkseye Velvet Tourmaline

Now is your moment.
It has arrived.
Something in you has always known it would come.

This is a moment of listening.

If you are just reading, then you will think,
'I listen every day.'
Your mind will jump ahead because you know all this.
You've done it all before.
You will barely touch the next words until
you light upon something new,
ever new
always new.
Because if you are not continually skipping to something
New
you may actually meet something in all your travels.
You may actually feel what's beneath the surface.
Your heart may join with another
and know its original tenderness.
That is listening.
You let go of the constant noise in your head,
the replaying of details,
the unconscious habits,
the clever defenses
and reactive judgments.

In listening you enter the moment
fully

while emptying yourself completely,
to be a conversation
where hearts mingle
though minds might disagree
with the inspiration of joined hearts and indescribable love
where all belong
with each other
and no one is asked to be lesser or greater.

Now is our moment.

Stone Combination Section

Listening More Deeply to/with the Stone Combinations

In the first part of this book, you began an adventure in listening to (with) the stories of individual Stonebeings. You allowed that into your heart and it felt...utterly unique ....compelling....and so thrilling that it was impossible not to ask: *"Where do I go from here?"*

Well, now you enter the next adventure – stones in very intentional combinations. When stones join their energies their intent grows exponentially and they give of themselves even more expansively. Their powerful vibrations flow off the page, right into your heart, making it even easier to listen to the stones and to receive their magnificent gifts.

So do it! Don't let the words just carry you. Listen for yourself. Walk in, enter the words, and offer your own heart, too. Any combining of respectful energies creates something amazing.....something wonderful......something that could never be predicted but suddenly is...a miracle. You are now officially being invited to add **your energy** to the Stonecombinations and to live in that exponentiality.

You'll find some new help, in the *"Stone Combinations"* Section, to truly support you integrating your energy with the stones. Each combination lists most of the same categories as the individual stones (in the A-Z section), like *"Physical Description"* and *"Affirmation of Support,"* but new categories have been added: **"Elemental Dance"** and *"Tools for Manifestation."* In the *"Elemental Dance,"* you feel the core of the energy of the stones themselves— the elements of Fire, Earth, Air, Water and Ethers/Spirit.

The constant movement of these elements is what makes up life and its forms, like stones. Just feeling the *"Elemental Dance"* welcomes you to the flow of life in everything, including yourself.

As for the *"Tools for Manifestation,"* here you find specific tasks/exercises to encourage you to directly take the wisdom that you have gained from the stones and to use it in your daily life. This way you truly and immediately join your energy with that of the stones and that exponential union helps you to work together in new ways to manifest as you choose.

One of the most wondrous gifts of Stonebeings is to inspire manifestation. With their bodies, they literally form most of the structure of this planet and therefore they give a physical foundation to everything we physically do. When you also combine with them, energetically (as you do in your listening), you join with their vast, inherent creativity. Together you and the stones can unite intent, energy, focus, and wisdom to co-create what you truly want in life.

So when you listen to the *"Tools for Manifestation"* inspirations, deepen your listening into an active participating. Do the suggested tasks, even if they don't always, exactly fit you. Do them because they will give you new wisdom to open your heart to what unlimited choices you have, and you will gain new ways to co-create the life you didn't dare to even imagine before. And when that gets scary or confusing, the stones will support you with their endless patience and perseverance. As you offer respect and a truly clear intent, Stonecombinations will facilitate you manifesting powerfully and miraculously.

To support your respectful, clear intent, we offer the following "Tools for Manifestation" in listening to and working with Stonecombinations: At the end of the stone combination you will see other combinations that work well with that one. Listen for yourself. Since each Stonecombination works exponentially, multiple Stonecombinations can expand energy even more beautifully. (Note: If you don't recognize any Stonecombinations suggested for combining, refer to "Stones Alive! 2 Volume 1."

More about
Stone Combinations..........

As you explore the "Stone Combinations" Section, you will find two specific types of combinations that we haven't talked about yet. The first one is called "**House as Teacher.**"

These stones come together to co-create a very special space that will keep allowing and activating the energies that you choose there. They are designed to be placed in your home, in your office (or to be respectfully carried during particular rituals/events), so that you can revel in vibrations that keep affirming you exponentially. For instance, when you put the "House as Teacher: Sweet Clarity" by your phone, you consciously co-create the biggest space possible for truthful, clear communications. The wondrous thing about joining with the Stonebeings for this is that they vibrate differently than we humans, so they present us with possibilities and awareness that we just couldn't get any other way, nor that we could even imagine.

When you place a "House as Teacher" combination in your home, you're empowering yourself to realize that even your house has energy and consciousness that you can learn from and that you can work with directly to co-create a space that will keep empowering, regenerating and honoring you. When you work with stones in this, they will hold your intent for you, even when you're too tired...too defensive...too confused. Together, you surround yourself with ongoing awareness and respect.

The other Stonecombination that we haven't talked about yet is an "**Act of Power Wand.**" There is only one in this book ("Conscious Joy"). It's here to catalyze something wondrous and unique. The "Act of Power Wand" Stonecombinations appear at exactly the moment when we need them so that we stand in our power and act upon it. So they will activate all of us completely differently.

This Stonecombination is utterly magical. Listen. How does it inspire you? We're not going to tell how it touches us, so that you can listen, for yourself, in your own clarity, with your own truth..........

Amazing Journey

"House as Teacher Stonecombination"

- ◆ **Wolframite** — I ready us for any adventure and for remembering that everything is an adventure.

- ◆ **Aquamarine** — I show us how to speak and how to listen to every other consciousness, with ease.

- ◆ **Phenakite** — I unite every step in our bodies with every dream and every flow of our Spirits.

Elemental Dance: The Earth, Water and Air Elementals balance out the natural fire of movement/travel, steadying the journey so that it can be as conscious and as enjoyable as possible.

Tools for Manifestation:

Whenever you go on a journey, take this combination with you.

Listen to its wisdom and let it kindly guide your steps.

Or let it live where it can bless continual journeys: your car, your garage, your mailbox etc.

Whenever you look upon it, focus on ease and efficiency of travel and communication and then relax.

Worry about nothing.

Tools for Combining:

Realize that this combination always promotes life and its constant movement.

So hang it in areas where movement is respected and greatly appreciated, just for its own sake!

- • Combine it with "Respectful Welcome" to honor all comings and goings.

- Combine it with "Sweet Clarity" and put near your phone/computer for clear, fruitful communications.

Blessed Responsibility

"House as Teacher Stonecombination"

♦ **Rutilated Quartz** — I stimulate your communication with your bodies and yourselves, first, so that you can respond easily and respectfully to all things and beings.

♦ **Azurite** — I free up lifeforce in us until our birthright creativity overflows.

♦ **Celestite** — I increase your clarity and your wisdom, simultaneously, so that you can recognize truth and act upon it.

Elemental Dance: The focus on the Air Elementals emphasizes your *intents* which birth all timely, respectful actions.

Tools for Manifestation:

Place this Stonecombination in your workplace so that everything you do unites with your spirit.

Let every act (no matter how mundane or small) reflect your deepest respect.

Periodically touch these stones and affirm, "I bless my responding to everything with love."

Place it upon a northern wall of your home to facilitate wisdom with action.

Tools for Combining:

This combination blesses any area of your life where you must ACT.

• Combine with "Earth Magic," in your outdoor spaces, to expand your respect of the earth and your ability to live peacefully with all its beings.

- Combine with "Bountiful Harvest" to attract all the resources needed to care for and honor your lifeforce.

Bountiful Harvest

"House as Teacher Stonecombination"

- ♦ **Copper** — I happily flow with the river of life, dancing in constant, ever unknown change.

- ♦ **Malachite** — I join our bodies with the Earth-body bounty.

- ♦ **Emerald** — I give thanks for the beauty of endless creation.

Elemental Dance: This combination enhances the profundity of the Earth Elemental to its fullest degree. When you work with it, you more deeply connect with the earth and therefore with its natural, continual bounty.

Tools for Manifestation:

Wherever you place this combination, it GROWS or expands things.

Place it near your garden to help you nurture the plants and enjoy a fruitful crop.

Place it near a nursery to support the healthy growth of children.

Place it where you handle money so that you can feel the sacredness of those transactions and expand their bounty.

Place it over where you eat to honor the harvesting of the earth's richness.

Place it in a SE corner of your home to emphasize ever abundant resources.

Tools for Combining:

- • Combine it with "Earth Magic" for greater appreciation of nature. With them both nearby, create rituals of thanksgiving and give-back when the earth and life have been good to you.

- Combine it with "Loving Family" for ever closer bonds between all the family members. Let it be in the center of any circle where you discuss things, especially things that ask for extra love and patience with all involved.

Center Stillness

♦ **Herkimer Diamonds** — We soothe your breathing until you keep coming back to yourselves, your fullness, your true divinity, as if you had never pretended to leave it……..

♦ **Una Oportunidad Sagrada Stonessence** (*"A Sacred Opportunity"*) — I welcome you to your truth. This celebrates your courage in being a divine human at this perfect moment and it supports you unconditionally, always, all ways.

Elemental Dance: "Una Oportunidad Sagrada" embraces the ability of Herkimer Diamonds to connect with both the earth and the skies (simultaneously) and profoundly expands it.

Physical, Emotional, Mental Integration: We truly welcome you to your body and being, just as they are in this moment. We embrace you. We love you for facing yourself. In that timeless space, you meet the center of you, your own perfect balance. It is unique to you. "Center Stillness" affirms that and allows you to keep going more deeply into yourself, into your body, into life, while ever being peace.

Electrical Body Alignment: We combine you with free energy.

Affirmation of Support: "I am myself and I love me just as I am."

Tools for Manifestation:

Hold "Center Stillness" while you meditate.

Know that it will draw you into the spiral of life, itself.

Accept it.

Go there with only your willingness.

Hold "Center Stillness" while you move intentionally.

Let it fill every part of your body until you can listen to each muscle

262

Personal Story

Thank you again and again. The Center Stillness is truly profound; it reminds me to do the necessary and needful things in a meaningful way: breathe with purpose, drink good water, eat more greens. It's a good friend to me already.

~ Jennifer S.

and bone's story.

Know the embrace of acceptance thoroughly.

Act upon it.

Hold "Center Stillness" when you feel challenged.

Feel all your feelings.

Let it breathe with you while you know yourself even more.

Know deeper and deeper breaths, until the challenge gives you its perfect story.

Accept everything.

Aligns with These Other Stonecombinations:

- Combines with "Leading with the Heart" for creatively manifesting with your spirit.

- Combines with "Connecting to your Guids" to inspire constant support and guidance.

Personal Story

One day, Tohmas spontaneously created a new Vibrational Jewelry necklace. It was full of Herkimer Diamonds in a Stonessence and just thrilling to look at. Well, actually it would normally have been thrilling to look at, but I was in a hurry that day. I really wanted to go to yoga class, and I had so much work to do, that it looked like it was going to be a real race to also go to class. But I was determined.

I was just about to run out the door (literally), when Tohmas put this new necklace in my hand and said, "Listen to it. Find out what it is."

Aaaarrrgggh! Wouldn't you know it? I had almost escaped. Okay, okay, I knew that if I was going to listen to this gorgeous new necklace, I had to stop. Stop. Then I had to relax and just listen— just let it happen. Okay.

So I listened to the stones and they twinkled at me. Their name was "Center Stillness." They told me that when I wore them, they would

---

Personal Story

This afternoon I used "Center Stillness" again during silent meditation. When I put it on I had goosebumps and during meditation I felt my heart centre open with much flowing of tears.

~Tim M.

amplify every affirming choice that I would make and act upon. Perfect! They were so quick with their words that I had been able to record their message and I still had time to make it to yoga. So I threw the necklace on and I raced out the door.

I just barely made it to the start of class. Normally I really like having time, in advance, to stretch, to relax— to really get there and to be in that space. Not today. I just started doing the poses that our teacher gave us to do.

My body moved very fluidly. I was extremely limber right away. I could just enter the asanas without a lot of effort. My mind was still. As I did the postures my body moved from one to the other as if they were a single dance. I had never felt that way before. Each move deepened my calm and my muscles softened noticeably. Awareness and breath just filled me, naturally. I casually wondered what I was doing that was making such a difference in my practice.

Then I heard these words, "We are called 'Center Stillness.' We will amplify every choice that you make and act upon." Perfect. I was wearing it! It was absolutely perfect that I had listened to "Center Stillness" and brought it with me to yoga class that day.

~ Marilyn T.

Conscious Joy

"an Act of Power Wand"

♦ **Amazonite** — I cover you with miraculous joy.

♦ **Aquamarine** — I grace all your connections with ease and bliss.

Shadow Integration: Reach into sadness when it comes over you. It is not you. It does not belong to you. It is a teacher, a voice of wisdom, bearing gifts. Inhale it all, accepting the perfection of the union of sadness and wisdom.

Everyday Embracing: Release the need to measure immeasurable lifeforce with linear: time, space, expectations, fears and others' opinions. Value yourself unconditionally and accept the miracles in playing with the clouds, brushing your teeth and smiling unreasonably.

Dreamtime Doorway: Find new passions every day. Delight in a single, perfect, calm breath. Allow life to gift you with anything, which is everything you ever needed or wanted, yet not imagined.

The Act of Power:

Make a list of whatever truly delights you. (Fill it with pictures, too.)

Place "Conscious Joy" on the list and declaring this is your life, now.

Note how much of the time of your precious life is or is not spent being happy.

When you find yourself unfulfilled by your own choices, go back to the list, touch "Conscious Joy" with full breath.

Personal Story

I love the work that we do. I love being a part of our business. The hardest part of my day is knowing when to stop, because I just want to keep doing more.

Stretching myself so thin started catching up to me, a bit. When I would go to bed at night, and was still, my mind would go wild, 'When are we going to get that catalog done? What if we don't make the deadline? What if Charlotte doesn't have time to do the graphics...' It went on and on, until even I got bored with it. But that didn't stop it.

One night before bedtime, I took one of the Act of Power Wands with me. I needed to write some more about it and I thought I could do it in bed— a change of scenery might help. So I sat with "Conscious Joy." I listened to it for my writing.

It didn't say anything. Not a word. We just sat in the silence together and I felt good. I didn't worry about a thing. It just didn't matter.

Well, the next day, I realized that I still hadn't written about "Conscious Joy." I had to do it.

(con't on next page)

Remember how happiness feels.

Fill yourself with it.

Now.

It is a choice.

Aligns with These Other Stonecombinations:

- Combine with "Freedom," as both combinations require full intent and impart empowerment immediately.

- Combine with "Impatience into Presence," to support you being utterly present in each act and choice.

My day was so full I couldn't do anything about it until bedtime that night. I held the "Conscious Joy" next to my heart. I breathed deeply and easily. I thought about my day. I thought about how happy I was doing this work. I remembered how honoring it was to be a part of AhhhMuse. I just reveled in it.

The next thing I knew it was morning and I still hadn't written about the wand. But I also realized that I had gone to sleep, peacefully, on the nights that I had sat with "Conscious Joy." That was what was most important to me and I appreciated it completely. I now keep a "Conscious Joy" next to our bed all the time.

~Marilyn T.

Concrete

I am Concrete, one of, if not the most, widely used combinations of stones on this planet. I am a combination of a wide variety of stones, gravel, slag, ashes, or sand (and possibly many other things depending on the inventiveness of humans and the immediate availability of material — for instance, pumice) mixed with cement and water. My cement these days is mostly what is considered Portland cement. Portland cement is 85 % lime and silica and some common materials used to produce it are limestone, shale, slag, shells, clay, silica sand and iron ore. Cement is so fine that it will pass through a sieve capable of holding water. One pound of cement is said to contain 150 billion grains. My hardness, as concrete, will vary depending on my mix and how I dry (curing and hydration). I touch so many hands and so many lives on this Earth Mother.

Elemental Dance: I support the strength of your structures and if you appreciate that, then you will find more strength and stamina in your being for your choices.

Electrical Body Alignment: I connect you to the full bounty of the earth as you wish.

Affirmation of Support: *"I create my space and my world in utter sacredness and joy."*

Tools for Manifestation:

Unlike the other Stonecombinations in this book

you do not wear this one.

Yet it does touch all of our lives, continually.

Of all the Stonecombinations that you encounter in your days,

this one may be the most common.

What does it mean to you?

Do you realize that you are surrounded by it continually?

Do you consider that it holds together the structures of your world?

Do you *feel* it and its gifts to you?

For one week, notice every time you see concrete.

Pause.

Give thanks for its presence in your life.

From then on, not only might you appreciate concrete

but all the other gifts of the Earth Mother that you may have ignored.

When you do this, you will be surrounded by never-ending bounty.

Disease into Vitality: Allergy Support

♦ **Snowflake Obsidian** — Know who you are— celebrate that now with every part of your being.

♦ **Moonstone** — Wherever you travel, you live in your center, balanced and whole.

♦ **Desert Snow Quartz** — All the changes you bring into your journey give you more freedom.

♦ **Herkimer Diamond** — Today you walk into the world with brand new joy!

Elemental Dance: The Earth and Water Elements in this combination balance wondrously with the Fire and Air, encouraging continual, new inspirations and the structures to hold them and make them so!

Physical, Emotional, Mental Integration: We offer a new perspective to see even more of who you are so you can walk and talk in that truth. This reminds you to accept your choices and to honor them deeply, even when you think they could have been wrong. We support you staying in the center of your body and being, in any circumstance. This frees you to release unneeded defenses/sensitivities/mucous.

Electrical Body Alignment: We link you to innocent acceptance.

Affirmation of Support: *"I am safe and whole in my world."*

Tools for Manifestation:

Stand in front of a mirror.

Look at yourself.

If you feel judgment, just feel it silently, unconditionally. Just let those words come and go freely.

When the judgment has sighed and left, smile at yourself.

Even if you don't quite feel like smiling, give this precious gift to all of you.

Smile at every part of your body, one at a time.

Smile especially at anything you have considered to be your imperfection.

Close your eyes.

Send a smile to every organ, every muscle, every bone – every inner part of you.

Give them extra smiles to carry with them while they do the work of living.

If any part of you feels uncomfortable with this, smile a few extra times for good measure.

Smile at judgment, fear, separation..... why not? Frowning with them certainly hasn't been that much fun............

Aligns with These Other Stonecombinations:

- Combines with "Should into Acceptance" for overall peace and relaxation.

- Combines with "Disease into Vitality: Respiratory Support" encouraging you to BREATHE through everything!

Disease into Vitality: Attention Support

- ♦ **Brookite** — I soften the ways of separation that you have practiced so long and truly welcome you into your body and divinity. Ho!

- ♦ **Malachite** — I smooth the wrinkles of stress and trauma and align your body's meridians in spontaneous celebration of life!

- ♦ **Azurite** — I draw upon the source of life within us to support you feeding your needs and magically fulfilling your desires.

- ♦ **Turquoise** — I lighten your mind. I invite your carefree innerchildren into all your experiences and decisions. Yes~

Elemental Balance: The Earth Element in Brookite and Malachite unite to concentrate and focus the airiness of Azurite and Turquoise. This roots your mind into the activity of your choice.

Physical, Emotional, Mental Integration: We easily, immediately welcome in the full magnificence of your being into every part of your reality and life. As you ground yourselves into your divinity, we Stonebeings show you the elegance of truly being present, every moment, and when you are not, we remind you to just accept everything— everything. We embrace your challenges and struggles so thoroughly that your strengths and weaknesses even out and balance into a complete union of body, mind, heart and spirit, now.

Electrical Body Alignment: We link with your wholeness and remind you of it, continually, in all of your realities, this moment.

Affirmation of Support: *"I am wondrous and I act upon that every moment of my life."*

Tools for Manifestation:

Whenever you feel tense, hold this Stonecombination to your forehead.

Breathe it in. Relax. Read the above words and breathe with every single word.

Breathe the words into your body. Let them land where they will. Watch them.

Feel how they invigorate your being while soothing you.

All is well.

Aligns with These Other Stonecombinations:

- Combines with "Focused Grounding" for extra physical presence and co-ordination.

- Combines with "Reality Creator" to emphasize creating your own reality.

Disease into Vitality: Bone Support

- ◆ **Red Calcite** — I clear confusion at the core.

- ◆ **Strawberry Quartz** — I affirm your desire to be the unique miracles you already are.

- ◆ **Malachite** — I show you the natural cycles of the earth inside and outside of you.

- ◆ **Azurite** — I offer unlimited creativity.

- ◆ **Howlite** — I show you the joy of responsibility.

Elemental Dance: All the Elements represent themselves beautifully so that their energy can be easily offered to anyone in any circumstance.

Physical, Emotional, Mental Integration: We support your bones and strength while helping you to increase your flexibility. We invite you to know the satisfaction of service.

Electrical Body Alignment: We link you to the ability to create divinity upon the earth.

Affirmation of Support: *"I love the strength of my wonderful bones."*

Tools for Manifestation:

No matter how busy you are, you must create time, space (and therefore, choice) in your life.

In a journal list how you spend your time now. List your constant activities and then list how much time you usually spend doing them.

Then write down how you are most likely to spend the rest of your time.

When you have thoroughly exhausted these possibilities, start over completely. Write with fresh inspiration (putting aside everything you have already written). Put down how you *want* to spend your time. Be completely fanciful. You have already recorded reality, now is the moment to record your finest imaginings.

Take a little something from your fun list and insert it into your daily list of activities. Just start very small. When you are doing something from your fun list, wear your "Disease into Vitality: Bone Support" necklace. It will support you. It will support you in spending your time doing what you really want to do.

Keep doing something from your list of dreams, regularly.

Aligns with These Other Stonecombinations:

- Combines with "Disease into Vitality" to provide a continual foundation for integration of vitality.

- Combines with "Turkll Delight" to ever inspire you towards fun!! (Now that's great homework!)

Disease into Vitality: Dream & Sleep Support

- ◆ **Brookite** — I honor the magicalchildren ever alive and ready within you, awake or asleep!

- ◆ **Smokey Quartz** — Let me remind you that you are ever safe, strong and well-loved......

- ◆ **Sodalite** — I offer to tone all parts of you including your body/mind.

- ◆ **Fluorite** — I walk you boldly into the dreamtime as the shaman you wish to be.

Elemental Dance: The Earth and Water Elements, here, soothe and relax continually and kindly.

Physical, Emotional, Mental Integration: Today is the day that you can embrace yourself. In the nighttime/the dreamtime, you face yourself at the core. We can help to protect and calm all parts of the body so that you can go readily to sleep, as you wish. This supports removing stiffness and promotes full-body amplitude and profoundly deeper, more peaceful, regenerating breathing.

Electrical Body Alignment: We offer to connect you with the certainty of peace.

Affirmation of Support: *"I am peace and joy, day and night, always."*

Tools for Manifestation:

This Stonecombination was listened to, embraced, and co-created on a very magical day when Mars was closer to the earth (8/27/03) than it will be for another 60,000 years.

Mars, in astrological language, kindly represents for us:

Sheer lifeforce

Vitality

Courage

Action ...and much more ...

Be active about creating a glorious, relaxing space from which to enter your sleep and dreamtime.

It is such a richly regenerative, kind, sacred time.

Honor it well.

Place this combination near your bed and let this be your signal to:

Stop. Breathe. Relax every part of your body. Visualize what you want to see in your life, not what you don't like.

Aligns with These Other Stonecombinations:

- Combines with "Arms of Michael" to affirm that you are safe and ever protected.

- Combines with "Faith's Embrace" so that you can leap, consciously and joyfully, into your dreams.

Disease into Vitality: Growths Support

♦ **Brookite** — Let me show you the utter magic of every day.

♦ **Apache Tear** — Remember to ever let go of hurts and pain.

♦ **Desert Snow Quartz** — Together we can catalyze complete transformation!

♦ **Crystal** — I want to lighten your mind, your heart, and fill your being with ongoing trust and joy.

Elemental Dance: The Etheric Elements come together to support expansion in your true choices.

Physical, Emotional, Mental Integration: We support your bodies and beings growing in continual and new balance. We ask to help to release unneeded feelings and struggles and we emphasize your natural vitality.

Electrical Body Alignment: We link to your innate balance and wholeness.

Affirmation of Support: *"I express my truth easily and immediately."*

Tools for Manifestation:

Hold this combination over any part of your body that feels unloved or somehow neglected.

Hold it there until you can feel vitality glowing and growing.

Breathe.

Breathe while your well-being expands.

Breathe while your body releases any stored fear or hurt.

Breathe acceptance.

Aligns with These Other Stonecombinations:

- Use with "Arms of Michael" to feel safe, protected and guided.

- Use with "Crystal Pleiadean Pyramid Alignment" to align all body meridians as quickly as possible.

Disease into Vitality: Heart Support

- ♦ **Sunstone** — I very happily connect your gut instincts and your tenacity for outright evolution with your sweet heart.

- ♦ **Malachite** — Let me soothe, tone, en-**courage** your heart and every part of your perfect wonder of a body.

- ♦ **Tourmaline** — Come to the peace of body and spirit joined. It supports every physical process as you wish.

- ♦ **Peridot** — I can bring you to the depths of what you cannot accept (of the exact things that you deny), with tenderness so that you can embrace absolutely everything, which is ever more life.

Elemental Dance: The Fire Element is the base of this combination so that we can stop being just "in our heads" and jump into our bodies and our hearts.

Physical, Emotional, Mental Integration: We bring you face-to-face with whatever you use to block life and invite you to ask yourself, *"How can I embrace this and be even more life and love?"*

Electrical Body Alignment: Let us align you with the true peace of an open and ever opening heart. Now.

Affirmation of Support: *"I love myself utterly and completely right now and always."*

Tools for Manifestation:

This Stonecombination was listened to, embraced, and co-created on a very magical day when Mars was closer to the earth (8/27/03) than it will be for another 60,000 years.

Mars, in astrological language, kindly represents for us:

Sheer lifeforce

Vitality

Courage

Action … and much more …

Trust that you have brought this Stonecombination to you right here, right now because you are a wise spirit-in-form. Your heart understands and knows what you need, whether or not you have words to explain this. Accept it. Welcome these stones into your life. They joyfully offer you their unique services to so love you that you open your heart, freely, to ever and ever and ever more wonders. Watch the affirmation of this in every single moment of your life. Celebrate it thoroughly as it happens.

Aligns with These Other Stonecombinations:

- Combines with "Fear into Love" so that you know you are supported when you feel challenged.

- Combines with "Bliss" for the sheer enjoyment of it all!

Disease into Vitality: Hormonal Support

- ♦ **Tasmanian Crocoite** — I touch all your extremes of being and bring them together by sheer acceptance.

- ♦ **Amblygonite** — I focus on supporting your free, true choices manifest in life.

- ♦ **Peridot** — I encourage the heart to take the lead, aligning the body with the spirit in full integration.

- ♦ **Brookite** — I allow, welcome, and support your new consciousness to manifest more life and more vitality in and around you.

Elemental Dance: The foundation of the Fire Element, here, urges you to connect with your instincts and your natural cycles with gusto and appreciation.

Physical, Emotional, Mental Integration: We encourage you to see and to directly experience the effects of your thoughts, beliefs and emotions upon your body and your reality. This invites you to increase your ability to respond in a conscious, free manner to all of life. It supports you living in your center and your power, in all moments. Watch for the continual expansion of all your realities.

Electrical Body Alignment: I unite you with immortality and with continual vibrancy in your body, right here, right now.

Affirmation of Support: *"I love my body and it loves me!"*

Tools for Manifestation:

Hold this Stonecombination in your hand.

Listen to its vibration.

Ask it to show you whatever energetic gifts that it has to offer you.

Personal Story

I've been using the Disease into Vitality: Hormone Support Stonessence.

Usually every other month I have to put up with about 3 weeks of PMS BEFORE I even start my period. Since I have been spraying the stone essence on my sacral charka I have now had two "normal" on time periods and without the migraines that I was having.

YEAH!

Thanks for the essences!

~Rhonda S.

Offer your respect and thanks.

After you have received its gifts and given thanks, often,

hold this jewelry on any part of your body that needs some kind of extra support.

Allow the support and give thanks.

Aligns with These Other Stonecombinations:

- Combines with "Infinite Intimacy: the Female Version" and "Infinite Intimacy: the Male Version" to encourage you to unite your inner female and male selves lovingly and kindly.

- Combines with "Death" to support you accepting and honoring the natural cycles of life and death and life......

- Combines with "Immortality," inviting you to consciously act upon the unlimited choices of your life.

Disease into Vitality: Nerve Support

- **Hematite** — I anchor all that you are, on all levels, with breath and endless vitality.

- **Blue Lace Agate** — I calm, soothe, and lift you into time-lessness where all is well.

- **Phenakite** — I align you with your true magnificence, your absolutely undeniable unlimitedness.

- **Silver** — I urge you to release the unnecessary focus on the mind-alone. This softens your world so that you can receive, abundantly, all the treasures that quietly, patiently await you.

Elemental Dance: This combination focuses on all the elements except Fire, to facilitate pure and continual regeneration and peace.

Physical, Emotional, Mental Integration: We sweetly inspire you so that you can see worlds where distractions and scattered thoughts do not control anything (not even themselves). This integrates you with the *feeling* of peace, so that you can act upon it and then know it, undeniably, for yourself, and free yourself.

Electrical Body Alignment: We welcome you to your spontaneous empowerment.

Affirmation of Support: *"I love the feel of energy moving in my life."*

Tools for Manifestation:

This Stonecombination was listened to, embraced, and co-created on a very magical day when Mars was closer to the earth (8/27/03) than it will be for another 60,000 years.

Mars, in astrological language, kindly represents for us:

Sheer lifeforce

Vitality

Courage

Action ...and much more ...

Choose to align with the energies that can be represented by nerves: welcoming change; etheric energies; freedom; knowing equality with all life; embracing the future ...and whatever else you intuit for yourself.

All is well.

Speak it.

Think it.

Feel it.

Act it.

Aligns with These Other Stonecombinations:

- Combines with "Center Stillness" to encourage peace as a way of life.

- Combines with "Stress into Centeredness" to release unneeded stimuli.

Disease into Vitality: Pancreas Support

- ♦ **Realgar** — I embrace every challenge and reveal their hidden treasures.

- ♦ **Sunstone** — I unbury the deepest wounds, freeing them.

- ♦ **Chrysoprase** — I accept you so unconditionally that you BREATHE.

- ♦ **Rhodonite** — Smile …it shows you how to live with your vulnerable, inner selves.

Elemental Dance: This dance of Elements in this combination joins your instincts and your reflexes with your heart.

Physical, Emotional, Mental Integration: Smile, life truly is wonderful …but it may not meet your expectations! We can show you where to look to find the treasures inside of all things, including disappointment: They inspire you. They uplift you. They bring you to the wonder and reality of it all (The rest is up to you.).

Electrical Body Alignment: I link you to the sweetness of being alive!

Affirmation of Support: *"I am rewarded richly for embracing life."*

Tools for Manifestation:

Make yourself a "Notebook of Wonders!"

Decorate it lavishly— just the way you exactly want it.

Then carry it with you everywhere.

No matter what happens to you, write down the wonder you see in every single event.

Stretch yourself until you are constantly in awe.

Be a "Wonder Reporter."

Aligns with These Other Stonecombinations:

- Use with "Hope's Call" or "Mary's Wonder" to feel your guardian angel helping you to find wonder.

- Combine with "Bliss" just for the fun of it.

Disease into Vitality: Respiratory Support

- ♦ **Tourmaline** — I root the body while you relax your heart and soul.

- ♦ **Lapis Lazuli** — I offer wisdom as the base for body and spirit, joined.

- ♦ **Iolite** — I unite intuition and wondrous mystery with your practical world.

- ♦ **Blue Lace Agate** — Remember, focus on your breath in all things.

Elemental Dance: The Air Element in this Stonecombination is beautifully utilized, encouraging you to do the same.

Physical, Emotional, Mental Integration: We offer the opportunity to BREATHE in every action, thought and feeling. You connect with prana and limitless fuel for all of your inspirations and dreams. Then you relax each part of your body and being, as needed.

Electrical Body Alignment: We link you with respect for all life.

Affirmation of Support: *"Abundant, glorious life flows through me in every breath."*

Tools for Manifestation:

Before you do anything else, RIGHT NOW.....breathe.

Just breathe.

Get used to the ease of it. Let it fill you just as it wants to and then **smile**.

Smile at the wonder of air and breath revitalizing your body and your wonder, too.

When you can, pause before each decision, each word, each action, and just breathe.

Let air and breath fill your every experience, first, foremost and always.

Aligns with These Other Stonecombinations:

- Use with "Relationship into All" to share your wonder at life with all other beings.

- Use with "Connecting to Your Guides" to grow your intuition into strong spontaneous wisdom.

Disease into Vitality: Stamina Support

- ♦ **Black Garnet** — I so admire your body and your brave choice to be in it, that it welcomes you into unimaginably full and overflowing life and energy.

- ♦ **Carnelian** — I so awaken your passions that your desire to act your dreams grows your body as strong as you can imagine, here, now.

- ♦ **Iolite** — I insistently, sweetly connect you to your intuition, allowing you to see the natural flows of life (beneath the surface) and how to dance with them………. as you wish~

- ♦ **Desert Snow Quartz** — I offer you untold, unknown transformation to wield as you will……to accept yourself as strong and perfect, even in the boldest faces of resistance.

Elemental Dance: The Elements and Elementals of these stones keep amplifying to help you to hold the space for anything.

Physical, Emotional, Mental Integration: When you *truly* want to feel the full tides of lifeforce move you, hold us to your heart and smile. That smile can open you to the acceptance of a truly grounded body and of sharper, clearer senses that will show you (in DELIGHT) your transformation to vitality. It will offer you the doorway to gratitude where all miracles reside just before manifestation.

Electrical Body Alignment: We link you to the power in your body.

Affirmation of Support: *"I accept full lifeforce in and through this body, now!"*

Tools for Manifestation:

This Stonecombination was listened to, embraced, and co-created on a very magical day when Mars was closer to the earth (8/27/03) than it will be for another 60,000 years.

Mars, in astrological language, kindly represents for us:

Sheer lifeforce

Vitality

Courage

Action............and much more...............

Align with this as you choose. Empty yourself and write a wish list of all the most magnificent, perfect dreams that you would like to act out. You are ready. Make it so.

Aligns with These Other Stonecombinations:

- Combines with "Lack into Allowability" to help you have all the energy you need to accept life.

- Combines with "Sweet Shield" so that you can focus on gathering and storing your own energy, first and foremost.

Earth Magic

"House as Teacher Stonecombination"

- ♦ **Pine Needles** — We are sacred offerings to the Earth Mother and to the Spirit within in all of us.

- ♦ **Chrysocolla** — I come from the heart of the Earth to accept us, and then affirm us with every breath, tear and smile.

- ♦ **Rubellite** — I join with the heart of the Earth Mother and with all her children upon the earth so that we co-create love in everything.

Elemental Dance: This combination delightfully enhances the Water, Earth and Fire Elementals to create a tool for tremendous nurturing and thrilling possibilities.....for whenever we thoroughly embrace anything it grows into unimaginable love and unpredictable magic.

Tools for Manifestation:

Wherever this combination is it awakens the magical and blissful union between us and all other things and beings upon the earth.

Place in your basement to enhance the rooting of your home/building into the earth with respect and love.

Place in any outdoor space to honor the earth spirits (and who knows what will happen then?).

Place by the garden to naturally reduce pests and to help the plants thrive.

Place by an eastern window to celebrate the rising sun and the birth of all possibilities.

Tools for Combining:

- Combine with "Sweet Companions" for continued, enhanced communication with other life forms.

- Combine with "Loving Family" for a greater appreciation of the cycles of earth and of the cycles of life within us all.

Evolutionary Grace

- ◆ **Boji®** — I anchor your body in time and space and multiple dimensions at once. This honors all your free, loving choices and supports them in all the worlds, with you.

- ◆ **Green Obsidian** — I reach into your heart and recognize it as the leader between all your selves and all your divine possibilities now. This warms your essence with constant, insistent affirmations of magnificence.

- ◆ **Ajoite** — I compassionately join you with the earth and your free choice to live here as a magnetic, loving co-creator. Ho!

- ◆ **Japanese Cherry Blossoms Essence** — I clearly welcome you into the realm of inexplicable, amazing miracles where you now belong, and yet, perhaps don't quite see yourself there.

Elemental Dance: This combination accentuates the Water Elemental to soothe you during the bumps of life's ride.

Physical, Emotional, Mental Integration: We bless you as the completely evolving earth being you are. Whatever you need to change even more, you will find. We support you in attracting your truth in full, non-judgmental love and acceptance. Each being will experience "Evolutionary Grace" uniquely. We invite you to dive into this extraordinary opportunity. Free yourself and all expectations and create an aura of utter transformation and just revel in whatever it is, as it is, when it is.

Electrical Body Alignment: We unite you with the self that holds all knowingness and loves, accepts and supports, fully, all that you are now.

Affirmation of Support: "*I am what I am becoming.*"

Celebrating the Auspiciousness: Welcome "Evolutionary Grace." This sacred stone and flower combination birthed itself during an April Full Moon. It not only heralded the ever wondrous spring, it affirmed all births, growth and evolution. Its perfect, timeless timing and intent allows us to step into acting upon the incredible, unconditional love we are, in all levels of existence.

"Evolutionary Grace" not only recognizes the full-scale evolution of consciousness that we have jumped into, it truly supports us. It does not offer us the conditional love and ways that we seem to be familiar with, it offers us the multi-dimensional acceptance and tools that we perhaps don't recognize yet. Even Einstein said that problems cannot be solved at the level that they were created. So this ever exponential stone union/support witnesses us as the evolving beings we are, helping us to release our attachment to what we have been and grow into what we choose to be and perhaps don't always recognize in ourselves.

Aligns with These Other Stonecombinations:

- Combines with "Leading with the Heart," giving us a foundation, within ourselves, to trust and to depend on continually.

- Combines with "Center Stillness," allowing us the constant peace to respond to everything from our spirits.

Gathering Respect

♦ **Ruby** — I honor your life force and your resonant field. From that point of respect all is possible.

♦ **Turquoise** — I affirm your truth clearly and declare it to all life, helping you to link to other respectful resonant fields.

♦ **Herkimer Diamond** — I smile! It offers a child-like ease that allows and attracts spontaneous manifestation of miracles.

Elemental Balance: The Elementals in this combination equally link heaven and earth, encouraging grounding <u>and</u> soaring!

Physical, Emotional, Mental Integration: We offer more clarity and focus to the core of lifeforce and possibilities. This aligns you with the Elementals spontaneously, as you choose. It connects you with the courage and commitment needed to keep growing every single now.

Electrical Body Alignment: We happily link you to other resonant fields of respect.

Affirmation of Support: *"I appreciate all of creation and it appreciates me."*

Tools for Manifestation:

Sit down quietly.

Breathe.

Ask that your basic intents in this life be spoken to you.

Revel in that and accept them freely.

Write them down.

Live with them.

Invite your sacred witness to observe them with you.

Do they fit you completely?

If so, give great thanks.

If not, re-write them, asking for the support of your loving spiritguides.

When they fit you, give great thanks.

Repeat this ritual continually to create a clear resonant field that attracts whatever is meant to support your unconditionally loving manifestations.

Aligns with These Other Stonecombinations:

- Combines with "Sweet Shield" just because they like each other!!

- Combines with "Evolutionary Grace" for more focus and dedication.

Innocent Child

"House as Teacher Stonecombination"

- ◆ **Kunzite** — I open your heart and free up your innocence and willingness.

- ◆ **Blue Apatite** — I remind us of every sweetness ever known. As we focus on that, all wonders find us at every turn.

- ◆ **Amazonite** — I laugh, just because …

Elemental Dance: This combination focuses on joining the heart (Water) with spirit (Ethers).

Tools for Manifestation:

Wherever you place this Stonecombination it encourages your inner child and a pure trust of life.

Place it in the spaces where you play.

Take it with you when you go on an outing just for fun.

Place it where children spend time.

Place it where you focus upon healing.

Place it on a western wall to spontaneously increase your intuition.

Tools for Combining:

- • Combine it with "Loving Family," just because!
- • Combine it with "Earth Magic," to create more miracles.

Leading with the Heart

♦ **Herkimer Diamonds** — We soften resistance and separation in you, until you soar through challenges and ease— gracefully... equally... with no thought of why...

♦ **Peridot** — I keep opening your heart, especially when fear comes to teach you about being unconditional.

♦ **Una Oportunidad Sagrada Stonessence** (*"A Sacred Opportunity"*) — We show you how to do what you don't know how to do yet— just when you need it.

Elemental Dance: This combination amplifies the Water Elemental, to focus on the heart and acceptance.

Physical, Emotional, Mental Integration: We offer to align your body, your mind, and your being with your heart. It shows you the truth that is always there and therefore, the endless support for you in any moment. It allows you to feel safe within yourself and urges you into constant newness and growth.

Electrical Body Alignment: We join you with your spirit in every thought, feeling and action. It aligns you with the original language of union.

Affirmation of Support: *"I speak and act from the truth of my heart."*

Tools for Manifestation:

Make a list right now. This list is the most important one of your entire life.

What do you most want to be?

Write as much and as fast as you can, so that your mind cannot edit.

Stop. Breathe. Relax. Look at the world. See what you admire about it and luxuriate in it. Think of no-thing. Just witness beauty.

Go back to your list. Does it say what you truly want to be? Does it speak with your most magnificent truth? There's no reason to be anything else.

Hold "Leading with Your Heart." Ask your heart, "Is this my truth?"

Change the list until it speaks of your true beauty.

Now wear those words in your heart, in "Leading with Your Heart," and act upon them.

Admire yourself.

Aligns with These Other Stonecombinations:

- Combines with "Fear into Love," encouraging your heart as the leader it is.

- Combines with "Gabriel's Dawn" and "Hope's Call" constantly renewing and re-energizing you.

Totem Stories from Hawkseye Velvet Tourmaline

Listening brings us together.

The same lines of communication exist in all of our bodies.

Not only do we wear color or brightness or shape,

they wear us!

And when they wear us they tell a page of our story

by showing how and why we formed.

All of our stories fit together

colorfully

brightly

geometrically.

They weave in a quilt of life

where every imagining or whim

shows off itself

and creates a whole earth

an earth of belonging.

All life forms in balance:

The blues calm the reds.

The tetrahedrons expand the lines.

You can feel it in the blues and the lines inside you

unless

you must judge the colors and the shapes.

If you must decide who they are without listening

then your precious listening will fade into the shouts of competition.

It will slip away

as if it had never been.

Then when you need it (like now)

you won't believe in it

because you will have shaped your world without respect

where listening does not belong.

Yet you always belong.

You belong with the earth and you belong with life.

Urge your heart open to every color, brightness and shape.

Decide nothing upon nothing

so that you will listen to the vastness of life

weaving within you and around you

forming us all.

Loving Family

"House as Teacher Stonecombination"

- ♦ **Kornerupine** — I join you with the family of your clear, free, conscious choices.

- ♦ **Aventurine** — I fill you with the joy of exponential love.

- ♦ **Rose Quartz** — I soften your need to be correct and encourage your heart to lead your life.

Elemental Balance: This combination focuses on the Earth, Water and Fire Elementals to ground loving, compassionate energy.

Tools for Manifestation:

Wherever you place this combination, it will support you finding special beings to love and to be loved by.

Place this wherever you gather with good friends and family.

Bring this combination to special celebratory events, like weddings.

Place this next to pictures of family and friends.

Tools for Combining:

- Combine with "Innocent Child" to facilitate inner child healing.

- Combine with "Sweet Clarity" for deeper family communication.

Perfect Purpose

◆ **Tibetan Tektite** — I anchor you so thoroughly and so peacefully in the here and now all you know is gratitude... and more ... ever more ...

◆ **Azurite** — I call forth creativity that you didn't even know existed.

◆ **Himalayan Quartz** — I join you with your loving guides on every dimension.

◆ **Astrophyllite** — I completely charge your core star essence with truth, poetry, unimaginability and earth support now.

Elemental Dance: This combination amplifies the Etheric with the Earth Elementals, giving you a glorious base from which to grow and thrive.

Physical, Emotional, Mental Integration: We quietly and continually ground your being and body with the earth. This releases unnecessary striving while simultaneously fostering simple **allowing** in every thought, word and deed. It increases immediate sensitivity to when and how you will change your surroundings, perspective and learning. It relaxes all physical and mental systems, focusing on intuition as a lifestyle choice in manifestation.

Electrical Body Alignment: We support you in accepting your own power and wisdom.

Affirmation of Support: *"I love myself and what I do for a living."*

Tools for Manifestation:

Make a list of what you usually do each day. Do this for a week, simultaneously making up a supplemental list of things you do semi-regularly. Place the two lists in an area where you work and simply let yourself feel their energy for a single day.

Now read the lists. Breathe through and meditate upon each item on the list, one by one. Then allow yourself to meditate upon (not "think" about) them, completely detached, for a day and a night.

Burn the lists with great joy and relish.

You are free. You can completely change any routine or any pattern you have. Let your mind and body wander into any new area you like. You are an explorer. See what finds you. Your life will transform itself unexpectedly. Affirm "I love myself and what I do for a living!"

Aligns with These Other Stonecombinations:

- Combines with "Welcome Home" to affirm that you belong here upon the earth.

- Combines with "Business Success," encouraging you to work at what fulfills you.

- Combines with "Connecting to Your Guides" helping you to clearly receive guidance when you need it.

Perfect Release

"House as Teacher Stonecombination"

- ◆ **Smokey Quartz—** I accept everything with such grace that whatever is not needed anymore simply slips away naturally, quietly.

- ◆ **Turquoise—** I embrace the independent, free spirit within us. It urges us to welcome the unknown as the adventure it always is.

- ◆ **Amethyst—** I connect us with our most freeing, gracious perspective.

Elemental Dance: The Earth and Ether Elements come together to embrace what is so that all Elements are free to express themselves, perfectly, with no unnecessary attachment.

Tools for Manifestation:

Wherever this Stonecombination is it keeps the energy moving. It encourages freedom and constant, continual change.

Place it wherever you release things—by the garbage, by the recycling, in the bathroom.

Place it by your entrance/exit areas to attract the energy you need and to let go of everything else.

Place by affirmations declaring the things that you wish to be free of in your life.

Tools for Combining:

- • Combine with "Sweet Clarity" to empower yourself to keep making continual decisions and to release the rest.

- • Combine with "Innocent Child" to let go of old traumas.

Respectful Welcome

"House as Teacher Stonecombination"

- ♦ **Ruby** — I connect with lifeforce at its core. This enriches you and revitalizes your body and spirit.

- ♦ **Hematite** — I link us with the earth. It deeply cares for your body and expands your strengths.

- ♦ **Herkimer Diamond** — I inspire you, uplift you, and urge you to leave behind the past and the future.

Elemental Balance: The underlying core of the Fire Elementals, here, honors births, beginnings and new arrivals of all kinds.

Tools for Manifestation:

Wherever you place this combination it fosters happiness, newness and honoring.

Place this near the dining table to bless the food.

Place this near the entryway of your space to greet all guests and events.

Take this with you on trips and place it in the entryway of where you are staying to honor and welcome YOU.

Tools for Combining:

- Combine with "Perfect Release," to support you being fully present in this moment.

- Combine with "Sweet Clarity" to show your full welcoming of everything, even the unknown.

Reality Creator

- **Wolframite** — I bring you to this body, this reality, to respond.

- **Crocoite** — I help you find the resources to fulfill dreams.

- **Sulphur** — I affirm you choosing consciousness, which hones awareness and allows everything else to just slip away freely.

- **Green Apatite** — I warm the heart, knowing that it leads the body and the mind.

- **Blue Apatite** — With you, I face the truth, confidently, innocently, joyfully.

- **Amethyst** — I share the wonder of it all with all life, in all forms and formlessness.

- **Amblygonite** — I stand in truth and love and reflect that in all realities, endlessly.

- **Evolutionary Grace Stonessence** — I help to catalyze all the change you need.

Elemental Dance: This Stonecombination links the Elementals with the Ethers so beautifully that it amplifies your possibilities and respond-abilities.

Physical, Emotional, Mental Integration: We remind you that you are free beings choosing each moment of your lives (or not). This supports you with stamina, motivation and the clarity to create whatever you choose. It balances you with continual breath and awareness. It attracts you to the truth so that you manifest immediately and powerfully with whatever resources you need.

Electrical Body Alignment: I link you to power.

Affirmation of Support: *"I create my life, as I lovingly choose, now."*

Tools for Manifestation:

Always explore yourself.

Witness all that you do and think and feel; this is the fuel of your reality.

Do you want to change your life?

Then focus on the changes as if they already were your life, right this moment.

Insist upon it.

If and when you resist these changes, just accept it (the resistance) and rejoice in it and love it for its chutzpah.

Nothing deflates resistance faster than enjoying it.

Live the life of your choice. It is so whether you accept it or not.

Aligns with These Other Stonecombinations:

- Combines with "Uriel's Wisdom," to help you create with vision and patience.
- Combines with "Disease into Vitality" to welcome in health and energy as a way of life.

Sacred Companions

"House as Teacher Stonecombination"

- **Stibnite** — I urge you to be and to accept who you truly are.

- **Topaz** — I respect all life and show you how to speak with and listen to anything.

- **Selenite** — I join our hearts with all other life forms.

Elemental Dance — This combination enhances the union of Air, Earth, and Water Elementals to increase telepathy and compassion with other life forms.

Tools for Manifestation:

"Sacred Companions" facilitates human connection with all other beings upon the earth, and specifically, with domesticated animals.

Place wherever your animal friends live, eat and sleep.

Place at the entryway of your space to welcome friendly animals.

Take with you when you take your animal friends to stressful places, like the vet's office, so you can clearly communicate with them what is happening and why.

Take with you when you go on walks with your animal friends so that you can learn from how they interact with the world and nature.

Tools for Combining:

- Combine with "Loving Family" to profoundly deepen your connection to animals, plants and stones.

- Combine with "Earth Magic" so that the animals, plants and stones that live with you will feel welcome.

Spontaneous Manifestation

- **Kornerupine** — The world comes to me and I stand in willingness. I open my heart more and more until I give and receive everything as an empowering gift.

- **Chrysoprase** — I soften myself. I care for all my being, even the parts that feel hard and afraid. Together we are whole.

- **Aventurine** — I warm my heart to feel every abundance and to accept it in a spiral of ever growing thrill and gratitude.

- **Raw Silver African Diamond** — All of life shapes me, which is how I live with more vitality and strength NOW.

Elemental Dance: This Stonecombination thoroughly and insistently connects all the Elementals with the heart and with instant integration (through a concentration upon Water and Earth).

Physical, Emotional, Mental Integration: We spontaneously align with the elementals and our union grows exponentially. We gracefully access all the energies that enhance life and fulfill true dreams and desires. Together we grow **into** every experience **instead** of away from it. All beingness flows into balance.

Electrical Body Alignment: We align with the full power of creating and manifesting with life in every dimension and form.

Affirmation of Support: *"I allow myself to attract whatever I truly need, want, and love."*

Spontaneous Manifestation:

This jewelry co-created itself (with us) spontaneously, one day.

It came completely naturally out of the practice of our life— respect.

In this ever growing resonant field, the Elementals and these stones came in answer to our vibration.

Together we co-created spontaneous manifestation.

It is the way of free, unconditional manifestation in the new earth paradigm.

In the old earth paradigm, we often created from separation and painful effort.

Aligns with These Other Stonecombinations:

- Combines with "Center Stillness" to make sure that you are manifesting from a clear, true intent.

- Combines with "Transformation, Prosperity & the Goddess," which supports the earth and the new earth paradigm of constant change and abundance.

- Combines with "Turkll Delight," uniting us with all our spirit help.

I had been working there on and off since I was ten. And all of a sudden I was released!!! Josh left his job about the same time. We went to California and the night before we left we found out I was pregnant! We started our spiritual jobs when we got back and things are going great!

So I have to say thanks to you for giving me such a fabulous tool to use in my life! It truly has been amazing to work with Spontaneous Manifestation!!!

~Noelle B.

Sweet Clarity

"House as Teacher Stonecombination"

- ♦ **Galena** — I reach into your natural bond with all life and translate it into every part of your life.

- ♦ **Desert Snow Quartz** — I unite you with infinity.

- ♦ **Himalayan Quartz** — I bring you the freshness and the instantaneous renewal of the mountains. I transport you to your truth now.

Elemental Balance: This combination focuses on the Earth and Etheric Elementals to profoundly increase natural earth telepathy and intuition.

Tools for Manifestation:

Wherever you place this combination it will clarify and heighten everything, while increasing your ability to respond to anything more efficiently and cheerfully.

Place next to your phone for easier communications.

Place next to your computer to receive information more efficiently.

Place next to your sacred places (or altars) to enhance your listening to and acting upon spirit.

Place at your place of work so that you can work with greater organization.

Bring with you to unknown places so that you can learn the ways and words of others more readily.

Tools for Combining:

- • Combine with "Perfect Release" when you need to let go of old misunderstandings and hurts.

- Combine with "Amazing Journeys" to encourage new, wondrous adventure.

Volcano Juice

or, if you prefer,
Affirming Your Path Now

- **Neodymium Crystal*** — I urge you to live and grow with joy as your constant wisdom.

- **Praseodymium Crystal*** — I insist that you embrace everything as easily and as compassionately as is possible.

- **Hawaiian Calcite** — I smooth over everything, balancing all with love and happy grace.

- **Argentina "Herkimer"** — I bless you enthusiastically and continually. Yes, yes, yes …

- **Argentina Meteorite** — I sum up this full combination of Stonebeings by opening you up to new worlds with their endless affirmation.

Elemental Dance: This combination focuses on the manifestation and continually growing of the Fire Elemental.

Physical, Emotional, Mental Integration: We invite you to be present with everything, which opens you up to endless worlds where there are new learnings, loves and challenges. We then invite you to be present there, as well, etc., etc. This reminds you to root yourself in the earth physically and spiritually and to stretch your heart into every newness possible so that you can root there, confidently, blissfully, and …

Electrical Body Alignment: We root and ground your highest aspirations and your most mysterious learnings and adventuring.

Affirmation of Support: *"I embrace the unknown as a way of glorious life."*

Tools for Manifestation:

Are you an adventurer?

Are you ready to leap into life

today?

Always?

Then these stones have found you with purpose and great bliss—you are one and the same.

Just know that your path cannot be affirmed, any longer, by the traditions of society.

No one that you have met can ever understand what you are doing.

You must look into the unknown for your support— for the certainty that being uncertain is one more miracle in the unfolding of EVERY-THING, of life, of gloriousness.

When you wear this necklace, know that you are here.

Trust that you have arrived

AND

that you are also endlessly traveling everywhere else and that you are well-loved in every step

Always

All ways.

Aligns with These Other Stonecombinations:

- Combines with "Wheel of Life" for perfect timeliness in all actions.
- Combines with "Center Stillness" to ground and integrate your new inspirations.

Note: This Stonecombination is sun sensitive.

Welcome Home

When we co-create new Stonecombinations, we sit down with that intent; we listen with empty minds and open hearts. Then we record whatever wisdom the Stonebeings offer us. This combination birthed itself spontaneously. It just came to us, because it was the time for it to be created—because the need for its energy is so great. Feel that when you wear this jewelry and remember that you are home, anywhere.

Personal Story

Welcome Home has been a favorite combination of mine since I first heard the name. Marilyn hadn't even told me the description or what was in it and the chills on my arms told me I had to get it. "Just send it to me." It has not left my body since it arrived. It helps connect me to the earth and the heavens simultaneously, without overwhelm, to where I can fully embrace who I am and the gifts I have to offer. Since wearing it, I have felt more present, aware, open to all the possibilities around me. My business has shifted to more clarity and abundance, my connection to Spirit is more active and vibrant, and the world just seems more unlimited than it used to be, because my limited mind has released the limits I placed on myself. I am more open to all the unlimitedness I can receive. What could be better?

~Jennifer S.

♦ **Calcite/Cuprite** — I connect you so deeply into the earth that you can surrender to her unlimited bounty and simultaneously, you can lift up to the skies.

♦ **Aqua Phenakite** — I know who you are. I watch as you find out who you are, not just as a human or even as an earth being. I celebrate that you are becoming a citizen of the cosmos.

Elemental Dance: The strong Etheric Elementals are beautifully grounded in this combination.

Physical, Emotional, Mental Integration: We offer you awareness. We offer you such awareness that you enter into trust and you don't have the need to leave any more. With us upon your heart, you can remember and **know** that wherever/whomever you are, you are home. We affirm your utter divinity. You belong to yourself and to life and you can act from that knowingness every moment.

Electrical Body Alignment: We link you to divine awareness, as you choose.

Affirmation of Support: *"I am a precious, loved, loving child of the universe."*

Tools for Manifestation:

Take this necklace with you while you sit outside in your favorite setting.

Show it the marvels of nature. Together, drink everything in.

When you are overflowing with wonder, touch this necklace to help you always remember the incredible generosity and miracles of the earth.

Do this until you feel that you belong to/with the earth, no matter what happens.

Then sit under the stars together and see yourselves traveling everywhere.

While you are doing this, root yourself more and more deeply into the earth.

Take along your earthbody and joy with you.

Travel freely and with respect.

Aligns with These Other Stonecombinations:

- Combines with "Transformation, Prosperity & the Goddess," to truly celebrate the earth while you simultaneously expand your consciousness beyond it.

- Combines with "Evolutionary Grace" so that you can personally evolve yourself during a profound time of evolution for all.

- Combines with "Relationship into All" encouraging you to share your growth with, and in, balance with others.

Wheel of Life

♦ **Sulphur** — Today you enter life. This moment you choose life or you deny it. Whatever you choose, I go with you, I walk with you. I touch your heart, for you **are** life, itself, and we are life, together, all ways, always.

♦ **Cinnabar** — Reach into the core of life. What do you find? You find your essence and you find mine— it is the same wave in the ocean of being. When you remember that, we join and vitality is undeniable.

Elemental Dance: This ancient combination of Stonebeings highlights the action of the Air Elemental and the inspiration of the Fire Elemental to manifest the perfect action at the perfect moment.

Physical, Emotional, Mental Integration: Sit. Listen. If you are going to receive this, then let your heart absorb this— not just your mind— and then you will live it— you will be the integration of these energies joined:

We are the Wheel of Life. Whatever way you turn us, we are life. Wherever we sit, in sun or in shade, we are life. Feel that so fully that lifeforce feeds you, and every inspiration that is yet unnoticed. Now you are life, too— not because we have said this, or even because you have felt it, it is simply the truth. No matter what you do, you BE. Whenever you listen to us, we will say this. We speak this without end and however you consider it today, it is so. So be it.

Electrical Body Alignment: When you align with us, you align with your body, a vehicle of choice and freedom *as you choose.*

Affirmation of Support: *"I am life and it is me."*

Tools for Manifestation:

Welcome.

It may seem coincidental that we meet.

Or you may not consider it important at all,

yet it is.

Every part of life, every movement of it within and around you

is significant. It signifies life.

You and all that you witness, speak, dance, breathe life.

You may take that for granted and even that is evidence that life is eternal.

It is so omnipresent, forever, that you get used to it.

Listen.

Life is happening. To be present means that you are touching life right now.

Blessing

Welcome to life.
Whenever you wish to join it, it will be there.
It is forever.
It does not need measurement or definition,
It is that it is.

Perhaps you will experience this many different ways.
You may want to show that you care for life well—
that you express it like an artist.
This allows you to deserve life
to earn breath.

And yet life is eternal.

It will wear different colors.
It will call out to you and it will sit in the silence never saying a
word
never needing anything.

When you welcome every moment as a gift and an illusion, equally,
you will meet life.

Aligns with These Other Stonecombinations:

- Combines with "Center Stillness," graciously inviting you to
  go more deeply into yourself, into life, to enjoy it.

- Combines with "World Peace," focusing on an ever bigger,
  broader, more loving perspective.

Personal Story

(Note from Twintreess: We often are honored to listen to
Stonecombinations that are specifically for certain people, and no one
else. When they work with those stones, they become totems for
them and powerful supports in their life. This is one of the stories of
our listening to stones to help co-create a customized combination
for someone.)

Custom Necklace: Rhodochrosite/Pink Sapphire/Lepidolite

*I have worked with stones off and on most of my adult life but more in-
tensely in the last couple of years and I have several of Ahhhmuse's pieces.
In my association with Marilyn, I have come to see that she and Tohmas
are awe-inspiring beings who have the wonderful gift of consciously speaking with the stones and they receive their messages with clarity and in a
very respectful way. And so trusting that relationship, I asked Marilyn if
she would help me co-create a "jewelry piece" that would incorporate the
attributes of unlimited love, surrender to the Divine, and I thought the
third attribute would relate to gratitude. I knew that Rhodocrosite vi-
brates to the energy of unlimited love, and that Pink Sapphire has been
called the "surrender" stone, so I knew that I definitely wanted those two
stones to be a part of this creation. I left it to Marilyn and Tohmas to hear*

which stone would make up the trinity of my pendant. I also knew that I wanted the necklace to be very feminine, and I wanted to feel soft, yielding, receptive and open to love and to my world when I wore it.

Finally, "she" arrived and the necklace is just spectacular. The Rhodocrosite came in the shape of a triangle or pyramidal shape with the point down. Three pink-lavendar stones are lined up across the top side of the triangle and a small bead of Lepidolite sits at the very top, all wired together in gold (masculine) wire. The message that came with the necklace describes Rhodocrosite in this combination as offering grounding and transformation quickly and easily; the Sapphires (three of them which again is symbolic for me of representing the trinity) assist in accessing the higher vibrations of unlimited love; and the Lepidolite reflects forgiveness, the gateway to transformation. How perfect! This very feminine necklace embodies all the attributes I asked for plus one of the most important–forgiveness— for unlimited love cannot exist and be expressed if I have not forgiven myself and others.

I am complimented on my necklace every time I wear it. I know its love draws people in. Many thanks and blessings to you, Marilyn and Tohmas, your wire wrapper, the Stonebeings, and our Gods-within for helping me bring forth this magnificent creation.

~ Bonnie W.

Blessing

Welcome to life.

Whenever you wish to join it, it will be there.

It is forever.

It does not need measurement or definition,

It is that it is.

Perhaps you will experience this many different ways.

You may want to show that you care for life well—

that you express it like an artist.

This allows you to deserve life

to earn breath.

And yet life is eternal.

It will wear different colors.

It will call out to you and it will sit in the silence never saying a
word

never needing anything.

When you welcome every moment as a gift and an illusion, equally,

You will meet life.

Totem Stories from Hawkseye Velvet Tourmaline

Now you've worn every Stonecolor

you've put on each shape.

You know what it is to be seeded in the stars

and grown upon the earth.

You have watched rainbows

dance across your skies

and you have painted your imagination

upon life's canvas.

Who are you?

A human crystal?

A shaman inventor?

Whatever you announce as you

I believe

for I am a human crystal,

a shaman inventor,

a rainbow dancer and an imagination painter.

I have been all these things with you

for as you listened to me

I listened to you

and our conversation is still forever.

About Us

Hi, we're Marilyn & Tohmas Twintreess. We're the Listeners forming the background of this book, translating Stonestories to human language. We're very honored to join you here.........

This is what we do and what we are (and combining those things certainly is a great privilege). Our life is made up of listening to the life all around us— so our days are very full. We have discovered that everything and every being has a story, right down to the rocks that we walk next to, and on, every single day.

Isn't that miraculous?

It is so miraculous that we spend our lifeforce sharing those stories, as they wish to be told. That's what this book is: the wish of the stones to be told. And your receiving of that wish is creating even more miracles. In our world, that kind of respectful exchange is evidence of the quantum evolution that humans are experiencing now as such dramatic, uncontrollable change, that it is undeniable. Yeehaw!!! *Hang on for the ride!*

We are fully aligned with that evolution for it means that humans will join the Earth Mother and all its beings in ways that maybe they have never done before: Instead of racing to dominate others, we are learning to live with them in respect. We are all becoming family.

Okay, okay, we know you're saying that these words are supposed to be "About us" and you're wondering where the personal stuff comes in. Well, this is it. Everything that we have talked about here (and anywhere else for that matter) is our life, day in, day out. Listening to life and jumping into planetary evolution are what we do for ourselves <u>and</u> for our work. That is the core of our business, AhhhMuse— whose name means to listen to our muses for the sheer joy and creativity of it all. And that's what we do. We co-create all sorts of amazing things (things we had never heard of before!) with our spirits.

Listening is also the core of our non-profit, Elementals of Life. For years, it put on a festival that brought together humans and the spirits of nature in such profound play and work that we helped to co-create new paradigms of work and play, in utter respect.

This is our life. We happily share it with you. Thank you so much for listening. We appreciate you joining us here, more than words can say (though we do keep trying!). We honor your journey and invite you to share adventures, as you wish. Thank you!

Tools and Services for your Listening and Support

Welcome

In listening to this book, you are on a grand adventure, and we're thrilled for you! Congratulations and blessings to you at every step along the way!

Listening like this changes your life in a single breath and it may never be the same again. We sure do appreciate the profound wonder and the challenge of that. After all, how do you keep exploring this path and keep affirming yourself along the way?

We have learned of and co-created so many tools and services that have helped us to keep listening. They have supported us so utterly, so thoroughly, that we have made listening our life. We share them with you, now, and that is our deepest, most glorious happiness. It's why we are here. Thanks. Enjoy~

Tools and Services for your Listening and Support

Books– *All of the books that we share comes from listening to the stories and the ways of our great teachers: stones; animals; plants; our guides and other willing humans. We thank them all, always. It is our honor to share that wisdom with anyone else in the world who wishes it.*

Stones– *Truly unique and glorious Stonebeings have always come into our life. In every way, they have supported us, co-created with us, rooted us into our bodies and the earth, and welcomed us as evolving, human friends. They have asked us to share them, respectfully, with other people. When you are ready to work with them, call us. Tell us what you want and/or we can listen to the Stonebeings to find out which ones can most support you right now. We so love doing that.*

Vibrational Jewelry– *Most all the Stonecombinations in the "Stones Alive!" books are Vibrational Jewelry necklaces. The Stonebeings asked us to co-create this specific jewelry with them as it would allow humans to actually carry the vibration of the earth and its generous support in a form that would* *unexpectedly get their attention (jewelry!) and invite them to appreciate those gifts. Also, they said that the small stones in the jewelry would show people that size does not determine **power**, and it would also **honor** the same, small stones that normally are just cast aside, in the mining business, without notice.*

Stonessences– *These also are Stonecombinations from the "Stones Alive!" books, that are in gem elixir sprays. We certainly knew nothing about creating Stonessences when the Stonebeings asked us to co-create these with them. Now we have found out that they need to be "brewed" during exact phases of the sun and the moon. Because of this, each creation of the Stonessences is completely unique and they come to us at exactly the right time, when we most need them. The whole grouping of "Disease into Vitality"combinations shows us that very clearly. For instance, the "Disease into Vitality: Hormone Support" came exactly at a time when many of the women in this country were entering menopause.*

The Rituals of Manifestation Deck– *We use this every day. It may be one of the most profound tools that has ever graced our life. One day when we were listening, we were shown that humans physically manifest everything, by using specific stages of energy. Those stages form the 52 cards/rituals of the Deck. Using them literally teaches us to daily claim our responsibility for creating our own life. For us, it has focused our intents, embraced our struggles and manifested miracles. Every time we use it, we manifest miracles. We envision a time and a paradigm on the earth when that's all any of us manifests.*

Life Enhancers (Lithium Clay Wearables)– *A geologist friend of ours hand harvests some of the highest content Lithium, in clay, in the world. What's profound about that is that Lithium in its natural state (not the drug) helps to balance virtually all of our metabolic processes, and it does it by stimulating or relaxing, according to whatever is needed in that moment! It's absolutely incredible. The safest, most efficient way we know of using it is by wearing it: anklebands; wristbands; caps; backbands; sleeping & meditation pads, (even dog collars) etc. We used the L.E. headbands while writing this book. They buoyed up our inspiration, our listening and our stamina, beautifully (thank you!).*

The Life Enhancers have given us the opportunity to co- create something from start-to-finish, that is done with complete respect at every stage: The Lithium clay is hand harvested. We listen to the Lithium and assemble the packets of clay, happily. The Life Enhancers are hand-sewn, locally, with organic fabrics. Then we use them in our lives so that we can pass on what we have learned of them- a completely respectful co-creation.

Deva's Gift Crystal Singing Bowls– *In 1995, we listened to the Deva of Crystals (their totem spirit) and asked her for a new crystal singing bowl design. She gave us one with a handle on the bowl, saying that humans are less likely to deny the full, empowering **vibration** of crystal sound, when they actually hold it in their hands! How true! We are immensely grateful for the gift of the Crystal Deva.*

Listening Service– *Yes. We all need affirmation and we all need to look at our journey from a freer, more loving view. Listening to our spirits has given us that many times over and the joy of that spills* *over into everything we are. We offer it to you, too, in whatever form truly supports you: listening to stones; animals; astrology; your guides— that's the wonder of listening, it forms to you as you need, not according to what we might think (after all, what would we know about it?).*

Spiritcoaching– *Wherever you are, whatever you are doing, we can support you to continually act upon your spirit, upon your special creativity, in your life. We would be honored to do that. There's no way to tell you in advance exactly how this would happen, because we have to listen for those parameters, once you offer your willingness to do this. Whatever program we would offer would come from our hearts, our commitment, and your open heart and likely would require time and rituals from you as well.*

Thank you. Thank you for letting us share this with you. It is our way of expanding upon the gifts that we have received and creates even more wonder and magic upon the earth mother. We love it all. If you want to see and know more, please visit our website: www.ahhhmuse.com and please give us a holler. We would so love hearing from you.

Please watch for "Stones Alive! Volume 3"

Meet you there......

When the Stonebeings first asked us to co-create a stones reference book with them, we felt utterly honored. Of course we would do it!!! How could we not......even though we didn't know specifically how we would do it (It was just a "human" moment!). So we just started, and let our hearts be led by the sheer wisdom and spontaneous manifestation of the stones in every single moment and circumstance.

Working with them landed upon us and our life like a living, walking, talking meditation— an altered state of reality that seamlessly wove into all other realities. They brought us along in their unique, sacred way of life — so much so, that when they told us, "This will be **three** books, a trilogy," we never even blinked. We quietly, utterly accepted it. We simply wove that into our reality, as well, even though we didn't then know how we would create even one book. It didn't matter; what mattered was that the stones had breathed it into our reality with their words and their love, and our part was to add our human manifestation.

As you already know, these "Stones Alive!" books are living, breathing meditations with the stones. They take you into other worlds that ever live alongside our human one, just waiting for a single word: Yes! We said, "Yes." We invite you to say "Yes," to "Stones Alive!, Volume 3" too. Do we know how we will co-create it? Not quite. But we have lived in the magic too long not to know that it will happen and it will present itself as a gloriously alchemical miracle.

"Stones Alive!, Volume 1" is a reference guide to stones that ask to help support us (humans) in this incredible, evolutionary leap we struggle and transform in. It invites us to see that the stones (and the other beings upon this planet) **as partners** in an evolution the likes of which has never happened before on this earth. If we just open our hearts to these possibilities, it shows us we are not alone.

"Stones Alive!, Volume 2" takes us deeper into the adventure. It urges us to grow trust and to even trust as **a way of life** (simple for stones, radical for humans). Surrounded by trust, the Stonebeings and the combinations in this book invite each of us, personally, to listen to stones for ourselves— to realize that we can partner with them (and the other beings upon the earth) in our lives, not just in a book: With our own hearts, we can listen to the stones, and bask in their timeless wisdom and recordkeeping, just when we most need it.

Yes, "Stones Alive!, Volume 3" takes us even more deeply into new worlds. It shows us how to trust our conversations with stones enough to co-create with them— to manifest the peaceful, gloriously loving lives and selves we have ever wanted. Yes. Listen with us in the final book of the "Stones Alive!" trilogy and together (remember, you're never alone) we will explore the tools and ways that will model for us how to spontaneously and joyfully co-create the earth of our true, peaceful hearts. How's that for an evolution.

Join us there. We send you love for the journey.

Index

Actinolite 21-22

Ajoite 122, 293

Allanite 23

Amazonite 265, 297

Amblygonite 25, 281, 307

Amethyst 27, 183, 187-198, 230

Anatase 28

Andalusite 30

Apache Tear 277

Apatite 31

Aqua Phenacite 316

Aquamarine 256, 265

Argentinian "Herkimer" 314

Argentinian Meteorite 314

Astrophyllite 33, 303

Aventurine 302, 310

Azurite 258, 269, 273, 303

Barite 35

Black Garnet 289

Blue Apatite 297, 307

Blue Lace Agate 283, 287

Boji® 293

Brookite 269, 275, 277, 281

Calcite 199-205

Calcite w/Realgar 38

Calcite/Cuprite 316

Carnelian 289

Carrolite 40

Cassiterite 41

Celestite 44, 258

Chalcopyrite 47

Chrysocolla 291

Chrysoprase 49, 285, 310

Cinnabar 51, 318

Columbite/Tantalite/Niobium 53

Copper 55, 260

Copper/Gold/Silver 56

Covellite 57

Crocoite 59, 281, 307

Desert Snow Quartz 62, 269, 277, 312

Diopside 68

Dravite 69

Dumortierite 71

Emerald 260

Erbium 73

Erythrite 74

Euclase 75

Eudialyte 77

Europium 79

Fluorite 206-213, 275

Fuchsite 81

Galena 312

Gold 83

Goshenite 85

Green Apatite 307

Green Kyanite 86

Green Obsidian 293

Hawaiian Calcite 314

Hawkseye Velvet Tourmaline 17, 89, 180, 251, 300, 323

Heliodor 90

Hematite 283, 306

Herkimer Diamond 262, 269, 295, 298, 306

Hessonite Garnet on Smokey Quartz 92

Howlite 273

Huebnerite 94

Iolite 287, 289

Ivoryite 96

Kornerupine 302, 310

Kunzite 297

Lapis Lazuli 287

Lepidolite 98

Lithium Clay 100

Lithium Crystal 101

Magnetite 104

Malachite 260, 269, 273, 279

Mangano Calcite 105

Meteorite 107, 314

Mookaite 108

Moonstone 269

Morganite 111

Mother Earth Spheres 113

Neodymium 314

Nepalese Quartz 116, 237, 303, 312

Neptunite 117

Orpiment 120

Papagoite 122

Pectolite 123

Peridot 279, 281, 298

Petalite 125

Phenakite 214-218, 256, 283

Pine Needles 291

Pipestone 127

Praseodymium 314

Prehnite 129

Psilomelane 130

Pyrite 219-225

Quartz 226-241

Quetzalcoatlite 132

Rainbow Boji® 134

Raw Diamond 310

Realgar 38, 285

Red Calcite 273

Rhodonite 285

Rhodozite 138

Rose Quartz 242-245, 302

Roselite 139

Rubellite 291

Ruby 295, 306

Rutilated Quartz 258

Rutile 140

Sahara Sand 143

Samarium 146

Scheelite 148

Selenite 246-250

Silver 149, 283

Smokey Quartz 275, 305

Snowflake Obsidian 269

Sodalite 275

Sphalerite 151

Sphene 153

Spinel 154

Stibnite 309

Stillbite 156

Strawberry Quartz 273

Sulphur 158, 307, 318

Sunstone 279, 285

Terbium 161

Thulium 162

Tibetan Tektite 303

Topaz 309

Tourmaline 279, 287

Turquoise 269, 295, 305

Vanadinite 164

Wolframite 166, 256, 307

Xenotine 170

YAG 172

Yttrium 173

Yttrium Fluorite 174

Zircon 176